Global Trade, Labour R
International Law

CW01431102

This book provides a set of proposals for how best to guarantee effective enforcement of labour rights worldwide.

The linkage between labour standards and global trade has been recurrent for some 200 years. At a time when the world is struggling to find a way out of crisis and is striving for economic growth, more than ever there is a need for up-to-date research on how to protect and promote labour rights in the global economy. This book explores the history of the field and also provides an overview of emerging trends and opportunities. It discusses the most recent problems including: the effectiveness and the role of the International Labour Organization (ILO) in the second century of its existence, the World Trade Organization (WTO) and its potential relevance in the protection of labour rights, the effectiveness of the US and the EU Generalised System of Preferences, the impact of corporate social responsibility (CSR) instruments on labour rights, and labour provisions in the international trade agreements concluded by the US and the EU. The book argues, inter alia, that trade agreements seem to be a useful tool to help pave the way out of the crisis and that the United States–Mexico–Canada Agreement (USMCA) can be perceived as a model agreement and a symbol of a shift in perspective from long global supply chains to a focus on regional ones, local production, jobs and a rise in wages.

The book will be essential reading for academics and students in the fields of human rights law, international labour law, industrial relations law, international sustainable development law, international economic law and international trade law. It will also be of interest to practitioners, non-government organisations (NGOs) and policy makers.

Aneta Tyc is Doctor of Law (2015) and Assistant Professor at the Department of European, International and Collective Labour Law at the Faculty of Law and Administration of the University of Lodz. She is author or co-author of 80 publications in the field of labour law in several languages and has authored several dozen papers presented at scientific conferences. She has been Principal Investigator on six research projects and is a winner of many prestigious awards, prizes and scholarships.

Studies in Modern Law and Policy
Series Editor: Ralf Rogowski
Professor of Law, University of Warwick

Also in the series

Networking the Rule of Law
How Change Agents Reshape Judicial Governance in the EU
Cristina Dallara and Daniela Piana
ISBN: 978-1-4094-3305-7

Social Systems Theory and Judicial Review
Taking Jurisprudence Seriously
Katayoun Baghai
ISBN: 978-1-4094-5402-1

The EU Economic and Social Model in the Global Crisis
Interdisciplinary Perspectives
Edited by Dagmar Schiek
ISBN: 978-1-4094-5731-2

Constitutional Evolution in Central and Eastern Europe
Expansion and Integration in the EU
Edited by Kyriaki Topidi and Alexander H.E. Morawa
ISBN: 978-1-4094-0327-2

Central and Eastern Europe After Transition
Towards a New Socio-legal Semantics
Edited by Alberto Febbrajo and Wojciech Sadurski
ISBN: 978-1-4094-0390-6

Democracy, Law and Governance
Jacques Lenoble and Marc Maesschalck
ISBN: 978-1-4094-0395-1

Global Trade, Labour Rights and International Law
A Multilevel Approach
Aneta Tyc
ISBN: 978-0-367-74798-5

Global Trade, Labour Rights and International Law

A Multilevel Approach

Aneta Tyc

Routledge
Taylor & Francis Group

LONDON AND NEW YORK

First published 2021
by Routledge
2 Park Square, Milton Park, Abingdon, Oxon OX14 4RN

and by Routledge
605 Third Avenue, New York, NY 10158

Routledge is an imprint of the Taylor & Francis Group, an informa business

© 2021 Aneta Tyc

British Library Cataloguing-in-Publication Data
A catalogue record for this book is available from the British Library

Library of Congress Cataloging-in-Publication Data
Names: Tyc, Aneta, author.
Title: Global trade, labour rights and international law : a multilevel
    approach / Aneta Tyc.
Description: Milton Park, Abingdon, Oxon ; New York, NY :
    Routledge, 2021. | Series: Studies in modern law and policy |
    Includes bibliographical references and index. | Contents: The
    history of development of workers' rights in the context of global
    trade rules — The ILO and its effectiveness — The WTO needs
    reforms : is there space for labour rights? — Generalised system of
    preferences : the US and the EU compared — The US's and the
    EU's international trade agreements — Private standard-setting :
    the impact of CSR instruments on labour rights — Conclusions.
Identifiers: LCCN 2020055598 (print) | LCCN 2020055599
    (ebook) | ISBN 9780367747985 (hardback) | ISBN
    9781032007236 (paperback) | ISBN 9781003159612 (ebook)
Subjects: LCSH: Labor laws and legislation, International. |
    International trade. | Foreign trade regulation.
Classification: LCC K1705 .T93 2021 (print) | LCC K1705 (ebook) |
    DDC 344.01—dc23
LC record available at https://lccn.loc.gov/2020055598
LC ebook record available at https://lccn.loc.gov/2020055599

ISBN: 978-0-367-74798-5 (hbk)
ISBN: 978-0-367-74801-2 (pbk)
ISBN: 978-1-003-15961-2 (ebk)

Typeset in Galliard
by Apex CoVantage, LLC

In Memory of my Grandmother, Adela Tyc, who was sent to a forced labour camp in Germany during the Second World War and Her Father, Władysław Siekierski, who was killed by the Germans at the Auschwitz-Birkenau concentration camp

Contents

Acknowledgements

The project was financed by the National Science Centre in Poland pursuant to the decision number DEC-2016/21/D/HS5/03849. The project's registration number is 2016/21/D/HS5/03849.

General introduction

Despite a long debate on the linkage between labour standards and global trade, and numerous attempts to answer the question of how to provide not only economic growth but also social justice and the effectiveness of fundamental labour rights, a response to the plight of many workers worldwide is still needed. This is particularly evident not only in the context of frictions between the US and China that are likely to continue under the Presidency of Joe Biden[1] but also in terms of the COVID-19 pandemic, which has resulted in an economic crisis, with skyrocketing unemployment and an uncertain future shape of the global division of labour and supply chains. The aim of the book is to re-identify opportunities to improve the regulation of global processes towards achieving economic growth, social progress and the protection of workers' rights. Under such difficult circumstances when we are facing the spectre of deep recession, the realisation of such an objective is needed more than ever.

The relationship between strengthening of labour standards and global trade was already a challenge for the creators of the Treaty of Versailles. For this reason, according to the International Labour Organization (ILO) Constitution: 'the failure of any nation to adopt humane conditions of labour is an obstacle in the way of other nations which desire to improve the conditions in their own countries'. In recent decades, factors such as low labour costs, the possibility of flexible employment reduction, lowering wages and reduction of duties related to social security have often determined the transfer of business to countries offering the most favourable conditions of its operating. Depletion of workers' rights and cheap labour have constituted incentives for international or cross-border employers to enter the market. The authorities of respective countries have created lower standards for the protection of workers in order to attract businesses. Such activities have translated into the infringement of human labour rights, for example, the use of forced labour or child labour, and have clearly refuted the ILO Declaration on Social Justice for a Fair Globalization adopted in 2008, according

---

1 Jacob M Schlesinger, 'What's Biden's New China Policy? It Looks a Lot Like Trump's' *The Wall Street Journal* (10 September 2020) <www.wsj.com/articles/whats-bidens-china-policy-it-looks-a-lot-like-trumps-11599759286> accessed 5 November 2020.

to which: 'the violation of fundamental principles and rights at work cannot be invoked or otherwise used as a legitimate comparative advantage and . . . labour standards should not be used for protectionist trade purposes'.

Until a little while ago, some would have said that a panacea to ensuring economic growth and social justice consisted in erasing barriers to free trade, fighting protectionist practices and finding solutions on how to avoid social dumping, which would distort free competition. Today, however, the scenario in which Joe Biden eliminates all Trump's tariffs is little probable. Besides, nothing in Biden's economic plans indicates a full withdrawal from protectionism. A recent change in circumstances will have an impact on solutions proposed in this book, for example, related to the need of concluding free trade agreements.

The relationship between labour law and trade policy should be the starting point for the debate. The main purpose of labour law is to combat injustices in the world of work. In addition, it can boost labour productivity, mitigate failures in labour markets, and facilitate economic production. By contrast, the fundamental objective of trade policy is connected with raising efficiency and income and providing more consumption possibilities. This is because it regulates cross-border flows of goods and services. Moreover, trade creates winners and losers thus deepening inequality. For this reason, it is crucial to realise if there is a mutual complementarity or a mutual conflict between labour law and trade policy in achieving development aims.[2] This prompts us further to ask a question: is the possibility of keeping a fair balance between economic growth and social progress still likely, and under which conditions?

This book employs a multilevel approach, thus its main themes are as follows: the history of development of workers' rights in the context of global trade rules, the effectiveness and the role of the ILO in the second century of its existence, the World Trade Organization (WTO) and its potential relevance in the protection of labour rights, labour rights under the Generalised System of Preferences programmes, labour provisions in international trade agreements and private standard-setting processes, including their impact on labour rights. Consequently, the book naturally covers diverse layers of social structure from the very micro to the very macro, for example, workers, employers, companies, industries, states, governments, international organisations, global economy. There are interactions between these layers and each of them is impacted by diverse processes and trends. A multilevel approach helps in identifying dimensions on which to address labour rights in the most efficient manner.

This book is based predominantly on legal research. Adopting a multilevel legal approach, it examines especially the WTO law, the ILO labour standards, specific chapters relating to labour in international trade agreements concluded by the

---

2 David Cheong and Franz Christian Ebert, 'Labour Law and Trade Policy: What Implications for Economic and Human Development?' in Shelley Marshall and Colin Fenwick (eds), *Labour Regulation and Development: Socio-Legal Perspectives* (Cheltenham, Northampton: Edward Elgar Publishing 2016) 83–84; see the cited literature.

EU and the US, the law governing the US and the EU Generalised System of Preferences (GSP) schemes, domestic laws, and self-regulation within the CSR framework.

A logical-linguistic method, which allows the exegesis and interpretation of the content of law and the removal of emerging doubts, is used. Besides, the author to a great extent uses a legal comparative method, which facilitates the formulation of de lege ferenda postulates. The analysis applies a variant of the traditional comparative method, which consists of comparing regulations in different countries, as well as a variant aptly characterised by Bogg and Ewing, according to whom:

> In a changed and changing world . . . the comparative exercise may have a new and different function, which in part is to identify trends and patterns in the regulation of labour globally. This is undertaken with a view to respond to these global trends, particularly where the latter are thought to challenge the values that underpin the study of labour law.[3]

A historical method is another method used in this research. It requires from the author to have a vision of law as a social phenomenon of a dynamic nature, which has a clear development path. The investigator should take into account not only changes in law but also the controversy about law, its application and interpretation. The reflection is accompanied by the search for links with certain social phenomena occurring in the history.

What is inevitable is the examination of law from the perspective of the need for realisation of fundamental workers' rights. An axiological legal method has been used in a natural way here. The study of law in axiological terms is a consequence of understanding the law as a set of standards of conduct in relations between people, built on the basis of some values to their implementation and protection. Positive law is not only a carrier of specific values but also their guarantee. The author of the book refers to them in the interpretation of law.

This book offers a new way of approaching the title theme. First, drawing not only on theoretical foundations but also on a problem-solving approach, the author offers an in-depth analysis of the history of development of workers' rights in the context of global trade rules. From a historical point of view, the linkage between labour standards and global trade has been recurrent for 200 years and it is crucial to clearly present conceptual underpinnings which stand behind the nexus.

Second, as the ILO celebrated its 100th anniversary in 2019, it is unavoidable to reflect on the great heritage of ten decades of its existence but, above all, it is timely to take stock of the effectiveness of the ILO's enforcement mechanisms. Although the ILO has proved its capacity to define, evaluate and monitor

---

3 Alan Bogg and Keith D Ewing, 'Freedom of Association' in Matthew W Finkin and Guy Mundlak (eds), *Comparative Labor Law* (Cheltenham, Northampton: Edward Elgar Publishing 2015) 298.

international labour standards, it lacks tools to enforce compliance with ILO agreements. Procedural compliance, concerned with formal obligations such as reporting, seems to be on the decline. Substantive compliance, that is, whether states have fulfilled obligations set out in an international instrument is also unsatisfactory, especially in terms that ILO appears to be unable to respond to cases of non-compliance. This book draws important lessons on what strategy the ILO should adopt in the next century and on how to shape the future direction of global labour governance.

Third, the book deals with the potential relevance of the WTO in the protection of labour rights, especially in the era of the WTO crisis, when the Organization needs reforms. By means of analysis and detailed criticism, the proposed conceptual framework addresses both what the author calls 'the institutional approach' and 'the integrated legislative approach'. On the one hand, this results from the reflection whether labour standards should be left to the ILO (e.g. Hepple[4]), encompassed by the WTO agenda (e.g. Cohan Baclawski;[5] Wolffgang and Feuerhake[6]) or both forces should be combined ('the institutional approach'), for example, the Agency for Trade and Labour Standards 'ATLAS' jointly governed by the WTO and the ILO (Barry and Reddy[7]); joint ILO-GATT/WTO Enforcement Regime (Ehrenberg[8]); the concept of a global labour and trade framework agreement 'GLTFA' (Addo[9]). On the other hand, the adopted conceptual framework results from the ideas of the integration of core labour standards (CLS) into the WTO through changes to law, for example, the view according to which the WTO should build on Article XX(e) of GATT by adding a provision that allows countries to sanction the specific sector of a country that has violated CLS, if the ILO has determined that there is a violation (e.g. Elliott and Freeman;[10] Plasa[11]) ('the integrated legislative approach').

4 Bob Hepple, 'The WTO as a Mechanism for Labour Regulation' in Brian Bercusson and Cynthia Estlund (eds), *Regulating Labour in the Wake of Globalisation: New Challenges, New Institutions* (Oxford, Portland OR: Hart Publishing 2008).
5 Brittany Cohan Baclawski, 'Re-Thinking the WTO's Relationship to International Labor Standards: Is It Finally Time for a Global Approach' (2016–2017) 48 *Georgetown Journal of International Law* 235.
6 Hans-Michael Wolffgang and Wolfram Feuerhake, 'Core Labour Standards in World Trade Law: The Necessity for Incorporation of Core Labour Standards in the World Trade Organization' (2002) 36(5) *Journal of World Trade* 883.
7 Christian Barry and Sanjay Reddy, *International Trade & Labor Standards: A Proposal for Linkage* (New York: Columbia University Press 2008).
8 Daniel S Ehrenberg, 'From Intention to Action: An ILO-GATT/WTO Enforcement Regime for International Labor Rights' in Lance A Compa and Stephen F Diamond (eds), *Human Rights, Labor Rights, and International Trade* (Philadelphia: University of Pennsylvania Press 1996).
9 Kofi Addo, *Core Labour Standards and International Trade: Lessons from the Regional Context* (Heidelberg, New York, Dordrecht, London: Springer 2015).
10 Kimberly A Elliott and Richard B Freeman, *Can Labour Standards Improve Under Globalization?* (Washington DC: Peterson Institute for International Economics 2003).
11 Wolfgang Plasa, *Reconciling International Trade and Labor Protection: Why We Need to Bridge the Gap Between ILO Standards and WTO Rules* (Lanham, Boulder, New York, London: Lexington Books 2015).

Fourth, the book contains the most recent developments in GSP programmes, especially in the context of the Trump administration's steps relating to certain beneficiary countries. The book provides an assessment of the effectiveness of this unilateral mechanism. In particular, the academic question connected to the impact of the GSP on social development and human rights in the beneficiary countries is the key issue. The question to what extent the threat of blocking imports or the withdrawal from the scheme can give rise to policy change regarding labour standards is also discussed. This book aims to analyse the legal basis, advantages and disadvantages of the GSP schemes and to compare the EU's and the US's GSP labour provisions.

Fifth, for the purposes of this book much attention has been paid to the limitations of labour provisions included in free trade agreements concluded by the US and the EU and towards the ways in which they may be strengthened to better promote ILO fundamental labour rights. Focusing specifically on the need to ensure compliance with international trade agreements in relation to ILO standards, this book has articulated some constructive proposals, especially taking into consideration that these instruments may be very useful to help pave the way out of this crisis. Importantly, the book contains the most up-to-date and comprehensive research on the newest agreements, including the EU–Korea, the EU–Japan, and the EU–Canada agreements. Moreover, the book explores the newest US–Mexico–Canada Agreement and argues that it can be regarded as a new model agreement and that its quick implementation can be a chance to alleviate economic depression and create a framework for economic growth.

Sixth, the book contains the most up-to-date research on the extent to which self-regulation within the CSR framework contributes to improving workers' rights worldwide. The book explores current problems related to transnational company agreements, corporate codes of conduct, NGOs' social accountability standards, ISO standards, the Dow Jones Sustainability Index and the Global Reporting Initiative, each of which has been critically analysed.

1 The history of development of workers' rights in the context of global trade rules

1 The pre-ILO era

The linkage between global trade and labour law was already assumed in David Ricardo's theory on comparative costs dating back to the eighteenth century. At that time, in 1788, minister of finance of King Louis XVI – Baron Jacques Necker – claimed in his 'De l'importance des opinions religieuses' that the abolition of Sunday as a day of rest could provide a competitive advantage to a country if other countries did not act in the same way. Necker, however, was not the originator of the idea of international agreements to protect workers, but he was the first to notice that the question of workers' protection was an international one. Then, many industrialists of the nineteenth century understood that countries that wished to improve the position of their working classes would be negatively affected by competition from other countries that did not. Some of them, for example, Daniel Legrand and Robert Owen, incited discussions about an international regulation of labour. Admittedly in the nineteenth century the state focused mainly on the legislation related to the reduction of working time in the civil service, where no risk of international competition existed, but some measures aimed at limiting child labour and night work by women in factories were taken.[1]

The Alsatian manufacturer Daniel Legrand was the first tenacious promoter of international labour legislation. His indefatigable activity was clearly visible between 1840 and 1848, when he addressed many appeals to British, Swiss, French and German statespeople and civil servants. He highlighted that the prosperity of a state was closely linked to the physical well-being and morality of its working class. He was also aware of the fact that compensation for abuses become a subject of negotiation between the governments of all industrial countries. Nevertheless, he warned that focusing all attention on wealth would lead to dramatic

---

1 Arturo Bronstein, *International and Comparative Labour Law: Current Challenges* (Geneva: Palgrave Macmillan, International Labour Office 2009) 86; see the cited literature. See also: William H Meyer, 'Testing Theories of Labor Rights and Development' (2015) 37(2) *Human Rights Quarterly* 414, 415 <https://doi.org/10.1353/hrq.2015.0036> accessed 2 August 2020.

consequences, including the great mass of people deprived of trust in state institutions or even hostile to their state.[2]

Subsequently, some individual philanthropic manufacturers such as Robert Owen, the clergy, educators, economists and legislators reacted to the plight of the working class. Similarly to Daniel Legrand, they pointed out that values such as family life, human dignity and the health of the nation are equally or even more important than profits. However, the employers' opposition was sufficient to defeat their efforts to introduce reforms. Attempts at justifying such opposition were related to economic grounds and were focused on the fact that 'the reduction of hours of work and the prohibition of persons under a certain age from working in factories would raise the price of goods to the consumers, and home trade and prosperity would thereby be affected adversely since the cheaper foreign goods would be imported and flood the market'. The reformers had to tackle the problem that the establishment of humanitarian national legislation was hampered by international competition. The solution seemed clear to them and consisted in finding a way to undermine unlimited international competition by establishing global minimum standards for living conditions below which the worker should not be allowed to fall yet leaving the theory of comparative advantage intact. There is a general conviction that Robert Owen was the pioneer of international labour legislation, however, he was rather an advocate of labour legislation practised at international level. Having spent time in Glasgow among the working poor, Owen was preoccupied and saddened by the living and working conditions of its people. The Industrial Revolution, which began in England in the 1800s, caused these to be intolerable in many European countries. Owen carried out an experiment in New Lanark in Scotland, which was a manufacturing community of about 2,500 people. He put a permanent end to the 'truck system', according to which workers were paid partly or entirely in script redeemable only at company stores and establishments. Owen's workers received wages. Moreover, he not only shortened hours of labour but also made provision for the workers' leisure and the education of their children, and established cooperative marketing. The local bakery and store were run on a cooperative basis and sold goods below market value. He prohibited the labour of children under the age of ten and introduced free health care. His village became famous and he began to dream of a world filled with model communities, presenting his idealistic conception in a book entitled *A New View of Society* (1813). In 1818, with the aim of promoting his theories, he approached the Congress of the Holy Alliance at Aix-la-Chapelle, where he presented two Memorials suggesting that the Congress appoint a commission to visit New Lanark, adopt his idea and thus eliminate causes 'which perpetually generate misery in human society'. Admittedly, initially the Congress did not take up his idea, but then he received a Bill

2 Antony Alcock, *History of the International Labour Organisation* (London, Basingstoke: Palgrave Macmillan 1971) 6; Nicolas Valticos, *Droit international du travail* (Paris: Dalloz 1983) 7–9.

passed by Parliament in 1819 limiting the hours in cotton factories that was 'the real beginning of industrial legislation in England'.[3] It was one of the most important pieces of legislation at that time, along with the Act passed by the English in 1802, which reduced to 12 hours a day the employment of children in the textile factories. This Act was the first one that introduced the principle of factory inspection, despite the fact that the predominant belief during that period promoted economic laissez-faire or free-for-all economic development.[4]

Notwithstanding the aforementioned, it should be indicated that Charles Frederick Hindley, a member of the British Parliament, is regarded as the founder of the idea of international labour legislation. He was described as having 'a clear insight into the interdependence between nations that was created by foreign trade and international competition'.[5] In 1833, Hindley proposed an international treaty on hours of work as a means of promoting such legislation in England. Shortly thereafter, in 1838–1839, Jérome Blanqui, a French liberal economist, wrote as follows about the need for harmonisation of labour legislation in European countries: 'There is only one way of accomplishing it [the reform] while avoiding its disastrous consequences: this would be to get it adopted simultaneously by all industrial nations which compete in the foreign market'.[6]

The solution according to which finding a way to undermine unlimited international competition means establishing global minimum standards for living conditions below which the worker should not be allowed to fall yet leaving the theory of comparative advantage intact, was not the sole one. Another, namely international working-class action for the eight-hour day and restrictions on juvenile and child labour, was advocated by Marx and his followers in the First and Second Internationals. This international working-class action would provide 'schools of class struggle' with the goal of winning political power and establishing socialism. One of the two conclusions made in 1864 in the First International was that the workers in different countries needed to stand together in order to achieve better conditions and to prevent governments playing upon national prejudices to 'squander in piratical wars the people's blood and treasure'. The famous 'Proletarians of all countries, Unite!' was a reflection of this. The First International broke up in 1872 mainly because of premature attempts at establishing an international organisation of workers before these had developed solid organisations in their own countries. When the Second International was formed

---

3 Alcock (n 2) 5–6; Robert E Weir, *Workers in America: A Historical Encyclopedia* (Santa Barbara, Denver, Oxford: ABC-CLIO 2013) 565, vol 1: A-L; Valticos (n 2) 6.
4 Kofi Addo, *Core Labour Standards and International Trade: Lessons from the Regional Context* (Heidelberg, New York, Dordrecht, London: Springer 2015) 79–80.
5 Virginia A Leary, 'Workers' Rights and International Trade: The Social Clause (GATT, ILO, NAFTA, U.S. Laws)' in Jagdish N Bhagwati and Robert E Hudec (eds), *Fair Trade and Harmonization: Prerequisites for Free Trade? Volume 2 Legal Analysis* (Cambridge, London: The MIT Press 1996) 184.
6 Jérome A Blanqui, *Cours d'économie industrielle 1838–1839* (Paris 1839), quoted from: Leary (n 5) 184.

in 1889, it was caught on the issue of reform or revolution. On the one hand, it was aimed at sharing the cultural aspirations of surrounding society and enjoying its goods; while on the other hand, showing loyalty to a new order that might be created in the future, it denied approval and sought the end of that society. Besides, the members of the Second International spoke as if they were citizens of a world republic, and not citizens of particular countries, even if their leaders were leaders of parties functioning in those countries. Against this background, the conflict between national interest and supranational solidarity arose.[7]

The increasing pressure of international competition resulted in governments considering the problems of international labour legislation. In March 1889, the Swiss government proposed to organise a conference on issues that should be regulated by international agreement. The proposal covered the following areas: limitation of the working day for minors, a minimum age for the admission of children into industry, Sunday labour, prohibition of the employment of women and minors in unhealthy and dangerous trades, limitation of night work for women and minors and the ways and means of implementing international conventions encompassing these issues. The conference was held not in Berne, as originally proposed, but in Berlin in March 1890. Only non-binding resolutions related to Sunday rest, underground employment of women or children, child labour in factories and in unhealthy or dangerous occupations were allowed to pass. Unfortunately, no convention was adopted and, in addition, a dispute arose over monitoring the implementation of the resolutions. The Germans were in favour of restricting this to each government appointing a number of officials to investigate and report once a year on the extent of implementation. A different position was taken by the Swiss, who not only wanted 'obligatory arrangements' (implicitly – conventions) to be concluded among the participating countries but also wanted a permanent bureau, which would be competent to coordinate and publish information and to organise further conferences. Finally, the German proposal was adopted.[8]

In 1897, delegates representing workers in 14 countries met in Zurich at the International Congress on Labour Protection and urged the Swiss government to invite other governments with the aim of setting up a labour office.[9] In the same year, at the instigation of the Swiss and Belgian governments, an International Congress of Civil Social Reformers was convened in Brussels and a resolution calling for the establishment of an international bureau for the protection of labour was adopted.[10] A special commission was appointed to draft the statutes of a private, but government-oriented, international association. The draft was discussed and accepted in Paris in July 1900 and a committee of six members

---

7 Alcock (n 2) 7–9.
8 Bob Reinalda, *Routledge History of International Organizations: From 1815 to the Present Day* (London, New York: Routledge 2009) 164–166.
9 Addo (n 4) 83.
10 Alcock (n 2) 11.

was appointed in order to prepare the first congress in Switzerland. In addition, in 1900 the International Association for Labour Legislation was established. It consisted of national sections and was provided with an executive organ, namely the International Labour Office, opened in Basel in 1901, whose functions included publishing all labour laws, reports and other document promoting the study of national labour laws and their harmonisation, and maintaining relations among reformers from different countries. The International Labour Office ceased its activity in 1919, when its tasks were taken over by the International Labour Organization in Geneva.[11]

Impressed by the work undertaken by the International Association for Labour Legislation, governments began to agree on labour issues in bilateral treaties. In 1904 Italy and France concluded a treaty which was triggered by the Italian economic competition on the one hand and the conditions of migrant workers on the other hand. According to this treaty, France offered Italian immigrant workers access to the social benefits received by French workers, and Italy had to reform its laws on hours of work and minimum age for entry to the labour market in order to bring them in line with France. The French-Italian treaty of 1904 served as an example for other countries in Europe and by 1914 there were already 27 such agreements.[12]

In 1905–1906, under the prompting of the Swiss government conferences were held which resulted in the first two international conventions, that is, the International Convention Respecting the Prohibition of Night Work for Women in Industrial Employment and the International Convention Prohibiting the Use of White (Yellow) Phosphorus in the Manufacture of Matches. Another conference of experts was organised by the Swiss government in 1913. As before, if agreement among experts seemed feasible, the conference of experts should be followed by a diplomatic one. This time, however, the conference of experts was attended by governmental representatives from 15 states, who drafted conventions prohibiting night work for all children under 14 and proposing a maximum working day of 10.5 hours and a working week of 60 hours, but the diplomatic conference did not take place due to the outbreak of the First World War.[13]

Interestingly, in the US, some attempts to create a nexus between labour rights and trade started in early 1890. On the one hand, the importation of slaves was prohibited, and on the other hand, foreign goods manufactured by convicted labour were banned. Subsequently, the Hawley-Smoot Tariff Act was passed in 1930 with the aim of banning the imports of goods made by forced labour or indentured labour under penal sanctions. This Act is still in force; however, it is only sporadically enforced.[14] It should be noted that the Smoot-Hawley Tariff Act exerted devastating effects on the world economy by shrinking international

11 Reinalda (n 8) 166.
12 ibid 167.
13 ibid 168–169.
14 Christine Kaufmann, *Globalisation and Labour Rights: The Conflict Between Core Labour Rights and International Economic Law* (Oxford, Portland OR: Hart Publishing 2007) 171.

trade and triggering industrial stagnation and unemployment up to the Second World War.[15]

The early milestones of the development of the trade-labour linkage in the US were also related to the Tariff Acts of 1922 and 1930 with what was called 'cost equalisation', that is, the principle according to which the tariff rate should equalise the foreign and domestic costs of production. This concept had its origins in alerts directed to the Congress and issued by the American Federation of Labor (established in 1881 as the Federation of Organized Trades and Labor Unions) against imports from low-wage countries.[16] In 1933, President Roosevelt signed into law the National Industrial Recovery Act, which was meant to 'promote cooperative action, eliminate unfair practices, increase purchasing power, expand production, reduce unemployment, and conserve natural resources'. Special attention should be paid to three titles of this Act that extended executive authority over labour relations and interstate commerce. First, title I ('Industrial Recovery') equipped the president with the power to impose 'codes of fair competition' to be drawn up by representatives of companies in major industries. Besides, it codified protections for the collective bargaining rights of unions and prohibited the so-called 'yellow dog contracts' forbidding workers from joining a union. The proposed addition in section 7(a) promised to equalise bargaining power in such a way that these codes granted employees the right to organise and bargain collectively. Second, title II ('Public Works and Construction Projects') established the Public Works Administration and dedicated $3.3 billion for construction projects of highways, bridges, roads and railways. Finally, under title III ('Amendments to Emergency Relief and Construction Act and Miscellaneous Provisions') new tax revenues were created to cover the Act's administrative costs. It is worth noting that the President's Reemployment Agreement contained incentives for employers to commit to maximum hours per working week and minimum pay scales.[17] In May 1935, key provisions of the Act were declared unconstitutional according to the Supreme Court case law (Schechter v. United States).[18]

2 The founding of the ILO

The Intelligence Department of the Ministry of Labour in Great Britain, in particular its expert on foreign questions, EJ Phelan, realised that the issue of

---

15 Edward E Potter, 'International Labour Standards, the Global Economy and Trade' in Werner Sengenberger and Duncan Campbell (eds), *International Labour Standards and Economic Interdependence: Essays in Commemoration of the 75th Anniversary of the International Labour Organization and the 50th Anniversary of the Declaration of Philadelphia* (Geneva: International Institute for Labour Studies 1994) 363; see also: Laura Phillips Sawyer, *American Fair Trade: Proprietary Capitalism, Corporatism, and the "New Competition,"* *1890–1940* (Cambridge: Cambridge University Press 2018) 245.

16 Potter (n 15) 363.

17 Phillips Sawyer (n 15) 272–274.

18 Mario R DiNunzio, *The Great Depression and New Deal: Documents Decoded* (Santa Barbara, Denver, Oxford: ABC-CLIO 2014) 135.

international labour standards would emerge as soon as the Peace Conference was organised. A Memorandum on character and status of an International Labour Commission (First Phelan Memorandum) of 9 October 1918 included the first analysis of the situation carried out by the department. The document reflected the need to establish an International Labour 'Commission', and that idea was supported by the Home Office and the Ministry of Labour at Cabinet level. It was well understood that once free competition had been rebooted it would be a tough challenge not only to maintain the present minimum standard of wages and working conditions in industries which depend on foreign markets but also to raise the general standard of wages and conditions, unless similar standards were applied in all competing markets. However, if it were possible to ensure that standards in Europe went in line with those in England, there would be nothing to worry about for British workmanship was held to be generally superior.[19]

E Phelan, together with H Butler, G. Barnes and M Delevingne (the subsequent labour section of the British delegation to the Peace Conference) were for the creation of a permanent organisation for international labour legislation. They contended that it should consist of representatives of workers, employers and governments.[20]

The Second Phelan Memorandum assumed that the future International Labour Organisation should consist of two organs, namely a Secretariat (Office) to collect and disseminate information, and an Annual Conference to negotiate international labour legislation. The document paid particular attention to the role of governments in the process of implementation of this legislation. It is worth stressing that Phelan put forward some important proposals. One of them was that the government delegates should have two votes at the Annual Conference and the non-governmental delegates one vote each. In the event that a government failed to send one of the non-governmental delegates, the other should have the right to sit but not vote. The second proposal which should be mentioned, argued that any conventions adopted by a two-thirds majority at the Conference had to be brought by governments before their national parliaments for implementation. Moreover, Phelan's idea was also to provide machinery for complaint against improper implementation of conventions. Importantly, however, the issue of imposing economic sanctions was left open. On the one hand, such sanctions, that is, discrimination against the goods produced in a country which had adhered to a convention but were found not to comply with its provisions, seemed logical. However, a question arose whether such discrimination against goods should not be practised also when a state had declined to adhere to a convention. It was realised that such a solution could make all the backward and smaller states to combine with the aim of preventing the conclusion of a convention, so that it might be better not to discriminate against goods produced by a country that had not adhered to a convention. Unfortunately, it should be noted that any executive organ was envisaged in the Second Phelan Memorandum.

19 Alcock (n 2) 18–19.
20 ibid 19.

This shortcoming was made up for in the second draft by H Butler. He created the basis for an executive organ, namely the future Governing Body. The Labour Commission of the Conference was set up on 31 January 1919 and was composed of 15 members, two each from the Big Five (Great Britain, France, the United States, Italy and Japan), and five representatives from the other countries. It was later determined that two of the latter should come from Belgium and one each from Poland, Cuba and Czechoslovakia. During the work of the Commission, the topic of sanctions was further raised by A Fontaine, substitute of the representative of France. He argued that all states should automatically be obliged to apply the economic sanctions recommended unless the Court excused them from doing so. However, E Vandervelde highlighted that such an obligation might make states refrain from joining the ILO and finally the proposal was rejected.[21] However, it should be noted that the Treaty of Versailles in its Article 419, offered the possibility of imposing 'the measures of an economic character', although on different bases (more on this in Chapter 2).

The ILO with its principle of universality and its unique tripartite structure was established by the Treaty of Versailles, which in Part XIII (Article 427) instead of establishing binding rules of international law introduced nine 'methods and principles . . . to be of special and urgent importance':

1 Labour should not be regarded merely as a commodity or article of commerce.
2 The right of association for all lawful purposes by the employed as well as by the employers.
3 The payment to the employed of a wage adequate to maintain a reasonable standard of life as this is understood in their time and country.
4 The adoption of an eight-hour day or a forty-eight-hour week as the standard to be aimed at where it has not already been attained.
5 The adoption of a weekly rest of at least twenty-four hours, which should include Sunday wherever practicable.
6 The abolition of child labour and the imposition of such limitations on the labour of young persons as shall permit the continuation of their education and assure their proper physical development.
7 The principle that men and women should receive equal remuneration for work of equal value.
8 The standard set by law in each country with respect to the conditions of labour should have due regard to the equitable economic treatment of all workers lawfully resident therein.
9 Each State should make provision for a system of inspection in which women should take part, in order to ensure the enforcement of the laws and regulations for the protection of the employed.[22]

21 ibid 21–31.
22 <https://www.ilo.org/wcmsp5/groups/public/---dgreports/---jur/documents/genericdocument/wcms_441862.pdf> accessed 13 February 2021.

It should be also indicated that the concept of class cooperation, which resulted from the work of the Labour Commission, was the key point about tripartism. As Alcock pointed out, the intention was to ensure the collaboration of all, the public authorities, workers and employers, in bringing about the 'prosperity and contentment of all classes in all nations' and the 'social justice' of the Preamble, rather than the triumph of any one class. In this regard, the cause of the revolutionaries was rejected. Vandervelde described it as follows:

> If I dared to express my thoughts in a tangible way, I should say there are two methods of making the revolution we feel is happening throughout the world, the Russian and the British method. It is the British method which has triumphed in the Labour Commission; it is the one I greatly prefer, and it is for that reason that with all my heart I support the conclusions of my friend Mr. Barnes in expressing the hope that they may be accepted by the Conference, and that the working classes, having been one of the decisive factors in winning the war, shall receive their due recompense at the moment in which we are about to make peace.[23]

The linkage between trade and labour was confirmed with the establishment of the ILO in 1919. The ILO's objective was to assure that the development of international trade would not hinder the achievement of progress in the field of labour rights.[24] According to its Constitution: 'the failure of any nation to adopt humane conditions of labour is an obstacle in the way of other nations which desire to improve the conditions in their own countries'. As pointed out by J-M Servais, it is possible to interpret this in reference to two (not necessarily mutually exclusive) things. The first is the risk that companies and countries will use labour costs to gain a competitive edge. The second is the danger of contamination by a 'poor example'. The former interpretation indicates that in the face of fierce international competition, international labour standards act as a 'firewall' against those who seek to earn profits from poor working conditions.[25]

The fact that the ILO had not been endowed with the competence to cope with economic affairs was a great drawback of the Organization and its future functioning. This had not happened, despite the fact that issues listed in the Preamble and 'Labour Charter' raised complicated economic questions which went beyond the mere labour legislation.[26]

---

23 James Shotwell, *Origins of the ILO* (New York: Columbia University Press 1934) I 208–209, quoted from: Alcock (n 2) 36–37.
24 Olivier De Schutter, *Trade in the Service of Sustainable Development: Linking Trade to Labour Rights and Environmental Standards* (Oxford, Portland OR: Hart Publishing 2015) 7.
25 Jean-Michel Servais, *International Labour Law* (4th edn, Alphen aan den Rijn: Kluwer Law International 2014) 24–25.
26 Alcock (n 2) 36.

During the pre-Second World War period, the International Labour Conference adopted 67 conventions and 66 recommendations. These were published jointly in 1939 as the International Labour Code.[27]

3 The post-Second World War era

The linkage between trade and labour was strengthened after World War II. The International Labour Conference used formulations that 'labour is not a commodity', 'poverty anywhere constitutes a danger to prosperity everywhere' and that 'freedom of expression and of association are essential to sustained progress' already in the Declaration of Philadelphia, which was adopted on 10 May 1944, stated the goals of the ILO, and was integrated to its Constitution. In this way, it highlighted the need to ensure that the growth of trade should not be at the expense of workers' rights.[28]

The Havana Charter on the International Trade Organization (ITO), agreed in March 1948, constituted an early attempt to include a comprehensive labour provision into the multilateral trade framework.[29] The ITO, a specialised agency of the United Nations, was seen as an organisation in which countries could gradually agree on how to support international trade in order to ensure that it would contribute to employment and development, and in close cooperation with the United Nations Economic and Social Council. According to its Article 7:

> The Members recognize that measures relating to employment must take fully into account the rights of workers under inter-governmental declarations, conventions and agreements. They recognize that all countries have a common interest in the achievement and maintenance of fair labour standards related to productivity, and thus in the improvement of wages and working conditions as productivity may permit. The Members recognize that unfair labour conditions, particularly in production for export, create difficulties in international trade, and, accordingly, each Member shall take whatever action may be appropriate and feasible to eliminate such conditions within its territory.

On 6 December 1950, President Truman communicated that the US would not ratify the ITO Charter. His decision was connected with the considerable opposition from the US Congress, which was afraid that the ITO would represent an excessive check on the US sovereignty. Meanwhile, the General Agreement on Tariffs and Trade (GATT) entered into force in January 1948. It was

---

27 Bob Hepple, *Labour Laws and Global Trade* (Oxford, Portland OR: Hart Publishing 2005) 31.
28 ibid 8.
29 David Cheong and Franz Christian Ebert, 'Labour Law and Trade Policy: What Implications for Economic and Human Development?' in Shelley Marshall and Colin Fenwick (eds), *Labour Regulation and Development: Socio-Legal Perspectives* (Cheltenham, Northampton: Edward Elgar Publishing 2016) 97.

initially planned to be provisionally applicable with the aim to avoid a sudden suspension of trade flows, but finally it was institutionalised.[30]

The Marrakesh Agreement of 15 April 1994 establishing the WTO reinforced the regime of international trade and constituted a step towards its autonomisation. It was the final phase in a process of gradual liberalisation of international trade that began in 1948, and was conducted through a series of trade negotiations organised formally outside the United Nations system, and without any explicit connection to other areas, for example, labour rights, environmental standards or human rights, that were subject to international cooperation.[31] The WTO Agreement (like the GATT) expressly took into account labour standards concerns only in an exception from the GATT obligations regarding prison labour.[32]

The Singapore Ministerial Declaration adopted at the first WTO Ministerial Conference on 13 December 1996 cut off any attempts to form a clear link between trade and labour rights at the multilateral level. It stated as follows:

> We renew our commitment to the observance of internationally recognized core labour standards. The International Labour Organization (ILO) is the competent body to set and deal with these standards, and we affirm our support for its work in promoting them. We believe that economic growth and development fostered by increased trade and further trade liberalization contribute to the promotion of these standards. We reject the use of labour standards for protectionist purposes, and agree that the comparative advantage of countries, particularly low-wage developing countries, must in no way be put into question. In this regard, we note that the WTO and ILO Secretariats will continue their existing collaboration.

Taking the position, within the WTO, that labour rights should not be seen as being related to trade, was the consequence of the tension between two conflicting views presented by the US and the EU on the one hand, and developing countries on the other hand. In response to the entry into force of the WTO Agreement in 1995, the US and the EU intended to establish a relation between global trade and labour standards, which was opposed by developing countries because of their concerns about a loss of their comparative advantage and concerns that this would constitute a justification for protectionism.[33]

Although it is true that the 1998 ILO Declaration on Fundamental Rights and Principles at Work set out certain fundamental labour standards, it repeated the viewpoint from Singapore on the inappropriateness of labour standards jeopardising comparative trade advantages. Moreover, it contributed to the creation of

---

30 De Schutter (n 24) 8–9.
31 ibid 9–10.
32 Cheong and Ebert (n 29) 98.
33 De Schutter (n 24) 11.

the World Commission on the Social Dimension of Globalization in 2001. The Commission's report of 2004 concentrated on the concept of 'social dimension of globalization' upon which it was much simpler to achieve an agreement in comparison with opting for the trade and labour linkage. Multilateral negotiations on labour standards have been moved away from the WTO and moved a bit closer to the ILO, with the eight ILO core labour conventions more frequently referred to in bilateral and regional trade agreements.[34]

Another important document is the 2008 ILO Declaration on Social Justice for a Fair Globalization. Its principal objective was to provide an effective promotion of the Decent Work Agenda. It has placed expectations on the ILO committed to ensure that other institutions would show support for the agenda.[35] The Declaration on Social Justice for a Fair Globalization, as one of the ILO's officials has pointed out, can be seen as the ILO's authoritative opinion on the relation between trade and labour. According to the document: 'the violation of fundamental principles and rights at work cannot be invoked or otherwise used as a legitimate comparative advantage and that labour standards should not be used for protectionist trade purposes'.[36]

The ILO Centenary Declaration for the Future of Work of 2019,[37] which marked the 100th anniversary of the ILO, also highlights that 'in conditions of globalization, the failure of any country to adopt humane conditions of labour is more than ever an obstacle to progress in all other countries'. It also introduces an assurance that:

> [o]n the basis of its constitutional mandate, the ILO must take an important role in the multilateral system, by reinforcing its cooperation and developing institutional arrangements with other organizations to promote policy coherence in pursuit of its human-centred approach to the future of work, recognizing the strong, complex and crucial links between social, trade, financial, economic and environmental policies.

However, evidence has already been given that the trade system and labour standards would develop separately. References to labour rights are nonetheless included in some trade agreements[38] for a number of rationales, that is, economic, social and human rights. The economic rationale is based on the assumption that labour provisions should be used as instruments against unfair competition. The social rationale mirrors concerns about guaranteeing social protection.

---

34 Pieter Leenknegt, 'EU Trade Policy and International Labour Standards: The View from the ILO' in Roger Blanpain (ed), Jan Wouters, Glenn Rayp, Laura Beke and Axel Marx (guest eds), *Protecting Labour Rights in a Multi-polar Supply Chain and Mobile Global Economy* (Alphen aan den Rijn: Kluwer Law International 2015) 75–76; see the cited literature.
35 De Schutter (n 24) 11.
36 Leenknegt (n 34) 76.
37 Adopted at the 108th International Labour Conference.
38 De Schutter (n 24) 11.

The human rights rationale perceives labour provisions as a measure generally to improve labour standards and to assure respect for human labour rights reflecting values universally accepted by the international community.[39]

4 The free trade versus protectionism debate

The concept of free trade is not a new topic. Already in medieval times, a confederation of commercial cities on or near the North and the Baltic Seas, namely the German Hanseatic League, ensured the merchants of its members, inter alia, freedom of trade.[40]

Adam Smith's contributions to economic thinking provided conceptual underpinnings for a free trade movement in the later XVIII century. His works constituted an answer to a dominant doctrine in XVI to XVIII century known as 'mercantilism' that manifested itself in an extensive state regulation of the economy. In 1776, Smith published his polemic against mercantilists in a book titled 'An Inquiry into the Nature and Causes of the Wealth of Nations (WN)', in which he wrote about the gains of free trade. He argued that 'If a foreign country can supply us with a commodity cheaper than we ourselves can make it, better buy it off with some part of the produce of our own industry, employed in a way in which we have some advantage'.[41] Adam Smith's thoughts on the division of labour whereby the same number of workers is able to produce more, played a crucial role in his theory on international trade. According to the author, the division of labour leads to an increase in the national wealth (economic growth). This means that international trade is advantageous to countries because it is characterised by an extension of the division of labour leading to an increase 'of the exchangeable value of the annual produce of the land and labour of the country, or [to an] increase of the annual revenue of its inhabitants'. Smith's gains from foreign trade consist of 'the increase of . . . enjoyments' and 'the augmentation of . . . industry'. There are 'two distinct benefits' that make international trade advantageous for nations:

> It gives a value to their superfluities, by exchanging them for something else, which may satisfy a part of their wants, and increase their enjoyments. By

---

39 Samantha Velluti, 'The EU's Social Dimension and Its External Trade Relations' in Axel Marx, Jan Wouters, Glenn Rayp, Laura Beke (eds), *Global Governance of Labour Rights: Assessing the Effectiveness of Transnational Public and Private Policy Initiatives* (Cheltenham, Northampton: Edward Elgar Publishing 2015) 43–44.

40 Matthias Herdegen, *Principles of International Economic Law* (Oxford: Oxford University Press 2016) 14.

41 Adam Smith, *An Inquiry into the Nature and Causes of the Wealth of Nations* (Kathryn Sutherlandm ed, Oxford: Oxford University Press 2008) 293, quoted from: Herdegen (n 40) 14. See also: Reinhard Schumacher, *Free Trade and Absolute and Comparative Advantage: A Critical Comparison of Two Major Theories of International Trade* (Potsdam: Welt-Trends 2012) 13.

means of it, the narrowness of the home market does not hinder the division of labour in any particular branch of art or manufacture from being carried to the highest perfection. By opening a more extensive market for whatever part of the produce of their labour may exceed the home consumption, it encourages them to improve its productive powers, and to augment its annual produce to the utmost, and thereby to increase the real revenue and wealth of the society.[42]

Subsequently, David Ricardo's theory of comparative advantage provided further support for the concept of free trade. The complete presentation of this theory was published in Chapter 7 of his book entitled *On the Principles of Political Economy and Taxation* (1817). In order to explain it, the author used an example of England and Portugal producing cloth and wine. To produce the cloth, England requires the labour of 100 men for one year, and to make the wine 120 men for the same time. It follows that England would be interested in importing wine and in purchasing it by the exportation of cloth. On the other hand, to produce the wine, Portugal requires only the labour of 80 men for one year, and to produce the cloth in the same country, requires the labour of 90 men for the same time. Portugal should thus draw the inference that it would be advantageous for her to export wine in exchange for cloth. Ricardo explained that this exchange might even take place, notwithstanding that the commodity imported by Portugal could be produced there with less labour than in England. The author further argued that although Portugal could make the cloth with the labour of 90 men, she would import it from England where it required the labour of 100 men to produce it, because it would be advantageous to her rather to employ her capital in the production of wine, for which she would obtain more cloth from her trading partner, than she could produce by withdrawing a portion of her capital from the cultivation of vines and moving it to the manufacture of cloth.[43]

Baron de Montesquieu was another defender of free international trade. He described his position in his famous words: 'L'effet naturel du commerce est de porter à la paix. Deux nations qui négocient ensemble se rendent réciproquement dépendantes: si l'une a intérêt d'acheter, l'autre a intérêt de vendre; et toutes les unions sont fondées sur des besoins mutuels'.[44] Montesquieu added that 'l'esprit de commerce unit les nations'.[45] According to the interpretation by Howse,

---

42 Smith (n 42), quoted from: Schumacher (n 41) 13–16.
43 David Ricardo, *On the Principles of Political Economy and Taxation* (2nd edn, London: John Murray, Albemarle-Street 1819) 145–146.
44 'The natural effect of commerce is to bring peace. Two nations that negotiate between themselves become reciprocally dependent, if one has an interest in buying and the other in selling. And all unions are based on mutual needs'. Baron de Montesquieu, Charles de Secondat, *Esprit des lois par Montesquieu: Avec les notes de l'auteur et un choix des observations de Dupin, Crevier, Voltaire, Mably, La Harpe, Servan, etc.* (Paris: Firmin Didot frères 1862) 272.
45 ibid.

commerce represents for Montesquieu the idea of human society based on mutual neediness and not on rule or domination. Any closed society (*chaque société particulière*) has the effect of making people forget their timidity or vulnerability and of making them feel forceful. Consequently, they adopt a belligerent attitude toward other closed societies and tend to dominate one another on the inside. On the contrary, commerce entails the dependency on others for meeting one's natural human needs. This dependency does not give this sense that one has the power to take from the other what one wants, but that one must win it freely.[46]

Richard Cobden, a cotton factory owner and an author of many pamphlets in favour of free trade, held the opinion that international free trade would diminish poverty, inequality and social discrepancies. He was a father of the Cobden-Chevalier Treaty signed on 23 January 1860, namely a free trade agreement between Great Britain and France, which preserved the credo of welfare accumulation and mutual benefits flowing from free trade characterising the classical period of economic liberalism.[47] Cobden argued that

> physical gain will be the smallest gain to humanity from the success of this principle. . . . I see in the free trade principle that which shall act on the moral world as the principle of gravitation in the universe, drawing men together, thrusting aside the antagonism of race and creed and language, and uniting us in the bonds of eternal peace . . . we should see, at a far distant period, the governing system of this world revert to something like the municipal system.[48]

It should be highlighted that Cobden has been considered as a father of globalisation by the US magazine *Forbes*.[49]

In parallel, the US, a country with a long tradition of protectionism, relied on tariffs. Initially, they were regarded as an important source of revenue and then (until the Second World War) they were used as a means of protection of domestic industries. Likewise, in the last decade of the nineteenth century, some of the European states, for example, Germany, France, Austria-Hungary and Italy decided to adopt protectionism. The liberal attitude towards international trade was over with the outbreak of the First World War. It was impossible to return to free trade in the interwar period due to protectionist tendencies and the instability of currencies.[50]

---

46 Robert Howse, 'Montesquieu on Commerce, Conquest, War, and Peace' (2006) 31(3) *Brooklyn Journal of International Law* 693, 707–708.
47 Herdegen (n 40) 15.
48 Richard Cobden, *Free Trade with all Nations: A Speech Delivered in Manchester, England, January 15, 1846* (The School of Cooperative Individualism 1846) 6, quoted from: Eric Sheppard, 'Constructing Free Trade: From Manchester Boosterism to Global Management' (2005) 30(2) Transaction of the Institute of British Geographers 151, 158–159.
49 Abel Adekola and Bruno S Sergi, *Global Business Management: A Cross-Cultural Perspective* (Aldershot: Ashgate 2007) 1.
50 Herdegen (n 40) 15.

After the end of the Second World War, the US became a leader, gathering some other liberal democracies and providing a principal contribution to the establishment of liberal regimes.[51] In July 1944, the Conference of Bretton Woods took place and led to the creation of the International Monetary Fund (IMF) and the World Bank. Incidentally, the aforementioned International Trade Organization (ITO) was envisaged to be one of the Bretton Woods institutions. Instead, current global trade rules function under the World Trade Organization, which will be discussed in more detail in Chapter 3.

A formal international system governing monetary and trading relations among independent states was thus established. The Bretton Woods system implied the attainment of sustained rates of domestic growth by raising the productivity of the national workforce of particular countries through participation in a broader division of labour. Besides, the system assumed the gradual removal of trade controls and impediments. All this was meant to achieve a wider goal, that is, the creation of an open multilateral system of international trade based on rules governing its conduct, fixed exchange values, a steady flow of international liquidity and mechanisms aimed at supporting the balance-of-payments adjustment process. Following several decades of considerable increases in world trade, in the late 1960s and 1970s the international monetary and trading system was clearly weakened. This involved misaligned and volatile exchange rates, difficulties in balance-of-payments adjustment, fluctuating commodity prices, accumulating external and internal imbalances, including increasing external debts of developing countries. In 1971, the US decided to put an end to the convertibility of the dollar into gold.[52] Rising tensions in international monetary relations increased even more due to the 1973–1974 oil price shock. However, a new international monetary system capable of fully replacing the old one established in Bretton Woods has never been created. No currency was able to replace the king dollar. The Bretton Woods mechanisms and the long-term lethargy of the Western world engaging into a deep integration agenda and economic liberalisation, have been used by China (and India), whose spectacular successes we are witnessing today.[53] China's admission to the WTO (11 December 2001) contributed much

---

51 José Luis Gil y Gil, 'Labour Standards in EU Mega-Regional Free Trade Agreements: Taking The Transatlantic Trade and Investment Agreement (TTIP) as a Model' in José Luis Gil y Gil (ed), Tayo Fashoyin and Michele Tiraboschi (series eds), *Trade and Labour Standards: New Trends and Challenges* in (ADAPT Labour Studies Series, Newcastle upon Tyne: Cambridge Scholars Publishing 2018) 93–94.

52 Douglas O Walker, 'World Development in Historical Perspective' in Rhona C Free (ed), *21st Century Economics: A Reference Handbook* (vol 1, Los Angeles, London, New Delhi, Singapore, Washington DC: Sage 2010) 457–458.

53 In 1992, the IMF pointed out that: '[s]ince the mid-1980s, there has been a marked shift in the orientation of the trade and industrial policies of most developing countries away from a heavy reliance on direct intervention and inward-looking industrial policies toward less controlled and more export-oriented trade regimes'. This change in policy continued in the 1990s. Quoted from: Helen V Milner and Keiko Kubota, 'Why the Move to Free Trade?

to her plans of becoming the world's first trading nation. It is a great paradox of our time that the rules created by the Americans play in China's favour.

Studying the literature, one gets the impression that many authors create an apotheosis around the Bretton Woods system. For example, according to Rodrik, 'The Bretton Woods regime was a shallow multilateralism that permitted policy makers to focus on domestic social and employment needs while enabling global trade to recover and flourish'. The author further argues that: 'The Bretton Woods compromise was a roaring success: the industrial countries recovered and became prosperous while most developing nations experienced unprecedented levels of economic growth. The world economy flourished as never before'.[54]

Some scholars charge, however, that Bretton Woods imposed a Western-style development plan on the newly independent countries, thus continuing economic colonial policies in the framework of a new institutional structure. Given this context, novel patterns of financial market regulation should be implemented for a return to the Bretton Woods arrangements is not possible. As a matter of example, those patterns could embrace effective measures to eliminate tax haven and the introduction of a global financial transaction tax.[55] Moreover, the curtailment of investor-state dispute settlement mechanisms could be accomplished, following exactly the same pattern as adopted in the United States–Mexico–Canada Agreement (USMCA).

5 Globalisation and social justice

There have been two globalisations in the world, both driven by the free trade policies of the major trading countries: the first ran from roughly the dawn of the Industrial Revolution in the mid-nineteenth century to the outbreak of the First World War,[56] and the second has run since approximately the end of the Second World War. However, a disclaimer should be made that since the era of the Trump administration and its protectionist policies, some deglobalisation processes have been visible and they have been even more intensified due to the COVID-19 pandemic.

Democracy and Trade Policy in the Developing Countries' (2005) 59(1) *International Organization* 107, 107–108.

54 Dani Rodrik, *The Globalization Paradox: Why Global Markets, States, and Democracy Can't Coexist* (Oxford: Oxford University Press 2011) xvi–xvii.

55 Andreas Bieler, Bruno Ciccaglione, John Hilary and Ingemar Lindberg, 'Conclusion: Towards Transnational Solidarity on "Free Trade" Policy?' in Andreas Bieler, Bruno Ciccaglione, John Hilary and Ingemar Lindberg (eds), *Free Trade and Transnational Labour* (London, New York: Routledge 2015) 159.

56 Robert J Flanagan, *Globalization and Labor Conditions: Working Conditions and Worker Rights in a Global Economy* (Oxford: Oxford University Press 2006) 3.

As regards the first wave of globalisation, Huberman tried to show that trade served as a main pathway in the spread of labour standards. The author pointed out that

> in the absence of international governance, decentralized market forces in the early epoch of globalization succeeded in harmonizing the regulatory environment. Without forsaking domestic concerns, countries had an incentive to adopt comparable labor standards to those of trading partners because they wanted to protect market access. But states also came to recognize that improved standards because of their salutary effects on the development of new product lines and export destinations deepened economic integration, enabling further improvements in well-being.[57]

Thus, 'the first great wave of globalization had enduring effects in the development of "social Europe" and "liberal America"'.[58]

The second wave of globalisation has involved new actors, such as the Bretton Woods Institutions, WTO, NGOs, multinational corporations and so forth. In the world of work, this has its consequence in that it provokes tensions between labour rights and international economic institutions. The latter are taking on tasks and responsibilities of governmental character. Placing economic arguments at the forefront may generate conflicts with core labour rights, as defined by the ILO.[59] Social issues are sidelined and the ILO, established to ensure that workers enjoy social justice, has no real tools to enforce compliance with core labour standards.

In other words, globalisation has involved significant growth in world trade, long-term direct foreign investment by multinationals, and cross-border financial flows, including flows of short-term portfolio capital. On the other hand, it has entailed the migration of jobs from developed to developing countries. This means that the global economy, moving at a fast rate, with the flows of capital becoming more and more globalised and mobile has certainly affected labour, which has remained static. As correctly observed by Addo, labour and capital are the two main primary factors of production falling within the labour–trade linkage debate. The author expresses his concern that 'although labour is the most vulnerable in the globalised world, it is capital that is the most protected'.[60]

57 Michael Huberman, *Odd Couple: International Trade and Labor Standards in History* (New Haven, London: Yale University Press 2012) 171.
58 ibid 3.
59 Kaufmann (n 14) 8, 10. Cf Hannah Murphy, 'The World Bank and Core Labour Standards: Between Flexibility and Regulation' (2014) 21(2) *Review of International Political Economy* 399 <https://doi.org/10.1080/09692290.2013.779591> accessed 16 November 2020.
60 Addo (n 4) 40–41.

Concerns about wage inequality, job losses in developed countries and social injustice have become inextricably linked with globalisation.[61]

In particular, these concerns have been formulated by workers and trade unions who have been afraid of a race to the bottom in labour standards. Bercusson and Estlund noted that these groups have become insecure about a globalised variant of the same 'race to the bottom' that induced states on both sides of the Atlantic in the twentieth century 'to assert control over largely unregulated labour markets, to put a floor on "destructive competition", and to foster the development of labour market institutions that could generate more socially acceptable labour and living conditions'. The authors contended that the globalised flow of goods, services and capital has increasingly run circles around the regulatory systems established in the last century. They described the result of this phenomenon as a 'race to the rising bottom'. Indeed, on the one hand, many developing countries have benefited from shifting production to them, but on the other hand, a deep gap in wages and living standards between workers in developing and developed countries exists and this 'rising bottom' does little to ease the latters' fears about 'the downward spiral'.[62]

A further concern, namely the fear of job losses, was glaringly visible when the American Federation of Labor and Congress of Industrial Organisations (AFL-CIO) lodged a complaint with the US Trade Representative in 2004, requesting the imposition of economic sanctions on China. As pointed out by the Federation, during the term of President George W Bush, America's workers lost 2.7 million manufacturing jobs and nearly 900,000 professional service and information sector jobs. Importantly, a significant number of these lost jobs went overseas. The AFL-CIO reminded that Congress introduced Section 301 of the Trade Act of 1974 to authorise the president to impose trade remedies to redress unfair trade practices by other countries, including persistent violations of workers' rights that give producers in violating countries an illegitimate cost advantage. The Federation's petition demonstrated the burden that China's serious abuses of workers' rights imposed on the US's trade relationship, namely that

---

61 See more: Gudrun Biffl and Joe Isaac, 'Globalisation and Core Labour Standards: Compliance Problems with ILO Conventions 87 and 98. Comparing Australia and Other English-Speaking Countries with EU Member States' (2005) 21(3) *The International Journal of Comparative Labour Law and Industrial Relations* 405, 406–408. For more about the specific ways in which globalisation threatens labour see also: Katherine VW Stone, 'Flexibilization, Globalization, and Privatization: Three Challenges to Labour Rights in our Time' in Brian Bercusson and Cynthia Estlund (eds), *Regulating Labour in the Wake of Globalisation: New Challenges, New Institutions* (Oxford and Portland, Oregon: Hart Publishing 2008) 119–121; Anke Hassel, 'Employment Relations, Welfare and Politics' in Carola Frege and John Kelly (eds), *Comparative Employment Relations in the Global Economy* (Abingdon: Routledge 2013) 141–144.

62 Brian Bercusson and Cynthia Estlund, 'Regulating Labour in the Wake of Globalisation: New Challenges, New Institutions' in Brian Bercusson and Cynthia Estlund (eds), *Regulating Labour in the Wake of Globalisation: New Challenges, New Institutions* (Oxford, Portland OR: Hart Publishing 2008) 4.

denials of workers' rights in China artificially depressed wages and export prices and that more than 727,000 jobs were lost in the US. The Bush administration, however, rejected the workers' rights petition in 2004 (and then in 2006). The AFL-CIO commented on this bitterly:

> The administration offered no substantive critique of the petition's arguments but refused to enforce the workers' rights provisions of the law on principle, claiming it would lead to 'economic isolationism.' If the administration will not enforce the workers' rights provisions of our trade law in the case of China, where well-documented and egregious abuses of workers' rights are undeniably putting U.S. workers at an unfair disadvantage, it is unlikely to ever enforce these provisions. . . . The Bush administration's refusal to accept the China workers' rights petition sends a clear message – it would rather render our trade law a dead letter than use it to defend workers' rights and protect American jobs.[63]

Already in the early 2000s, it became clear that pro-globalisation moods were dominant in the poor countries of the South, whereas opponents of globalisation were prevalent in the rich countries of the North. Bhagwati calls this the 'ironic reversal' for the situation was exactly the opposite during the 1950s and 1960s. He meticulously compiled many views of authors arguing at the time against international integration of the rich countries and against trade liberalisation, investments and capital flows. Bhagwati cites, for example, the Chilean sociologist Osvaldo Sunkel, who said that 'integration into the international economy leads to disintegration of the national economy'. In the same vein, the sociologist Fernando Henrique Cardoso is also cited. He is the father of the 'dependencia' thesis, clearly showing how the poor countries would wind up in the international economy with a dependent status.[64] These voices were then not heard.

In the 1980s and 1990s, in the US there was a significant employment shift to low-paying sectors that resulted mainly from deindustrialisation, trade deficits and falling productivity growth in service-sector industries. The 18.1 million jobs created in the period 1979–1989 involved an increase 19.3 million jobs in the service sector and a loss of some 1.2 million manufacturing and mining jobs. It should be added that retail trade and services related to business, health and personnel, that is, the two lowest paying service-sector industries, noted the biggest job growth – 14.2 million. Subsequently, this trend continued in the 1990s and, consequently, almost an equal number of jobs was lost in industries producing goods in the period 1989–1995. Again, new jobs were created in low-wage

---

63 AFL-CIO, *The Bush Record on Shipping Jobs Overseas* (Washington DC 2004) <http://digitalcommons.ilr.cornell.edu/laborunions/13/> accessed 16 November 2020.
64 Jagdish Bhagwati, 'Coping with Anti-Globalization' in Horst Siebert (ed), *Global Governance: An Architecture for the World Economy* (Berlin, Heidelberg: Springer 2003) 26.

sectors.[65] It is worth stressing that virtually all new service-sector jobs created in the 1990s paid on average 20% less than manufacturing jobs.[66]

In a historical context, the advocates and opponents of globalisation and trade liberalisation always emphasised the effects of these phenomena on relative wages. This was connected to concerns that trade with low-wage developing countries will depress wages in industrialised countries.[67]

One of the best-known theories in this regard is the Heckscher-Ohlin economic theory, dating back to 1933. It assumes that free trade would trigger a convergence in labour conditions across the world. The reason for this is that countries would tend to specialise in the production of commodities requiring inputs that were abundant and cheap in the country. This would provide a comparative advantage in international markets over countries in which that input was in short supply and thus expensive. Similarly, countries with relatively abundant unskilled labour would specialise in unskilled labour intensive products, and so forth. Consequently, free trade increases the price of a country's abundant inputs and lowers the price of inputs in short supply. Thus, trade brings about an international convergence in factor prices. Let us imagine the situation in which there are two countries, A and B. Country A is endowed with an abundance of land, but has few workers. On the other hand, country B has many workers, but not much land. What would happen with no trade? Naturally, labour would generate high wages and low land rents in country A while it would cause low wages and high land rents in country B. By contrast, with international trade, countries will import goods made by their scarce input and will export goods made by their abundant factor. Country A will import from country B products requiring much labour and will export to country B land-intensive products. Wage rates will rise more rapidly in country B than in country A whereas land rents will rise more rapidly in country A than in country B. Therefore, a convergence of labour conditions will appear. The analogous reasoning explains how international migration leads to a convergence of working conditions.[68]

In contrast, according to the competing Stolper-Samuelson economic theory, any interference with trade that drives up the local import price must benefit the productive factor used intensively in producing the import-competing goods. This theory expected labour, the scarce factor of production, to be less scarce

65 Lawrence Mishel, Jared Bernstein and John Schmitt, *The State of Working America: 1996–97* (Armonk, London: M.E. Sharpe 1997) 184.
66 Sarah Anderson and John Cavanagh, 'In the United States: The Issue Is Jobs' in John Cavanagh and Jerry Mander (eds), *Alternatives to Economic Globalization: A Better World Is Possible* (San Francisco: Berrett-Koehler Publishers 2004) 46.
67 Tim Harcourt, 'Last Line of Resistance or a Golden Opportunity: Australian Trade Union Responses to Globalization' in Chris Rowley and John Benson (eds), *Globalization and Labour in the Asia Pacific Region* (London, Portland OR: Frank Cass 2000) 77.
68 Flanagan (n 56) 6. See also: Robert J Flanagan, 'European Wage Equalization Since the Treaty of Rome' in Lloyd Ulman, Barry Eichengreen and William T Dickens (eds), *Labor and an Integrated Europe* (Washington DC: The Brookings Institution 1993) 170.

in the absence of trade barriers. This provides an explanation why labour would benefit from tariff protection as regards real wages.[69] However, something else has been proven in practice. As reported by Addo, in the 1980s, the US manufacturing companies substituted towards skilled labour notwithstanding its increasing costs. If such an approach is accompanied by technological change contributing to more productive skilled labour, the costs will be reduced. This may indicate that instead of the international trade, a skill-oriented technological change is the main driving force behind changes in the relative wages.[70]

6 The labour-trade linkage debate

The main purpose of labour law is to combat injustices in the world of work. In addition, it can boost labour productivity, mitigate failures in labour markets and facilitate economic production. By contrast, the fundamental objective of trade policy is connected with raising efficiency and income and providing more consumption possibilities. This is because it regulates cross-border flows of goods and services. Moreover, trade creates winners and losers thus deepening inequality. For this reason, it is crucial to realise if there is a mutual complementarity or a mutual conflict between labour law and trade policy in achieving development aims.[71]

In the light of the subsections set out earlier, the coupling of trade and labour standards has been debated for some time, with many supporting the argument that international trade regulation should ensure that the goods traded are not produced in violation of labour standards.[72]

Two influential OECD studies of 1996[73] and 2000[74] have strongly affected the pro-linkage side of the debate. In the 1996 study, the Organisation presented findings according to which 'any fear on the part of developing countries that better core standards would negatively affect either their economic performance or their competitive position in world markets has no economic rationale. On the contrary, it is conceivable that the observance of core standards would strengthen the long-term economic performance of all countries'.[75] The OECD sought to explain that proper implementation of some core labour standards can support economic development, allowing trade to expand. It was argued that better

---

69 Harcourt (n 67) 77.
70 Addo (n 4) 46.
71 Cheong and Ebert (n 29) 83–84; see the cited literature.
72 See: Jordi Agustí-Panareda, Franz Christian Ebert and Desirge LeClercq, 'ILO Labor Standards and Trade Agreements: A Case for Consistency' (2015) 36 *Comparative Labor Law & Policy Journal* 347, 349.
73 OECD, *Trade, Employment and Labour Standards: A Study of Core Workers' Rights and International Trade* (Paris: OECD Publishing 1996) <https://doi.org/10.1787/9789264104884-en> accessed 16 November 2020.
74 OECD, *International Trade and Core Labour Standards* (Paris: OECD Publishing 2000) <https://doi.org/10.1787/9789264188006-en> accessed 16 November 2020.
75 OECD (n 73) 105.

enforcement of anti-discrimination standards might increase economic efficiency by ensuring that the allocation of labour resources moves closer to a free-market mechanism. As regards elimination of forced labour and child labour exploitation, it can likewise contribute to the improvement of allocative efficiency. In addition, exploitation of child labour 'is likely to undermine long-term economic prospects to the extent that it hampers children's education possibilities and degrades their health and welfare'. Referring to the economic effects of freedom of association and the right to collective bargaining, the Organisation showed that they are determined according to a number of factors. These rights cannot only contribute to upgrading production processes but also to raising workers' motivation and productivity. Besides, they can generate new market disturbance if unionised workers succeed in raising their working and pay conditions above market levels. It was further argued that the final effect on economic efficiency depends on the relative importance of these two effects.[76] The findings presented in the 1996 study were as follows: the more successful the trade reform in respect of the degree of trade liberalisation achieved, the greater is the respect of association rights in a given country. On the contrary, the more restrictive the trade regime in a country, the worse is its level of compliance with the ILO respective conventions. This means that one of the most important findings in the 1996 document was in favour of a mutually supportive relationship between improvements in bargaining and association rights and successfully sustained trade reforms. The OECD indicated that this positive, two-sided relationship appeared to be strongest after trade reforms had been in place for several years. Not taking into account countries with insufficient information, it was discovered that in any case the erosion of association rights followed trade reforms. There was also no case where trade liberalisation was impeded due to the promotion of the freedom of association and bargaining rights.[77] The OECD document of 2000 sustained that there was no evidence that countries with low core labour standards enjoyed a better global export performance compared to countries with high standards. However, it was further clarified that the difference between core labour standards and other labour standards was crucial for the purpose of analysing effects on trade performance. Admittedly, core labour standards do not have a negative impact on comparative advantage and may even have a positive effect, but standards such as minimum wages and working time can affect patterns of comparative advantage, for example, negatively affecting trade performance.[78]

---

76 ibid 11–12.

77 ibid 111–112.

78 OECD (n 74) 33. More about the impact of OECD documents: James Salzman and Julio Bacio Terracino, 'Labor Rights, Globalisation and Institutions: The Role and Influence of the Organisation for Economic Cooperation and Development' in Virginia A Leary and Daniel Warner (eds), *Social Issues, Globalisation and International Institutions: Labour Rights and the EU, ILO, OECD and WTO* (Leiden, Boston: Martinus Nijhoff Publishers 2006) 343 et seq.

In fact, supporters of the linkage between labour standards and global trade argue that countries that do not respect the ILO labour standards gain competitive advantage that can result in a 'race to the bottom' phenomenon.[79]

Besides, advocates of the nexus pose questions about the effectiveness of the ILO's enforcement mechanisms. Hence, they take the view that the introduction of economic sanctions and their imposition on countries that do not respect the core labour standards should be received positively since it could exert influence on those countries, making them extend the fundamental rights of workers to their citizens.[80]

Supporters of the trade-labour linkage argue that core labour standards should be considered as basic human rights as reflected in the United Nations Conventions.[81] As pointed out by McDougall, a claim to positive legal necessity is often a starting point for the human rights case for the linkage. The author cites Ernst-Ulrich Petersmann's famous words 'Human rights law requires adjusting international law and international organisations so that they protect human rights more effectively', and further highlights that it might be a claim that the WTO should be forced to obey Article 1(3) of the UN Charter in the light of which one of the purposes of the UN is to achieve international cooperation by 'promoting and encouraging respect for human rights and for fundamental freedoms for all'. Alternatively, 'it might be that states themselves have a legal obligation to "promote and protect" (and hence presumably to incorporate) human rights in their negotiation of trade treaties'.[82]

Last but not least, according to 'the solidarity argument', industrial countries will be perceived as participating actively in the exploitation of workers in developing countries if they do not insist on the adoption of universal minimum labour standards.[83]

On the other hand, anti-linkage proponents not only claim that labour standards and international trade are unrelated and should be kept separate,[84] but they also argue that protectionism and false humanitarianism is hidden

79 International Organisation of Employers, *The Evolving Debate on Trade & Labour Standards* (Geneva: IOE 2006) 2 <www.wto.org/english/forums_e/ngo_e/posp63_ioe_e.pdf> accessed 16 November 2020.
80 Addo (n 4) 21.
81 ibid 19–20.
82 Pascal McDougall, 'Keynes, Sen, and Hayek: Competing Approaches to International Labor Law in the ILO and the WTO, 1994–2008' (2017) 15(1) *Northwestern Journal of Human Rights* 32, 60; see the cited literature.
83 Louis Emmerij, 'Contemporary Challenges for Labour Standards Resulting from Globalization' in Werner Sengenberger and Duncan Campbell (eds), *International Labour Standards and Economic Interdependence: Essays in Commemoration of the 75th Anniversary of the International Labour Organization and the 50th Anniversary of the Declaration of Philadelphia* (Geneva: International Institute for Labour Studies 1994) 323.
84 Addo (n 4) 21.

behind the concept of such a nexus.[85] They point out that trade-labour linkage proponents

> are merely pushing a thinly disguised protectionist agenda and are seeking to deny developing countries the opportunity to realise their competitive and comparative economic and trade advantages and that if restrictions were to be placed on developing countries' ability to export their goods then, sadly, it would be the most vulnerable in society that would pay the heaviest price.[86]

They also add another argument against the linkage that market-based economic policies are adequate tools in order to improve labour practices in developing countries as they 'offer superior policy settings for lifting the pace and breadth of economic development'.[87]

Critics of the trade-labour nexus perceive that linkage as an invasion of sovereignty for it takes away the nation state's autonomy over the production processes within its jurisdiction and dictates universal standards without paying attention to local conditions or preferences.[88] Some linkage opponents even highlight that the solution lies not in trade sanctions but in international agreements on core labour standards, with voluntary compliance.[89]

Trade sanctions that may only worsen the situation of workers in targeted countries constitute an important argument against linkage. Howse and Trebilcock put it as follows:

> Trade restrictions raise the prices of imports, thus imposing a welfare cost at home, while at the same time worsening the labor situation in the target country. Demand for labor services will fall, and plants will downsize or close. Trade sanctions are akin to a tax on employment of low-skilled workers. Using trade remedies to enforce labor standards would worsen the problems at which they are aimed (by forcing workers in targeted countries into informal or illegal activities). Unemployment will rise and, given the absence or weakness of social safety nets (unemployment insurance), can be expected to have a detrimental impact on poverty.[90]

---

85 See, for example: Jagdish Bhagwati, 'Trade Liberalisation and "Fair Trade" Demands: Addressing the Environmental and Labour Standards Issues' (1995) 18(6) *The World Economy* 745, passim.

86 International Organisation of Employers (n 79).

87 ibid.

88 Luke L Arnold, 'Labour and the World Trade Organization: Towards a Reconstruction of the Linkage Discourse' (2005) 10(1) Deakin Law Review 83, 87; see the cited literature.

89 Stephen S Golub, 'International Labor Standards and International Trade' (1997), *International Monetary Fund Working Paper* WP/97/37, passim <www.imf.org/external/pubs/ft/wp/wp9737.pdf> accessed 16 November 2020.

90 Michael J Trebilcock and Robert Howse, *The Regulation of International Trade* (3rd edn, London, New York: Routledge 2005) 451.

Bibliography

Abel Adekola and Bruno S Sergi, *Global Business Management: A Cross-Cultural Perspective* (Aldershot: Ashgate 2007).

AFL-CIO, *The Bush Record on Shipping Jobs Overseas* (Washington DC 2004) <http://digitalcommons.ilr.cornell.edu/laborunions/13/> accessed 16 November 2020.

Andreas Bieler, Bruno Ciccaglione, John Hilary and Ingemar Lindberg, 'Conclusion: Towards Transnational Solidarity on "Free Trade" Policy?' in Andreas Bieler, Bruno Ciccaglione, John Hilary and Ingemar Lindberg (eds), *Free Trade and Transnational Labour* (London, New York: Routledge 2015).

Anke Hassel, 'Employment Relations, Welfare and Politics' in Carola Frege and John Kelly (eds), *Comparative Employment Relations in the Global Economy* (Abingdon: Routledge 2013).

Antony Alcock, *History of the International Labour Organisation* (London, Basingstoke: Palgrave Macmillan 1971).

Arturo Bronstein, *International and Comparative Labour Law: Current Challenges* (Geneva: Palgrave Macmillan, International Labour Office 2009).

Baron Montesquieu, Charles De Secondat, Esprit des lois par Montesquieu: Avec les notes de l'auteur et un choix des observations de Dupin, Crevier, Voltaire, Mably, La Harpe, Servan, etc. (Paris: Firmin Didot frères 1862).

Bob Hepple, *Labour Laws and Global Trade* (Oxford, Portland OR: Hart Publishing 2005).

Bob Reinalda, *Routledge History of International Organizations: From 1815 to the Present Day* (London, New York: Routledge 2009).

Brian Bercusson and Cynthia Estlund, 'Regulating Labour in the Wake of Globalisation: New Challenges, New Institutions' in Brian Bercusson and Cynthia Estlund (eds), *Regulating Labour in the Wake of Globalisation: New Challenges, New Institutions* (Oxford, Portland OR: Hart Publishing 2008).

Christine Kaufmann, *Globalisation and Labour Rights: The Conflict Between Core Labour Rights and International Economic Law* (Oxford, Portland OR: Hart Publishing 2007).

Dani Rodrik, *The Globalization Paradox: Why Global Markets, States, and Democracy Can't Coexist* (Oxford: Oxford University Press 2011).

David Cheong and Franz Christian Ebert, 'Labour Law and Trade Policy: What Implications for Economic and Human Development?' in Shelley Marshall and Colin Fenwick (eds), *Labour Regulation and Development: Socio-Legal Perspectives* (Cheltenham, Northampton: Edward Elgar Publishing 2016).

David Ricardo, *On the Principles of Political Economy and Taxation* (2nd edn, London: John Murray, Albemarle-Street 1819).

Douglas O Walker, 'World Development in Historical Perspective' in Rhona C Free (ed), *21st Century Economics: A Reference Handbook* (vol 1, Los Angeles, London, New Delhi, Singapore, Washington DC: Sage 2010).

Edward E Potter, 'International Labour Standards, the Global Economy and Trade' in Werner Sengenberger and Duncan Campbell (eds), *International Labour Standards and Economic Interdependence: Essays in Commemoration of the 75th Anniversary of the International Labour Organization and the 50th Anniversary of the Declaration of Philadelphia* (Geneva: International Institute for Labour Studies 1994).

Eric Sheppard, 'Constructing Free Trade: From Manchester Boosterism to Global Management' (2005) 30(2) *Transaction of the Institute of British Geographers* 151.

Gudrun Biffl and Joe Isaac, 'Globalisation and Core Labour Standards: Compliance Problems with ILO Conventions 87 and 98. Comparing Australia and Other English-Speaking Countries with EU Member States' (2005) 21(3) *The International Journal of Comparative Labour Law and Industrial Relations 405.*

Hannah Murphy, 'The World Bank and Core Labour Standards: Between Flexibility and Regulation' (2014) 21(2) *Review of International Political Economy 399* <https://doi.org/10.1080/09692290.2013.779591> accessed 16 November 2020.

Helen V Milner and Keiko Kubota, 'Why the Move to Free Trade? Democracy and Trade Policy in the Developing Countries' (2005) 59(1) *International Organization 107.*

International Organisation of Employers, *The Evolving Debate on Trade & Labour Standards* (Geneva: IOE 2006) <www.wto.org/english/forums_e/ngo_e/posp63_ioe_e.pdf> accessed 16 November 2020.

Jagdish Bhagwati, 'Trade Liberalisation and "Fair Trade" Demands: Addressing the Environmental and Labour Standards Issues' (1995) 18(6) *The World Economy* 745.

Jagdish Bhagwati, 'Coping with Anti-Globalization' in Horst Siebert (ed), *Global Governance: An Architecture for the World Economy* (Berlin, Heidelberg: Springer 2003).

James Salzman and Julio Bacio Terracino, 'Labor Rights, Globalization and Institutions: The Role and Influence of the Organisation for Economic Cooperation and Development' in Virginia A Leary and Daniel Warner (eds), *Social Issues, Globalisation and International Institutions: Labour Rights and the EU, ILO, OECD and WTO* (Leiden, Boston: Martinus Nijhoff Publishers 2006).

Jean-Michel Servais, *International Labour Law* (4th edn, Alphen aan den Rijn: Kluwer Law International 2014).

Jordi Agustí-Panareda, Franz Christian Ebert and Desirge LeClercq, 'ILO Labor Standards and Trade Agreements: A Case for Consistency' (2015) 36 *Comparative Labor Law & Policy Journal* 347.

José Luis Gil y Gil, 'Labour Standards in EU Mega-Regional Free Trade Agreements: Taking the Transatlantic Trade and Investment Agreement (TTIP) as a Model' in José Luis Gil y Gil (ed), Tayo Fashoyin and Michele Tiraboschi (series eds), *Trade and Labour Standards: New Trends and Challenges* (ADAPT Labour Studies Series, Newcastle upon Tyne: Cambridge Scholars Publishing 2018).

Katherine VW Stone, 'Flexibilization, Globalization, and Privatization: Three Challenges to Labour Rights in our Time' in Brian Bercusson and Cynthia Estlund (eds), *Regulating Labour in the Wake of Globalisation: New Challenges, New Institutions* (Oxford, Portland OR: Hart Publishing 2008).

Kofi Addo, *Core Labour Standards and International Trade: Lessons from the Regional Context* (Heidelberg, New York, Dordrecht, London: Springer 2015).

Laura Phillips Sawyer, *American Fair Trade: Proprietary Capitalism, Corporatism, and the 'New Competition,' 1890–1940* (Cambridge: Cambridge University Press 2018).

Lawrence Mishel, Jared Bernstein and John Schmitt, *The State of Working America: 1996–97* (Armonk, London: M.E. Sharpe 1997).

Louis Emmerij, 'Contemporary Challenges for Labour Standards Resulting from Globalization' in Werner Sengenberger and Duncan Campbell (eds), *International Labour Standards and Economic Interdependence: Essays in Commemoration of the 75th Anniversary of the International Labour Organization and the 50th Anniversary of the Declaration of Philadelphia* (Geneva: International Institute for Labour Studies 1994).

Luke L Arnold, 'Labour and the World Trade Organization: Towards a Reconstruction of the Linkage Discourse' (2005) 10(1) *Deakin Law Review* 83.

Mario R DiNunzio, *The Great Depression and New Deal: Documents Decoded* (Santa Barbara, Denver, Oxford: ABC-CLIO 2014).

Matthias Herdegen, *Principles of International Economic Law* (Oxford: Oxford University Press 2016).

Michael Huberman, *Odd Couple: International Trade and Labor Standards in History* (New Haven, London: Yale University Press 2012).

Michael J Trebilcock and Robert Howse, *The Regulation of International Trade* (3rd edn, London, New York: Routledge 2005).

Nicolas Valticos, *Droit international du travail* (Paris: Dalloz 1983).

OECD, *Trade, Employment and Labour Standards: A Study of Core Workers' Rights and International Trade* (Paris: OECD Publishing 1996) <https://doi.org/10.1787/9789264104884-en> accessed 16 November 2020.

OECD, *International Trade and Core Labour Standards* (Paris: OECD Publishing 2000) <https://doi.org/10.1787/9789264188006-en> accessed 16 November 2020.

Olivier De Schutter, *Trade in the Service of Sustainable Development: Linking Trade to Labour Rights and Environmental Standards* (Oxford, Portland OR: Hart Publishing 2015).

Pascal McDougall, 'Keynes, Sen, and Hayek: Competing Approaches to International Labor Law in the ILO and the WTO, 1994–2008' (2017) 15(1) *Northwestern Journal of Human Rights* 32.

Pieter Leenknegt, 'EU Trade Policy and International Labour Standards: The View from the ILO' in Roger Blanpain (ed), Jan Wouters, Glenn Rayp, Laura Beke and Axel Marx (guest eds), *Protecting Labour Rights in a Multi-Polar Supply Chain and Mobile Global Economy* (Alphen aan den Rijn: Kluwer Law International 2015).

Reinhard Schumacher, *Free Trade and Absolute and Comparative Advantage: A Critical Comparison of Two Major Theories of International Trade* (Potsdam: WeltTrends 2012).

Robert E Weir, *Workers in America: A Historical Encyclopedia* (vol 1, Santa Barbara, Denver, Oxford: ABC-CLIO 2013) A-L.

Robert Howse, 'Montesquieu on Commerce, Conquest, War, and Peace' (2006) 31(3) *Brooklyn Journal of International Law* 693.

Robert J Flanagan, 'European Wage Equalization Since the Treaty of Rome' in Lloyd Ulman, Barry Eichengreen and William T Dickens (eds), *Labor and an Integrated Europe* (Washington DC: The Brookings Institution 1993).

Robert J Flanagan, *Globalization and Labor Conditions: Working Conditions and Worker Rights in a Global Economy* (Oxford: Oxford University Press 2006).

Samantha Velluti, 'The EU's Social Dimension and Its External Trade Relations' in Axel Marx, Jan Wouters, Glenn Rayp and Laura Beke (eds), *Global Governance of Labour Rights: Assessing the Effectiveness of Transnational Public and Private Policy Initiatives* (Cheltenham, Northampton: Edward Elgar Publishing 2015).

Sarah Anderson and John Cavanagh, 'In the United States: The Issue is Jobs' in John Cavanagh and Jerry Mander (eds), *Alternatives to Economic Globalization: A Better World Is Possible* (San Francisco: Berrett-Koehler Publishers 2004).

Stephen S Golub, 'International Labor Standards and International Trade' (1997), *International Monetary Fund Working Paper* WP/97/37 <www.imf.org/external/pubs/ft/wp/wp9737.pdf> accessed 16 November 2020.

Tim Harcourt, 'Last Line of Resistance or a Golden Opportunity: Australian Trade Union Responses to Globalization' in Chris Rowley and John Benson (eds), *Globalization and Labour in the Asia Pacific Region* (London, Portland OR: Frank Cass 2000).

Virginia A Leary, 'Workers' Rights and International Trade: The Social Clause (GATT, ILO, NAFTA, U.S. Laws)' in Jagdish N Bhagwati and Robert E Hudec (eds), *Fair Trade and Harmonization: Prerequisites for Free Trade? Volume 2 Legal Analysis* (Cambridge, London: The MIT Press 1996).

William H Meyer, 'Testing Theories of Labor Rights and Development' (2015) 37(2) *Human Rights Quarterly* 414 <https://doi.org/10.1353/hrq.2015.0036> accessed 2 August 2020.

2 The ILO and its effectiveness

1 Introduction

'A daughter of the war'[1] – the ILO – celebrated its 100th anniversary in 2019. It is therefore unavoidable to reflect on the great heritage of ten decades of its existence. This chapter highlights important achievements of the Organization, particularly a system of international labour standards 'aimed at promoting opportunities for women and men to obtain decent and productive work, in conditions of freedom, equity, security and dignity'. The ILO's anniversary is also an opportunity to take stock of the effectiveness of its supervisory machinery and enforcement mechanisms. A multilevel approach on which this book is based requires us to devote considerable attention to the ILO's activity, particularly in the context of the Preamble of the ILO's Constitution, according to which: 'the failure of any nation to adopt humane conditions of labour is an obstacle in the way of other nations which desire to improve the conditions in their own countries'. The wording reflects one of the key drivers that led to the creation of the ILO, that is, the need to protect workers from the adverse effects of international competition.[2]

Apart from the ILO's rich heritage, this chapter will deal with the supervisory procedures of the ILO, namely regular supervision and special procedures. The ILO reporting machinery and the activity of the Committee of Experts on the Application of Conventions and Recommendations and the Conference Committee on the Application of Standards will be discussed and assessed in the framework of the former procedures. On the other hand, research on special procedures will naturally include the procedures relating to representations and complaints concerning non-observance of ratified conventions, and the procedure for

1 Bruno Cabanes, *The Great War and the Origins of Humanitarianism, 1918–1924, Studies in the Social and Cultural History of Modern Warfare* (Cambridge: Cambridge University Press 2014) 79. Quoted from: Daniel Maul, *The International Labour Organization: 100 Years of Global Social Policy* (Berlin, Geneva: De Gruyter Oldenbourg in Association with International Labour Office 2019) 15.
2 Breen Creighton, 'The Future of Labour Law: Is There a Role for International Labour Standards?' in Catherine Barnard, Simon Deakin and Gillian S Morris (eds), *The Future of Labour Law: Liber Amicorum Bob Hepple QC* (Oxford, Portland OR: Hart Publishing 2004) 254.

complaints with respect to freedom of association. Moreover, special attention will be paid to technical cooperation, which is an important aspect of the ILO's work. The chapter evaluates the ILO supervisory machinery and includes some concluding remarks on the ILO's effectiveness. Besides, it draws lessons on what strategy the ILO should adopt in the next century and on how to shape the future direction of global labour governance.

2 The ILO and its heritage

The ILO is the Methuselah of international institutions[3] and its Constitution (Chapter XIII of the Treaty of Versailles) occupies a leading position among the sources of international labour law. This document refers mainly to the functioning of the Organisation itself and its bodies, but also establishes a number of general principles, in some respects perceived as direct sources of law. These principles, for example, freedom of association, equal opportunities and treatment, protection of child labour, were included in the Preamble to the ILO Constitution and in the Declaration concerning the aims and purposes of the International Labour Organization, adopted at Philadelphia on 10 May 1944, the text of which was incorporated into the ILO Constitution in 1946[4] with the intention of strengthening the system of conventions and recommendations.[5] The ILO Constitution creates obligations between the member states of the ILO and between the member states and the Organization itself.[6]

Collectively, the ILO conventions and recommendations form international labour standards, otherwise known as the 'international labour code'.[7] The latter

---

3   Kimberly A Elliott and Richard B Freeman, *Can Labour Standards Improve Under Globalization?* (Washington DC: Peterson Institute for International Economics 2003) 93.

4   Nicolas Valticos, *International Labour Law* (Dordrecht: Springer 1979) 43.

5   Nicolas Valticos, 'The ILO: A Retrospective and Future View' (1996) 135(3–4) *International Labour Review* 473, 476.

6   Neville Rubin, *Code of International Labour Law: Law, Practice and Jurisprudence: Vol. I, Essentials of International Labour Law* (Consultation with Evance Kalula and Bob Hepple, Cambridge: Cambridge University Press 2005) 3.

7   Werner Sengenberger, 'International Labour Standards in a Globalized Economy: The Issues' in Werner Sengenberger and Duncan Campbell (eds), *International Labour Standards and Economic Interdependence: Essays in Commemoration of the 75th Anniversary of the International Labour Organization and the 50th Anniversary of the Declaration of Philadelphia* (Geneva: International Institute for Labour Studies 1994) 3; Adalberto Perulli and Vania Brino, *Manuale di diritto internazionale del lavoro* (Turin: Giappichelli 2015) 29; Alessandra Zanobetti, *Diritto internazionale del lavoro: Norme universali, regionali e dell'Unione europea* (Milan: Giuffrè 2011) 34 et seq.; Nicolas Valticos, 'Fifty Years of Standard-Setting Activities by the International Labour Organisation' (1996) 135(3–4) *International Labour Review* 393, 398; André Raynauld and Jean-Pierre Vidal, *Labour Standards and International Competitiveness: A Comparative Analysis of Developing and Industrialized Countries* (Cheltenham, Northampton: Edward Elgar Publishing 1998) 17; Marilyn J Pittard and Stuart Butterworth, 'The Rich Panoply of Sources of Labor Law: National, Regional and International' in Matthew W Finkin and Guy Mundlak (eds), *Comparative Labor Law* (Cheltenham, Northampton: Edward Elgar Publishing 2015) 49.

term became popular mainly because of a publication issued by the ILO in Montreal in 1941, entitled 'International Labour Code, 1939: A systematic arrangement of the Conventions and Recommendations adopted by the International Labour Conference, 1919–1939'. This work, amended and supplemented, was reissued in Geneva in 1954 (The 'International Labour Code, 1951: A systematic Arrangement of the Conventions and Recommendations adopted by the International Labour Conference, 1919–1951', with appendices embodying other standards of social policy framed by or with the cooperation of the International Labour Organisation, 1919–1951). However, it was not an official codification, but rather a methodological presentation of the subject matter of the conventions and recommendations adopted by the ILO General Conference from 1919 to 1951. Explanatory notes and annexes containing resolutions, protocols and reports supplemented the collection of texts.[8]

The ILO has so far adopted 190 conventions, 206 recommendations and six protocols.[9] While conventions are legally-binding international agreements creating obligations for member states, the recommendations only provide guidance on issues of policy, legislation and practice,[10] and are adopted in 'circumstances where the subject, or aspect of it, dealt with is not considered suitable or appropriate at that time for a Convention' (Article 19.1(b) of the ILO Constitution). Ratified ILO conventions may be directly applied in individual disputes in monistic systems (e.g. in Poland, France, Spain and most Latin American countries), while in dualistic systems they require further implementation into national law (e.g. in Australia, Canada, Scandinavian countries, Great Britain and the United States).[11] Recommendations, on the other hand, do not bind member states and are mainly used to supplement the convention, to suggest in detail how the provisions of the convention can be given effect or to propose higher standards.[12] Due to their nature, recommendations are not subject to ratification. Each of the Members undertakes that it will, within a period of one year and in no case later than 18 months after the closing of the Conference, bring the recommendation before the authority or authorities within whose competence the matter lies for the enactment of legislation or other action. Moreover, it will not only inform the Director-General of the International Labour Office of the measures taken to bring the recommendation before the said competent authority or authorities

---

8 Zanobetti (n 7) 35–36; Martine Humblet and Monique Zarka-Martres, 'ILO Standards Policy' in Jean-Claude Javillier and Alberto Odero (eds), *International Labour Standards: A Global Approach. 75th Anniversary of the Committee of Experts on the Application of Conventions and Recommendations* (Preliminary version, Geneva: International Labour Office 2001) 10.

9 <www.ilo.org/global/standards/introduction-to-international-labour-standards/international-labour-standards-creation/lang–en/index.htm> accessed 17 November 2020.

10 Christine Kaufmann, *Globalisation and Labour Rights: The Conflict Between Core Labour Rights and International Economic Law* (Oxford, PortlandOR: Hart Publishing 2007) 50.

11 Arturo Bronstein, *International and Comparative Labour Law: Current Challenges* (Geneva: Palgrave Macmillan, International Labour Office 2009) 7.

12 Lee Swepston, 'International Labour Law' in Roger Blanpain (ed), *Comparative Labour Law and Industrial Relations in Industrialized Market Economies* (11th edn, Alphen aan den Rijn: Wolters Kluwer 2014) 159.

with particulars of the authority or authorities regarded as competent, and of the action taken by them but also report to the Director-General, at appropriate intervals as requested by the Governing Body, the position of the law and practice in their country in regard to the matters dealt with in the recommendation (Article 19.6 of the ILO Constitution).

The ILO conventions and recommendations have certain characteristics that are classified in the literature into three groups. First, they are adopted within the institutional framework of an international organisation. Therefore, they are not subject to diplomatic negotiations typical for the adoption of international treaties. Interpretation of conventions does not rest with the member states, but with the International Court of Justice (Article 36 of the ILO Constitution). Second, in line with the principle of tripartism, the composition of the state delegations attending the sessions of the General Conference of the ILO – the body solely empowered to vote on the adoption of a convention or recommendation – does not only include government representatives but also employers and workers' representatives. Third, the efforts to give effect to these instruments explain their further characteristics: a two-thirds majority of the present delegates is sufficient for the adoption of a convention or recommendation in a final vote; members undertake to submit convention or recommendation to the competent authorities; members are required to report on the state of their legislation and practice on an issue that is the subject of a convention that has not been ratified; to report on compliance with ratified conventions, and to apply ratified conventions to non-metropolitan territories. Moreover, the withdrawal of a member state from the ILO does not affect the obligations arising from the ratified convention (Article 1 (5) of the ILO Constitution). An important characteristic of the ILO conventions and recommendations is also related to the complex system of supervision over compliance by the member states with international labour standards.[13]

Not all conventions have equal weight.[14] Within the ILO, they have traditionally been divided into three categories: those that protect fundamental human rights; those that require the maintenance of key tools of social policy formation and those that set basic labour standards.[15] The ILO especially emphasises the

---

13 Valticos (n 4) 44–45. Among the characteristics of the international labour code, Keith D Ewing distinguishes: The subject and scope of conventions and recommendations (which have grown very much since 1919); too many instruments, irrelevant to many countries, and flexibility. Keith D Ewing, 'International Regulation: The ILO and Other Agencies' in Carola Frege and John Kelly (eds), *Comparative Employment Relations in the Global Economy* (Oxon: Routledge 2013) 429–430.

14 See also: Raynauld and Vidal (n 7) 19 et seq.; David G Collings, Jonathan Lavelle and Patrick Gunnigle, 'The Role of MNEs' in Michael Barry and Adrian Wilkinson (eds), *Research Handbook of Comparative Employment Relations* (Cheltenham, Northampton: Edward Elgar Publishing 2011) 412.

15 Janice R Bellace, 'Who Defines the Meaning of Human Rights at Work?' in Edoardo Ales and Iacopo Senatori (eds), *The Transnational Dimension of Labour Relations: A New Order in the Making?* (Turin: Giappichelli 2013) 115; Philip Alston, '"Core Labour Standards" and the

need to ratify and implement conventions ensuring fundamental human rights.[16] The core labour conventions include:

1 Freedom of Association and Protection of the Right to Organise Convention, 1948 (No. 87);
2 Right to Organise and Collective Bargaining Convention, 1949 (No. 98);
3 Forced Labour Convention, 1930 (No. 29) (and its 2014 Protocol);
4 Abolition of Forced Labour Convention, 1957 (No. 105);
5 Minimum Age Convention, 1973 (No. 138);
6 Worst Forms of Child Labour Convention, 1999 (No. 182);
7 Equal Remuneration Convention, 1951 (No. 100);
8 Discrimination (Employment and Occupation) Convention, 1958 (No. 111).

Due to their importance from the standpoint of the functioning of the system of international labour standards and from the viewpoint of governance, four ILO conventions have been designated by the governing body as priority (or governance) instruments. These are as follows:

1 Labour Inspection Convention, 1947 (No. 81);
2 Employment Policy Convention, 1964 (No. 122);
3 Labour Inspection (Agriculture) Convention, 1969 (No. 129);
4 Tripartite Consultation (International Labour Standards) Convention, 1976 (No. 144).[17]

The other conventions are referred to as technical. However, this name does not mean that they are less important in relation to the protection of workers. It only proves that the conventions concern a specific professional group or a given phenomenon. The technical conventions include, for example:

1 Violence and Harassment Convention, 2019 (No. 190);
2 Domestic Workers Convention, 2011 (No. 189);
3 Work in Fishing Convention, 2007 (No. 188);
4 Promotional Framework for Occupational Safety and Health Convention, 2006 (No. 187);
5 Maritime Labour Convention, 2006 (MLC, 2006);
6 Maternity Protection Convention, 2000 (No. 183);

Transformation of the International Labour Rights Regime' in Virginia A Leary and Daniel Warner (eds), *Social Issues, Globalisation and International Institutions: Labour Rights and the EU, ILO, OECD and WTO* (Leiden, Boston: Martinus Nijhoff Publishers 2005) 37.

16 See also: Virginia A Leary, 'The Paradox of Workers' Rights as Human Rights' in Lance A Compa and Stephen F Diamond (eds), *Human Rights, Labor Rights, and International Trade* (Philadelphia: University of Pennsylvania Press 1996) 28.

17 <www.ilo.org/global/standards/introduction-to-international-labour-standards/conventions-and-recommendations/lang–en/index.htm> accessed 17 November 2020.

7   Part-Time Work Convention, 1994 (No. 175);
8   Termination of Employment Convention, 1982 (No. 158).[18]

International labour standards have a number of limitations. They are charac-terised by flexibility, which, on the one hand, makes them suitable for widespread use, but on the other hand, allows states to adapt to less demanding standards, which in turn may limit the possibility of influencing practice in the member states.[19] For instance, standards on minimum wages do not require member states to establish a specific minimum wage but to organise a system and the machin-ery to fix minimum wage rates in line with their economic development. Other standards contain 'flexibility clauses' that allow states 'to lay down temporary standards that are lower than those normally prescribed, to exclude certain cat-egories of workers from the application of a Convention, or to apply only certain parts of the instrument'.[20] However, flexibility has its limit. It is not possible to set different standards for individual countries or introduce regional stand-ards.[21] Another limitation is the insufficient pressure on member states to ratify ILO conventions and the lack of a mechanism to oblige them to do so. Even if the state ratifies the convention, there are no tools to enforce its application in national law.[22] The ILO does not have significant enforcement powers[23] or an

18 For the full list see: <www.ilo.org/dyn/normlex/en/f?p=1000:12000;;;:NO:::> accessed 17 November 2020.
19 Pittard and Butterworth (n 7) 49–50. Universalism has been 'narrowed' in the ILO Con-stitution itself, according to which: 'In framing any Convention or Recommendation of general application the Conference shall have due regard to those countries in which climatic conditions, the imperfect development of industrial organization, or other special circum-stances make the industrial conditions substantially different and shall suggest the modifica-tions, if any, which it considers may be required to meet the case of such countries' (Article 19(3)). See: Jill Murray, *Transnational Labour Regulation: The ILO and EC Compared* (The Hague: Kluwer Law International 2001) 39.
20 ILO, *Rules of the Game: A Brief Introduction to International Labour Standards* (3rd revised edn, Geneva: International Labour Office 2014) 19 <www.ilo.org/wcmsp5/groups/public/-ed_norm/-normes/documents/publication/wcms_318141.pdf> accessed 17 November 2020. See more: Antonio Ojeda-Avilés, *Transnational Labour Law* (Alphen aan den Rijn: Wolters Kluwer 2015) 103–104.
21 Kofi Addo, *Core Labour Standards and International Trade: Lessons from the Regional Con-text* (Heidelberg, New York, Dordrecht, London: Springer 2015) 111.
22 Pittard and Butterworth (n 7) 50. On the large gap between the ratification and implemen-tation of the convention, see: Manfred Weiss, 'International Labour Standards: A Complex Public-Private Policy Mix' (2013) 29(1) *The International Journal of Comparative Labour Law and Industrial Relations* 7, 9, 19.
23 See: Richard Locke, Thomas Kochan, Monica Romis and Fei Qin, 'Beyond Corporate Codes of Conduct: Work Organization and Labour Standards at Nike's Suppliers' (2007) 146(1–2) *International Labour Review* 21, 22; Leary (n 16) 40–41; Harry C Katz, Thomas A Kochan and Alexander JS Colvin, *Labor Relations in a Globalizing World* (Ithaca, Lon-don: Cornell University Press 2015) 58; Raynauld and Vidal (n 7) 19; Anne CL Davies, *Perspectives on Labour Law* (Cambridge, New York, Melbourne, Madrid, Capetown, Sin-gapore, São Paulo, New Delhi: Cambridge University Press 2009) 59; Brian A Langille,

enforcement body[24] (this point will be developed in paragraphs that follow). Thus, the literature emphasises that the system of creating and enforcing international labour standards requires 'revitalisation'.[25] Already in 1994, the Director-General of the ILO, Michel Hansenne, aptly communicated to the General Conference of the ILO: 'It is not enough merely to produce standards. For standards must be ratified and applied'.[26]

Raison d'être of the ILO is related to its normative function, but as highlighted by F Maupain, by issuing conventions and making use of the supervisory mechanism, the Organization has yet to implement another two complementary, overlapping functions: magisterial function and regulatory function. The former helps give authoritative, precise significance to purposes which are only generally stated in the Preamble to the ILO Constitution and in the Philadelphia Declaration. The second, on the other hand, aims to overcome the 'prisoner's dilemma' caused by global economic interdependence, which could prevent member states from promoting social progress for fear of losing their competitive advantage[27] (according to the Preamble to the ILO Constitution: 'the failure of any nation to adopt humane conditions of labour is an obstacle in the way of other nations which desire to improve the conditions in their own countries').

Since 1919, the International Labour Conference has also adopted seven declarations. The word 'declaration' is intended to emphasise, in a solemn manner, the importance of the content covered by the document.[28] With the exception of the already mentioned Declaration of Philadelphia (1944), declarations are

---

'Core Labour Rights: The True Story' in Virginia A Leary and Daniel Warner (eds), *Social Issues, Globalisation and International Institutions: Labour Rights and the EU, ILO, OECD and WTO* (Leiden, Boston: Martinus Nijhoff Publishers 2005) 94; Anil Verma, 'Global Labour Standards: Can We Get from Here to There?' (2003) 19(4) *The International Journal of Comparative Labour Law and Industrial Relations* 515, 519; Thomas Payne, 'Retooling the ILO: How a New Enforcement Wing Can Help the ILO Reach Its Goal Through Regional Free Trade Agreements' (2017) 24(2) *Indiana Journal of Global Legal Studies* 597, 608–610; Collings, Lavelle and Gunnigle (n 14) 412.

24 Michael W Toffel, Jodi L Short and Melissa Ouellet, 'Codes in Context: How States, Markets, and Civil Society Shape Adherence to Global Labor Standards' (2015) 9(3) *Regulation & Governance* 205, 207 <https://doi.org/10.1111/rego.12076> accessed 17 November 2020.

25 Creighton (n 2) 253. See also: Murray (n 19) 47.

26 See: Lucio Baccaro and Valentina Mele, 'Pathology of Path Dependency? The ILO and the Challenge of New Governance' (2012) 65(2) *Industrial & Labor Relations Review* 195, 199–200.

27 Francis Maupain, 'ILO Normative Action in Its Second Century: Escaping the Double Bind?' in Adelle Blackett and Anne Trebilcock (eds), *Research Handbook on Transnational Labour Law* (Cheltenham, Northampton: Edward Elgar Publishing 2015) 301; Francis Maupain, *The Future of the International Labour Organization in the Global Economy* (Oxford, Portland OR: Hart Publishing 2013) 6–7.

28 Jean-Michel Servais, *International Labour Law* (4th edn, Alphen aan den Rijn: Kluwer Law International 2014) 80.

promotional in nature and do not constitute legally binding instruments.[29] The other declarations are as follows:

- Declaration concerning the Policy of Apartheid of the Republic of South Africa, adopted in 1964;
- Declaration on Equality of Opportunity and Treatment for Women Workers, adopted in 1975;
- Tripartite Declaration of Principles concerning Multinational Enterprises and Social Policy (MNE Declaration), adopted in 1977;
- ILO Declaration on Fundamental Principles and Rights at Work, adopted in 1998;
- ILO Declaration on Social Justice for a Fair Globalization, adopted in 2008;[30] and
- ILO Centenary Declaration for the Future of Work, adopted in 2019.[31]

The core ILO conventions form the basis of the 1998 Declaration,[32] which unifies the understanding of fundamental human rights enshrined in the ILO Constitution and its standards.[33] The 1998 Declaration provides that

> all Members, even if they have not ratified the Conventions in question, have an obligation arising from the very fact of membership in the Organization to respect, to promote and to realize, in good faith and in accordance with the Constitution, the principles concerning the fundamental rights which are the subject of those Conventions,[34] namely:
>
> (a) freedom of association and the effective recognition of the right to collective bargaining;
> (b) the elimination of all forms of forced or compulsory labour;

---

29 Kaufmann (n 10) 50.
30 See interesting considerations in this respect by Jean-Michel Servais, 'A New Declaration at the ILO: What for?' (2010) 1(2) *European Labour Law Journal* 286, 286–300 <https://doi.org/10.1177/201395251000100210> accessed 17 November 2020.
31 <www.ilo.org/global/about-the-ilo/how-the-ilo-works/departments-and-offices/jur/legal-instruments/WCMS_428589/lang-en/index.htm> accessed 17 November 2020.
32 At the time of the adoption of the Declaration, there were seven conventions, the eighth (Worst Forms of Child Labour Convention) was adopted, as indicated, in 1999.
33 Swepston (n 12) 160.
34 Their special nature is revealed, inter alia, in the fact that they are 'enabling rights' – basic preconditions for other activities for which further guidance is provided in standards and strategic documents. See: Kari Tapiola, 'Global Standards: The Policy of the ILO' in Ulrich Becker, Frans Pennings and Tineke Dijkhoff (eds), *International Standard-Setting and Innovations in Social Security* (Alphen aan den Rijn: Wolters Kluwer 2013) 44; Maupain, ILO (n 27) 306.

(c) the effective abolition of child labour; and

(d) the elimination of discrimination in respect of employment and occupation[35].

In this connection, it should be concluded that since the 1998 Declaration binds the ILO member states,[36] it must be accorded greater importance than instruments of a purely promotional nature.

It would be impossible not to mention other soft law acts, which include the 1999 Decent Work Agenda that was built on four pillars: promoting employment by creating a sustainable institutional and economic environment, strengthening social protection, promoting social dialogue and tripartism, and promoting the fundamental principles and rights at work. These elements are inseparable, consistent and complement each other.[37] In September 2015, during the UN General Assembly, decent work and the four pillars of the Decent Work Agenda were integrated with the new 2030 Agenda for Sustainable Development. Goal 8 of the 2030 Agenda aims at promoting sustained, inclusive and sustainable economic growth, full and productive employment and decent work for all. In addition, the key facets of decent work are inherent in many of the other 16 goals.[38] Among other soft law instruments, one should distinguish the founding act of the World Commission on the Social Dimension of Globalization (2002), which then developed the aforementioned Declaration on Social Justice for a Fair Globalization,[39] the ILO resolutions, such as the resolution of 19 June 2009 enti-

---

35 The literature emphasises that the core standards should be reconstructed. See reflections on adding the right to just and favourable working conditions to this list: Anthony Woodiwiss, 'Globalization and Labour: Putting the ILO in Its Places' in Bryan S Turner and Robert J Holton (eds), *The Routledge International Handbook of Globalization Studies* (2nd edn, London: Routledge 2016) 534 et seq.; Anthony Woodiwiss, *Making Human Rights Work Globally* (London, Sydney, Portland OR: Routledge-Cavendish 2003) 78. Some authors believe that the ILO's designation of the four selected standards as 'core' suggests that other standards, such as minimum wages and occupational health and safety, are not equally fundamental. Accordingly, certain standards, even if not covered by the 1998 Declaration, should also be considered core. See: Katz, Kochan and Colvin (n 23) 58. About the need to update standards on an ongoing basis and to adapt them to the rapidly changing world of work (also in the context of the economic crisis that started in 2008) see: Giuseppe Casale, 'International Labour Standards and EU Labour Law' in Nicola Countouris and Mark Freedland (eds), *Resocialising Europe in a Time of Crisis* (Cambridge: Cambridge University Press 2013) 84.

36 See: Pittard and Butterworth (n 7) 48.

37 For more, see: Weiss (n 22) 11; Raquel Vela Díaz, 'El trabajo decente como prioridad para la OIT y para la Agenda 2030 de desarrollo sostenible: ¿una realidad para el futuro del trabajo?' in Martha E Monsalve Cuéllar (ed), *El futuro del trabajo: Análisis jurídico y socioeconómico* (Cuenca: Alderabán 2017) 378 et seq.

38 <www.ilo.org/global/topics/decent-work/lang–en/index.htm> accessed 18 November 2020.

39 According to this document, 'the violation of fundamental principles and rights at work cannot be invoked or otherwise used as a legitimate comparative advantage and that labour standards should not be used for protectionist trade purposes'.

tled 'Recovering from the crisis: A Global Jobs Pact' (the so-called Global Jobs Pact),[40] and ILO codes of good practice, such as the ILO Code of Good Practice on HIV/AIDS in Employment.[41]

3 The supervisory machinery of the ILO

3.1 Regular machinery of supervision

3.1.1 Examination of periodic reports

When an ILO member ratifies a convention,[42] it is obliged to submit reports according to Article 22 of the ILO Constitution: 'Each of the Members agrees to make an annual report to the International Labour Office on the measures which it has taken to give effect to the provisions of Conventions to which it is a party. These reports shall be made in such form and shall contain such particulars as the Governing Body may request'. Every year, the Office sends on a regular basis to each member state a single request for all the simplified reports which are due that year. Moreover, reports are requested every three years for fundamental[43] or governance[44] conventions, and every six years for the other conventions. It is also possible that reports on the application of a ratified convention may be requested outside of the regular reporting cycle. This may take place in the following cases:

- when the Committee of Experts on the Application of Conventions and Recommendations (CEACR) or the Conference Committee on the Application of Standards so requests (for details on these committees see what follows);

---

40 More see: Perulli and Brino (n 7) 36.

41 Swepston (n 12) 161. More see: Justyna Sobeyko, 'Konwencje i zalecenia Międzynarodowej Organizacji Pracy dotyczące postępowania w miejscu pracy wobec osób żyjących z HIV/AIDS' in Andrzej Kijowski (ed), *HIV/AIDS: Prawa człowieka w miejscu pracy* (Warsaw: UNDP Poland 2003) 56–57.

42 The analysis of the supervisory machinery of the ILO is based mainly on data from the ILO website, i.e.: ILO, *Handbook of Procedures Relating to International Labour Conventions and Recommendations* (Centenary edn, Geneva: ILO 2019) <www.ilo.org/wcmsp5/groups/public/-ed_norm/-normes/documents/publication/wcms_697949.pdf> accessed 18 November 2020.

43 Fundamental Conventions:

- freedom of association and collective bargaining: Conventions Nos 87 and 98;
- abolition of forced labour: Convention No. 29 and its Protocol, and Convention No. 105;
- equality of opportunity and treatment: Conventions Nos 100 and 111;
- child labour: Conventions Nos 138 and 182.

44 Governance Conventions:

- employment policy: Convention No. 122;
- labour inspection: Convention No. 81 and its Protocol, and Convention No. 129;
- tripartite consultations: Convention No. 144.

- when the Governing Body so requests, following proceedings instituted under articles 24 or 26 of the ILO Constitution or before the Committee on Freedom of Association (for details on this committee see below);
- when a report requested is not submitted or when no reply is provided to comments made by the supervisory bodies.

How does the mechanism of addressing failure to report function? First of all, the respect by member states of their reporting obligations is supervised by the Committee of Experts and the Conference Committee. The latter examines cases of failure to comply with reporting obligations on an annual basis, taking into consideration the information provided in the report of the Committee of Experts, as updated at the time of the Conference. The Conference Committee conducts examination with particular reference to:

- failure to supply reports for the past two years or more on the application of ratified conventions;
- failure to supply first reports on the application of ratified conventions;
- failure to supply information in reply to the comments of the Committee of Experts;
- failure to submit to the competent authorities the instruments adopted by the Conference during at least seven sessions;
- failure to supply reports for the past five years on unratified conventions and recommendations.

In recent years, especially during its 88th (2017) and 89th (2018) sessions, the CEACR has established a new practice of 'urgent appeals' with the aim of enhancing supervision of ratified ILO conventions.[45] This idea applies to a situation in which there are several years of omissions in submitting reports. More specifically, if reports due under Article 22 have not been received for three consecutive years, the Committee of Experts will be issuing urgent appeals to the governments in question. Consequently, repetitions of previous comments will be restricted to a maximum period of three years, after which the Convention's application will be examined in substance by the Committee on the basis of publicly available information, even if the government concerned has failed to send a report, thus ensuring a review of the application of ratified conventions at least once in the framework of the regular reporting cycle. The grave omissions in submitting reports and the urgent appeal will be of interest to the Conference Committee when examining compliance with reporting obligations.

---

45 See also: Committee on the Application of Standards, *Work of the Committee* (Document C.App./D.1 reproduced in Annex 1 of the report of the Conference Committee on the Application of Standards, 107th Session of the International Labour Conference, Geneva, May–June 2018) 5.

In addition to what was discussed earlier, there are some reporting obligations concerning non-ratified conventions. This is apparent from Article 19, paragraph 5(e), of the Constitution, according to which

> if the Member does not obtain the consent of the authority or authorities within whose competence the matter lies, no further obligation shall rest upon the Member except that it shall report to the Director-General of the International Labour Office, at appropriate intervals as requested by the Governing Body, the position of its law and practice in regard to the matters dealt with in the Convention, showing the extent to which effect has been given, or is proposed to be given, to any of the provisions of the Convention by legislation, administrative action, collective agreement or otherwise and stating the difficulties which prevent or delay the ratification of such Convention.

Similarly, it is incumbent on Members to report on recommendations. This is laid down in Article 19 (6d) of the ILO Constitution:

> apart from bringing the Recommendation before the said competent authority or authorities, no further obligation shall rest upon the Members, except that they shall report to the Director-General of the International Labour Office, at appropriate intervals as requested by the Governing Body, the position of the law and practice in their country in regard to the matters dealt with in the Recommendation, showing the extent to which effect has been given, or is proposed to be given, to the provisions of the Recommendation and such modifications of these provisions as it has been found or may be found necessary to make in adopting or applying them.

3.1.2 *The CEACR and the Conference Committee on the Application of Standards*

The CEACR and the Conference Committee on the Application of Standards were designated in the resolution adopted by the Eighth Session of the International Labour Conference in 1926 as being responsible for regular supervision of the observance by member states of their standards-related obligations.

The Committee of Experts consists of 20 independent members from all over the world who are appointed for renewable periods of three years by the Governing Body on the proposal of the Director-General. This body examines

- the annual reports referred to in Article 22 of the ILO Constitution on the measures taken by Members to give effect to the provisions of conventions to which they are parties, and the information provided by Members concerning the results of inspection;

- the information and reports concerning conventions and recommendations communicated by Members in accordance with Article 19 of the ILO Constitution;
- information and reports on the measures taken by Members pursuant to Article 35 of the ILO Constitution.

The final findings of the Committee of Experts take the form of

- a 'general report' that gives a panorama of the Committee's work and draws the attention of the Governing Body, the Conference and member states to matters of general interest or special concern;
- individual 'observations' on: the application of ratified conventions in member states; the compliance with reporting obligations; and the submission of conventions and recommendations to the competent national authorities;
- a series of 'direct requests', namely individual comments directed to governments by the Committee of Experts;
- a series of 'replies received to the issues raised in a direct request which do not give rise to further comments' (when a government has responded to a direct request and there is no need for further comment);
- a 'General Survey' of national law and practice in ILO member states in regard to the instruments on which reports have been supplied on unratified conventions and on recommendations in accordance with Article 19 of the ILO Constitution.

In the first place, the report of the Committee of Experts is submitted to the Governing Body for information and subsequently it is submitted to the Conference, which meets in June.

More specifically, the document goes to the Conference Committee on the Application of Standards, which is a tripartite body consisting of representatives of governments, employers and workers. It is regulated in Article 7 of the Standing Orders of the International Labour Conference. That provision reads as follows:

1 The Conference shall, as soon as possible, appoint a Committee to consider:

    (a) the measures taken by Members to give effect to the provisions of Conventions to which they are parties and the information furnished by Members concerning the results of inspections;

    (b) the information and reports concerning Conventions and Recommendations communicated by Members in accordance with Article 19 of the Constitution, except for information requested under paragraph 5 (e) of that article where the Governing Body has decided upon a different procedure for its consideration;

    (c) the measures taken by Members in accordance with Article 35 of the Constitution.

2 The Committee shall submit a report to the Conference.

The proceedings of the Conference Committee constitute an occasion for representatives of governments, employers and workers to meet and review how states discharge their obligations under and relating to conventions and recommendations. In particular, this is an opportunity for governments not only to extend information previously supplied, but also to indicate further measures proposed, draw attention to difficulties met regarding the fulfilment of obligations, and ask for help in finding the means of overcoming all obstacles and difficulties.

The Committee's role is also, inter alia, to examine cases of serious failure by member states to respect reporting or other standards-related obligations. The discussion of the Committee, including any explanations of difficulties that may have been provided by the governments in question, and the conclusions adopted by the Committee are contained in its report. The Committee's report is submitted to the Conference and discussed in plenary. In order to improve the visibility of the Committee's work, since 2007, the report of the Committee has been published both in the Record of Proceedings of the Conference and as a separate publication.[46] It is worth stressing that since 1968, a procedure of 'direct contacts' has been in force, which consists of personal visits by the ILO's representatives or independent experts to a member state to discuss difficulties in the implementation of the ILO standards and to assist in resolving them. This mechanism has certainly contributed to improvements in national law as well as practice 'in thousands of recorded instances and in many more cases which have not been noted formally'.[47]

3.2 Special procedures

The ILO Constitution includes provisions related to making a representation or a complaint.

3.2.1 Procedure for representation in applying ratified conventions

Article 24 reads:

> In the event of any representation being made to the International Labour Office by an industrial association of employers or of workers that any of the Members has failed to secure in any respect the effective observance within its jurisdiction of any Convention to which it is a party, the Governing Body may communicate this representation to the government against which it is made, and may invite that government to make such statement on the subject as it may think fit.

46 ibid 1.
47 Swepston (n 12) 179.

PACKING LIST

Taylor & Francis Group
an **informa** business

Informa UK Limited, 5 Howick Place, London, SW1P 1WG

Delivery Reference: 7000206294

Deliver to:
Laura Colucci-Gray
13 Hillpark Grove
EDINBURGH
EH4 7AP

Shipped From:
GB - United Kingdom

Document Date: 10.11.2022

A copy of your invoice for this delivery has been sent to the email address provided.

Item	Product	Description	RRP('£')	Edition	Your Reference	Quantity
The following items are from our order number: 2003304931						
00001	9780367630386	Writing STEAM	34,99	PB	TFGR0598564	1
00002	9780415651882	Space and Sense	46,99	PB	TFGR0598564	1

Please send remittances to: ReceiptsRemittances@informa.com. Any payment queries please contact the Credit Control team: TFCreditControl@informa.com or +44 (0) 208 052 2080 PAYMENT METHODS (Please ensure you quote your account number).

For UK customers all claims for shortages and damages must be made within 14 days of date of invoice.
For export customers (non-UK) all claims for shortages and damages must be made within 90 days of date of invoice.
Terms and conditions of supply are available on request. Legal and beneficial title to the goods set out remains with Taylor & Francis Group, a trading name of Informa UK Limited, until payment has been received in full from the Customer for any and all such goods supplied by Hachette UK Distribution Ltd on behalf of Taylor & Francis Group and any other amounts whatsoever due to Taylor & Francis Group.

Supplied by Informa UK Limited 1072954, Registered in England and Wales,Registered Office: 5 Howick Place, London, SW1P 1WG. VAT No:GB365462636 EORI No:GB365462636000

A closer look on the procedure for the examination of representations shows that, first of all, the Office acknowledges receipt of communications submitted pursuant to Article 24 of the ILO Constitution and informs the government in question. Then, the matter is brought before the Officers of the Governing Body, who report to the Governing Body on the receivability of the representation. Taking into consideration the criteria for receivability, the Governing Body makes a decision on the receivability without discussing the substance of the matter. If it is found that the representation is receivable, the Governing Body sets up a tripartite committee with the aim of examining the matter. However, if the matter refers to a convention dealing with trade union rights, the Governing Body may refer it to the Committee on Freedom of Association. In its report, the ad hoc Committee presents conclusions and gives recommendations for decisions to be taken by the Governing Body. According to Article 25 of the ILO Constitution, if no statement is received within a reasonable time from the government concerned, or if the statement when received is not deemed to be satisfactory, the Governing Body decides whether or not to publish the representation and any government statement made in reply to it. Moreover, it notifies the complainant organisation and government in question.

In November 2018, the Governing Body approved a number of measures concerning the operation of the representations procedure under Article 24 of the ILO Constitution.[48] Among other things, these measures include the following:

- arrangements to allow for optional voluntary conciliation or other measures at the national level, leading to a temporary suspension for a maximum period of six months of the examination of the merits of a representation by the ad hoc committee. The suspension would be subject to the agreement of the complainant as expressed in the complaint form, and the agreement of the government. These arrangements would be reviewed by the Governing Body after a two-year trial period; and
- ratification of the conventions concerned as a condition for membership of governments in ad hoc committees unless no government titular or deputy member of the Governing Body has ratified the conventions concerned.

Since 1919, fewer than 200 representations have been submitted, but there has been a noticeable increase in the use of this instrument in recent years.[49] As rightly pointed out by Swepston, on the one hand, this is a reflection of growing difficulties in a number of countries in securing observance of ratified conventions.

48 Governing Body, *Institutional Section* (Document GB.334/INS/PV, 334th Session, Geneva, 25 October–8 November 2018) 65.
49 <www.ilo.org/dyn/normlex/en/f?p=1000:50010:15184436955090::::P50010_DISPLAY_BY:1> accessed 18 November 2020.

On the other hand, the procedure contributes to real improvements in the application of conventions.[50]

3.2.2 Complaints as to the observance of ratified conventions

This special procedure is governed by Articles 26–34 of the ILO Constitution. The key point about the complaints procedure is that it gives a member state the right to file a complaint with the International Labour Office if it is not satisfied that another member state is securing the effective observance of any convention which both have ratified. The Governing Body may or may not communicate the complaint to the government concerned. Then, such a complaint is referred to a Commission of Inquiry, which considers it and reports on it.

There are currently no standing orders for the procedure of Commissions of Inquiry. This means that the Governing Body leaves the matter to the Commission of Inquiry itself, subject only to the Constitution's and its own general guidance. Reports prepared by Commissions of Inquiry tend to be fairly detailed for they describe the procedure adopted for the examination of complaints. This includes the procedure for receiving communications from the parties and other interested persons or organisations, as well as the procedure for holding hearings. It should be highlighted, however, that a document entitled 'The Standards Initiative: Implementing the workplan for strengthening the supervisory system'[51] makes it clear that consideration is being given to the possible codification of the procedure governed by Article 26. For the time being, however, the tripartite informal consultations revealed divergent views regarding the usefulness and urgency of developing such standing orders. Some members expressed the view that in some cases the lack of standing orders resulted in greater flexibility enjoyed by the Governing Body, which could effectively look for alternatives to the establishment of a Commission of Inquiry. Other members took the position that, in other cases, the investigation of such alternatives had been excessively protracted. Besides, it caused uncertainty and lack of transparency for governments in preparing for their participation in the procedure, and consequently, a Commission of Inquiry ultimately did not examine some meritorious cases.

During the existence of the ILO, the Governing Body has appointed a Commission of Inquiry in 34 cases,[52] some of which have achieved high visibility. Those cases include, inter alia:

- the observance of certain international labour Conventions by the Dominican Republic and Haiti with respect to the employment of Haitian workers

---

50 Swepston (n 12) 180.
51 Governing Body (n 48) 2–3.
52 <www.ilo.org/dyn/normlex/en/f?p=1000:50011:27873500108941::::P50011_DIS-PLAY_BY:1> accessed 18 November 2020.

on the sugar plantations of the Dominican Republic (report of the Commission of Inquiry of 1983);

- the observance by Poland of the Freedom of Association and Protection of the Right to Organise Convention (No. 87), and the Right to Organise and Collective Bargaining Convention (No. 98) (report of the Commission of Inquiry of 1984);
- the observance by the Federal Republic of Germany of the Discrimination (Employment and Occupation) Convention (No. 111) (report of the Commission of Inquiry of 1987);
- the observance by Nicaragua of the Freedom of Association and Protection of the Right to Organise Convention (No. 87), the Right to Organise and Collective Bargaining Convention (No. 98), and the Tripartite Consultation (International Labour Standards) Convention (No. 144) (report of the Commission of Inquiry of 1991);
- the observance by Romania of the Discrimination (Employment and Occupation) Convention (No. 111) (report of the Commission of Inquiry of 1991);
- and the recent concerning the observance by the Government of the Bolivarian Republic of Venezuela of the Minimum Wage Fixing Machinery Convention (No. 26), the Freedom of Association and Protection of the Right to Organise Convention (No. 87), and the Tripartite Consultation (International Labour Standards) Convention (No.144) (report of the Commission of Inquiry of 2019).

Two particularly high-profile cases concerned the observance by Myanmar of the Forced Labour Convention (No. 29) (report of the Commission of Inquiry of 1998), and the observance by the Government of the Republic of Belarus of the Freedom of Association and Protection of the Right to Organise Convention (No. 87) and the Right to Organise and Collective Bargaining Convention (No. 98) (report of the Commission of Inquiry of 2004). In the former case, the Commission of Inquiry gathered

> abundant evidence . . . showing the pervasive use of forced labour imposed on the civilian population throughout Myanmar by the authorities and the military for portering, the construction, maintenance and servicing of military camps, other work in support of the military, work on agriculture, logging and other production projects undertaken by the authorities or the military, sometimes for the profit of private individuals, the construction and maintenance of roads, railways and bridges, other infrastructure work and a range of other tasks.

The call-up of labour, provided for in very wide terms under the Village Act and the Towns Act, was found to be incompatible with the Forced Labour Convention (No. 29). The Commission of Inquiry detected that in actual practice, the manifold exactions of forced labour in many cases led not only to the extortion of money in exchange for a temporary alleviation of the burden but also to threats to the life and security and extrajudicial punishment of those unwilling, unable or slow to comply with a demand for forced labour. Such punishment or reprisals ranged from money demands to physical abuse, beatings, torture, rape and even murder.

It is worth noting that the Myanmar case was the first in which Article 33 of the ILO Constitution was used. That provision deals with the Governing Body recommendation as to action by the Conference in the event of failure to carry out recommendations of the Commission of Inquiry or the International Court of Justice (see more information in what follows).

As regards the case of Belarus, a large number of violations prompted the Commission of Inquiry to group its conclusions included in the report under six headings:

- Decree No. 2: Registration of trade unions;
- External interference in trade union affairs;
- Anti-union discrimination, harassment and retaliatory acts;
- Legislation affecting trade unions;
- Social dialogue; and
- General considerations.

3.2.3 Procedure for complaints with respect to freedom of association

In 1950, the ILO established a special supervisory procedure in the field of freedom of association and, in this context, the Committee on Freedom of Association was set up in 1951 as a tripartite organ of the Governing Body. It is composed of nine members of the Governing Body (three representatives each of governments, employers and workers) and nine deputy members sitting in a personal capacity, plus an independent chairperson.[53] The Committee deals with complaints of violations of freedom of association and collective bargaining principles. Such complaints can be investigated irrespective of whether the country in question has ratified any of the Conventions in the field of freedom of association. The Committee's decisions are taken by consensus, its working documents are confidential, and sittings are private. Its conclusions and recommendations are submitted to the Governing Body.

Any complaint comes from organisations of employers or workers or from governments. In view of the special procedures for the examination of complaints alleging infringement of freedom of association, the Committee remains free to decide whether an organisation may be considered to be an employers' or workers' organisation within the meaning of the ILO Constitution. Additionally,

---

53 See more: <www.ilo.org/global/standards/applying-and-promoting-international-labour-standards/committee-on-freedom-of-association/lang–en/index.htm> accessed 18 November 2020.

taking into consideration that the Committee does not feel bound by any national definition of the term, it enjoys complete freedom of decision in relation to the receivability of complaints regarding the applicant.

With a view to the organisation of the Committee's work, it is worthwhile highlighting that it meets three times a year and decides whether to investigate the complaint and reach a conclusion or, alternatively, ask the government in question for additional information. The Committee may ask the Governing Body to draw the attention of the government in question to the Committee's recommendations, which may include requests to take countermeasures and to keep it informed of any developments.

It should be observed that there are three types of reports that the Committee produces. 'Definitive' reports are issued when the Committee becomes convinced that the matters do not require any further investigation. On the other hand, the Committee draws up 'interim' reports in circumstances in which further information is required from the parties to the complaint, and 'follow-up' reports where it asks to be kept informed of developments. Follow-up cases are subsequently 'closed' in cases where the matters have been settled or the Committee decides that they do not require further investigation.

Special machinery in the field of freedom of association encompasses also a second body, that is, the Fact-Finding and Conciliation Commission on Freedom of Association, to which the Committee on Freedom of Association may refer the case. It consists of nine independent members appointed by the Governing Body and examines complaints of violations of freedom of association addressed to it by the Governing Body, including at the request of a government against which allegations are made. As regards the Commission's procedure, it may be compared to that of a Commission of Inquiry.

3.3 Technical cooperation

Apart from the regular system for supervising the application of standards and special procedures mechanisms, the ILO also provides assistance in drafting national legislation and helps countries address problems in legislation and practice in line with international labour standards. As already highlighted, another form of technical assistance includes advisory and direct contact missions involving meetings between ILO officials and government officials to discuss problems in the application of standards and to find solutions to problems encountered in the application of standards. Moreover, technical assistance encompasses promotional activities, such as seminars and national workshops aiming at raising awareness of international labour standards, developing the ability of national actors to use them, and offering technical advice on how to apply them for the benefit of all. It is worth stressing that there is a global network of international labour standards specialists undertaking many of these technical assistance activities. They are assigned to ILO offices situated across the world. International labour standards specialists meet employers' and workers' organisations, as well as government officials in order to provide assistance with problems emerging in the region, new ratifications of conventions and reporting obligations, to discuss possible ways forward for problems highlighted by the ILO supervisory bodies and to review draft legislation with the aim of ensuring that it complies with international labour standards.[54]

From a historical standpoint, already in the 1930s technical assistance missions were sent to different parts of the world to further disseminate international labour standards. Not only did those missions have connection with the geographical expansion of the ILO's work, but they also indicated that a stronger pressure was put on the relationship between economic planning and social legislation in the context of economically backward countries. They included such countries as Greece and Romania in the beginning of the 1930s, China in 1931, Egypt in 1932, Cuba in 1934[55] and – after the first Labour Conference of American States held in Santiago de Chile in 1936 – Venezuela, Brazil and other Latin American countries.[56]

Expansion of the ILO's technical services gained momentum with the Marshall Plan focusing on the increased productivity, and then during the era of David Morse – Director-General of the ILO in the period 1948–1970. For that is when the ILO experienced the enormous growth in membership that resulted from decolonisation. The number of its member states increased from 55 countries in 1948 to 121 in 1970, and almost all the new ones formerly were colonies in Africa and Asia. In the 1960s, the ILO was provided a further spur to expand its technical functions when it turned out that a majority of its member states consisted of developing countries. It should be also noted that the technical assistance missions started to be based largely on the services of external experts and not only the ILO officials just like during the interwar period. Over the period from 1950 to 1965, the ILO sent almost 2,000 experts from 78 nations on 3,000 expert missions to some 100 countries.[57]

Another problem was related to finances. In 1950, the ILO became one of the executive organs of the UN's Expanded Programme of Technical Assistance (EPTA) created in 1949, which was the main source of funding for the majority of Technical Assistance Programmes projects. For almost a decade after that, the ILO was not able to satisfy all needs resulting from the demand for technical assistance. Under the EPTA, the ILO received just over US$25 million between 1950 and 1960, whereas UNESCO was given US$35 million, the WHO US$45 million, and the Food and Agriculture Organization (FAO) US$68 million. Fortunately, in 1958, the opportunity for additional sources of funding appeared with the creation of the UN Special Fund. The situation generally improved with the establishment of the United Nations Development Programme in 1965, which

54 <www.ilo.org/global/standards/applying-and-promoting-international-labour-standards/technical-assistance-and-training/lang–en/index.htm> accessed 18 November 2020.
55 Maul (n 1) 106.
56 Guy Fiti Sinclair, *To Reform the World: International Organizations and the Making of Modern States* (Oxford: Oxford University Press 2017) 89.
57 Maul (n 1) 145, 156, 161.

facilitated fundraising for longer-term development programmes.[58] By compari-son, in 2008, the ILO had funding for technical cooperation projects in the amount of US$302 million, of which US$185 million were deployed to carry out programmes and projects in more than 100 countries.[59]

Technical cooperation underwent further reinvigoration of funding and expenditure at the beginning of the 1990s. This resulted from the establishment of the International Programme for the Elimination of Child Labour in 1992, with financing from the German government.[60] Then, the ILO Declaration on Fundamental Principles and Rights at Work of 1998 was adopted, in which the International Labour Conference recognised the obligation on the Organiza-tion to assist its Members, in response to their established and expressed needs, by offering technical cooperation and advisory services to promote the ratifica-tion and implementation of the fundamental conventions. Plenty of technical cooperation projects have been implemented so far with the aim of addressing identifiable needs in relation to the Declaration and strengthening local capacities thereby translating principles into practice. Some of the examples include:

- From Protocol to Practice: A Bridge to Global Action on Forced Labour – Bridge Project (2015–2020);
- Improving Labour Law Compliance and Building Sound Labour Practices in the Export Oriented Shrimp Sector in Bangladesh – Project (2013–2015);
- Promoting Workers' Rights and Labour Relations in Export Oriented Indus-tries in Bangladesh – Project (2013–2015);
- Eradicating Forced Labour from Global Supply Chains Through Social Dia-logue (2010–2011);
- Promoting Freedom of Association and Social Dialogue in Myanmar – Pro-ject (2013–2015).[61]

4 Concluding remarks

4.1 Evaluation of the ILO's standard setting framework

Criticism is sometimes invoked against the ILO's standard setting framework. As observed by Weiss, there are many outdated conventions that do not match current conditions prevailing in the world of work.[62] However, in 1997, the ILO

---

58 ibid 162.
59 Lars Thomann, *Steps to Compliance with International Labour Standards: The International Labour Organization (ILO) and the Abolition of Forced Labour* (Wiesbaden: Springer 2011) 62.
60 ibid 62.
61 The full list can be found at: <www.ilo.org/declaration/follow-up/tcprojects/lang–en/index.htm> accessed 18 November 2020.
62 Manfred Weiss, 'Re-Inventing Labour Law?' in Guy Davidov and Brian Langille (eds), *The Idea of Labour Law* (Oxford: Oxford University Press 2011) 52.

General Conference adopted an amendment to the ILO Constitution allowing the abrogation of outdated conventions according to 'acte contraire' procedure (the procedure for the abrogation of an outdated convention is the same as the procedure for its conclusion).[63] This amendment added paragraph 9 to Article 19 of the ILO Constitution, according to which:

> acting on a proposal of the Governing Body, the Conference may, by a majority of two-thirds of the votes cast by the delegates present, abrogate any convention adopted in accordance with the provisions of Article 19 of the ILO Constitution if it appears that the convention has lost its purpose or that it no longer makes a useful contribution to attaining the objectives of the Organization.[64]

At its 106th session in June 2017, the International Labour Conference abrogated, for the first time, obsolete international labour conventions: Night Work (Women) Convention, 1919 (No. 4), Minimum Age (Trimmers and Stokers) Convention, 1921 (No. 15), Night Work (Women) Convention (Revised), 1934 (No. 41), Hours of Work and Rest Periods (Road Transport) Convention, 1939 (No. 67).[65] Moreover, two conventions, namely Protection against Accidents (Dockers) Convention, 1929 (No. 28) and Minimum Age (Non-Industrial Employment) Convention (Revised), 1937 (No. 60) were withdrawn, whereby withdrawal procedure must be distinguished from the procedure for abrogation. The latter applies to conventions which are in force whereas the former applies to conventions which have never entered into force or are no longer in force due to denunciations, and to recommendations.[66] It would be fair to say that both procedures and the ILO's clear will to use them contribute to up-to-dateness of labour standards.

It is sometimes raised in the literature that international labour standards are often shaped paying particular attention to the needs of highly industrialised countries, and without taking into account the situation of developing countries.[67] What is, however, certain is that the ILO's concept of fundamental principles and rights at work must be considered its great achievement. There is,

63 Servais (n 28) 46, 54; Swepston (n 12) 159.
64 <www.ilo.org/global/about-the-ilo/how-the-ilo-works/departments-and-offices/jur/legal-instruments/WCMS_442248/lang-en/index.htm> accessed 18 November 2020.
65 Further outdated conventions were abrogated at the 107th session in 2018 <www.oit.org/wcmsp5/groups/public/-ed_norm/-relconf/documents/meetingdocument/wcms_616376.pdf> accessed 18 November 2020.
66 <www.ilo.org/global/about-the-ilo/how-the-ilo-works/departments-and-offices/jur/news/WCMS_563275/lang-en/index.htm> accessed 18 November 2020.
67 Weiss (n 62) 52.

however, still much to be done – in both industrialised and developing countries – today, in the world:

- 40.3 million people are in modern slavery, including 24.9 in forced labour
  and 15.4 million in forced marriage. According to the current figures available, one in four victims of modern slavery are children.
- 152 million children aged 5–17 are victims of child labour; 72 million of
  them are in hazardous work and other worst forms of child labour. Almost
  half of all 152 million children victims of child labour are aged 5–11 years.
- On average, women are paid 23% less than their male counterparts are and in
  many countries are effectively excluded from some occupations. Hundreds
  of millions of people face discrimination in the world of work because of the
  colour of their skin, ethnicity or social origin, religion or political beliefs,
  age, gender, sexual identity or orientation, disability or because of their HIV
  status.
- More than 40% of the world's population lives in countries that have ratified
  neither of the freedom of association and collective bargaining conventions.[68]

It is a shame, really, that not all core ILO conventions forming the basis of the
1998 Declaration have been ratified by all members holding non-elective seats in
the Governing Body. Looking at the composition of the ILO Governing Body,
it must be noted that ten of the titular government seats are permanently held
by states of chief industrial importance, that is, Brazil, China, France, Germany,
India, Italy, Japan, the Russian Federation, the United Kingdom and the United
States.[69] It would seem that these countries should lead by example. Unfortunately, with regard more specifically to the number of ratifications, Brazil has
ratified seven out of eight fundamental conventions, China four, India six, Japan
six, and the United States only two.[70] What is most striking about this is that
the total population of countries with a non-elected seat in the ILO Governing
Body, which have not ratified all eight core labour conventions, accounts for
44.77% of the world population,[71] and their share of the world GDP is 51.04%.[72]
Incidentally, signs of hypocrisy manifest themselves also in many other activities.
For example, on the one hand, China wants to be well received and places great

68 ILO, *Integrated Strategy on Fundamental Principles and Rights at Work 2017–2023* (Geneva:
    International Labour Office 2019) 3.
69 <www.ilo.org/wcmsp5/groups/public/@ed_norm/@relconf/@reloff/documents/meet-
    ingdocument/wcms_083528.pdf> accessed 18 November 2020.
70 <www.ilo.org/dyn/normlex/en/f?p=NORMLEXPUB:10011:::NO:10011:P10011_DIS-
    PLAY_BY,P10011_CONVENTION_TYPE_CODE:1,F> accessed 18 November 2020.
71 <www.worldometers.info/world-population/population-by-country/> accessed 18
    November 2020.
72 <www.worldometers.info/gdp/gdp-by-country/> accessed 18 November 2020.

emphasis on financing many of the ILO's projects,[73] but on the other hand, it organises concentration camps and forced labour for the Uighurs.[74] It is best to be clear about this – of course, there are many other such examples.

Members holding non-elective seats in the Governing Body do not set a good example as regards ratifications, but the problem is broader and does not concern only fundamental conventions. There is generally a great number of countries reluctant to ratify the ILO conventions. Moreover, the ratification itself does not guarantee full compliance with the provisions of a convention. Quite the contrary, it is a long way from ratification to implementation, and – as observed by Weiss – many countries are devoid of the administrative mechanisms for such implementation.[75]

4.2 Evaluation of the ILO's supervisory machinery

It may be argued that although the ILO has generally proved its capacity to define, evaluate, and monitor international labour standards, it lacks tools to enforce compliance with ILO agreements. Procedural compliance, concerned with formal obligations such as reporting, seems to be on the decline. Added to that is the fact that substantive compliance, that is, whether states have fulfilled obligations set out in an international instrument, is also unsatisfactory, especially in terms that ILO appears to be unable to respond to cases of non-compliance.[76]

As explained by Thomann, the procedural dimension of compliance includes the fulfilment of the reporting requirement but does not embrace the ratification of international agreements.[77] As regards the procedural dimension of compliance, based on the most recent data for 2019, a total of 2,007 reports (1,788 reports under Article 22 of the Constitution and 219 reports under Article 35 of the Constitution) were requested from governments on the application of Conventions ratified by member states. According to the report of the Committee of Experts on the Application of Conventions and Recommendations of 2020, the proportion of reports received by 1 September 2019 was low (795 reports corresponding to 39.6% of reports received). After this deadline, 624 more reports were submitted (30.6%). In total, 1,419 reports were received by the office representing 70.7% of the reports requested.[78] This is not an impressive result and

---

73 <www.ilo.org/wcmsp5/groups/public/-dgreports/-exrel/documents/publication/wcms_550919.pdf> accessed 18 November 2020.

74 Jen Kirby, 'Concentration Camps and Forced Labor: China's Repression of the Uighurs, Explained' *Vox Media* (25 September 2020) <www.vox.com/2020/7/28/21333345/uighurs-china-internment-camps-forced-labor-xinjiang> accessed 18 November 2020.

75 See: Weiss (n 62) 52.

76 Thomann (n 59) 179.

77 ibid 26.

78 The Committee of Experts on the Application of Conventions and Recommendations, *Application of International Labour Standards 2020* (Report, ILC.109/III(A), 109th Session of the International Labour Conference, Geneva 2020) 13–14.

the analysis of previous reports[79] leads to the conclusion that there is a general declining trend as regards reporting compliance. For example, in 1957, 95% of the reports requested were received and in 2009 it was only 70.24%.[80]

Similar conclusions can be drawn if one focuses solely on data concerning Article 22 of the Constitution. For example, in 1932, 447 reports were requested, and 423 reports were registered for the session of the Conference (94.6%). With some exceptions, the approximate 90% figure was maintained until the end of the 1950s. Thus, a closer look on data tells us that in 1933, 522 reports were requested, and 453 reports were registered for the session of the Conference (86.7%). In the following years, the figures were, respectively, as follows: in 1934, 601/544/90.5%; in 1935, 630/620/98.4%; in 1936, 662/604/91.2%; in 1937, 702/634/90.3%; and in 1938, 748/635/84.9%. After the war there was some decline by a few percent noticeable between 1945 (725/523/72.2%) and 1952 (981/826/84.2%), but then the percentage in question was oscillating even around 95% (e.g. in 1958, 1,558 reports were requested and 1,509 were registered for the session of the Conference, i.e. 96.8%).[81] The number of submissions generally decreased (below 90%) over the period 1960–1990, but 1964 and 1980 were exceptional years with 1,356 reports registered for the session of the Conference out of 1,495 reports requested (90.7%) in 1964, and 1437 reports registered for the session of the Conference out of 1,581 reports requested (90.8%) in 1980. Subsequently, since 1991, the percentage did not exceed 80%, except for years 1994 and 2013. In 1994, 2,290 reports were requested, and 1,879 reports were registered for the session of the Conference (82.0%) and in 2013, the figures were 2,176/1,755/80.6%, respectively. In the other years, the percentage ranged between a maximum of 78.9% in 2012 and a minimum of 68.06% in 2019. In 2012, 2,207 reports were requested, and 1,742 reports were registered for the session of the Conference and in 2019 the figures were 1,788 and 1,217, respectively.[82] The figures of 2019 are the most telling of all for this is the second time in history that the result dropped below 70% (the first time was in 1944–53.9%).

A noticeable downward trend in the number of submitted reports under Article 22 is said to be related to the constant increase in the number of members and ratifications of ILO Conventions, especially since 1989/1990. Clearly, many member states struggle with administrative problems, which prevent them from fulfilling their reporting obligations. Not astonishingly, some other states just want to avoid being assessed by the CEACR. A lack of political will or indifference overshadow the procedural aspect of compliance.[83]

---

79 <www.ilo.org/public/libdoc/ilo/P/09661/> accessed 18 November 2020.
80 See also: Thomann (n 59) 69.
81 The Committee of Experts on the Application of Conventions and Recommendations (n 78) 637 et seq.
82 ibid.
83 Thomann (n 59) 175, 341.

As pointed out by Thomann, the other aspect of compliance, i.e. substantive compliance, relates to all obligations other than procedural ones, namely to the legislative as well as practical implementation of the treaty's requirements. Cases of substantive non-compliance have most frequently been detected due to the comments on the situation by workers' and employers' organisations. On numerous other occasions, the CEACR strictly adheres to its legal analysis without taking account of the factual situation. The author stressed that the institutionalisation of the CEACR as a body of legal experts contributes to this deficit because of its lack of investigatory capabilities in the sense that the examination is based on written information only.[84]

One can infer from the number of observations the CEACR makes on the application of ratified Conventions that there are many regions in which cases of substantive non-compliance tend to increase. The number of infringements of international labour standards seems to be rising, even if one takes into consideration the increase in members and ratifications. Thomann expressed regret, saying that

> it seems that the supervisory bodies and organs have only in a few cases been able to provide an assessment of the factual situation beyond mere legal analysis. Non-compliance however not only refers to the correct legal application of ratified Conventions, but primarily that they are applied and implemented correctly and fully on the ground'. In his opinion, means which the ILO has at its disposal 'do not always allow that the actual obedience of international labour standards in national, regional or local context is ensured.[85]

On the other hand, some authors consider the ILO supervisory mechanism to be effective. For example, according to Addo, the ILO's supervisory roles are 'more highly developed' than in the case of other international organisations. One reason for such an opinion is related to the expertise and independence of the members of the supervisory bodies. The other reason is one of the ILO's tripartite structure, in which government, trade union and employer representatives work together.[86] However, is this enthusiasm justified? Certainly, the answer would be 'yes' when the respondent assesses the situation from the perspective of an ILO insider. It should be noted, however, that more objective arbitrators display sceptical attitudes towards this tripartite composition. They ask the following question: 'The narrowness of the labor interests represented, often consisting of what is sometimes described as a "labor aristocracy", may limit the ILO's apparent legitimacy. Will the interests of those most likely to be adversely

84 ibid 26, 176–177.
85 ibid 179.
86 Addo (n 21) 93.

affected by globalization (the poor, the unorganized, minority groups, women) have a place at the table?'.[87] Besides, it seems that the principle of tripartism is considerably weakened in cases in which there are no independent trade unions or employers' organisations in a given country or such bodies are not strong enough to defend their interests.

Without trying to settle this difficult issue at this stage, one must admit that there were also many cases regarding ILO member states for which the CEACR has expressed its satisfaction on specific conventions. Based on data since 2009, in a nutshell, satisfaction has been expressed in relation to: 38 countries in 2009, 50 countries in 2010, 40 countries in 2011, 56 countries in 2012, 30 countries in 2013, 25 countries in 2014, 29 countries in 2015, 18 countries in 2016, 26 countries in 2017, 23 countries in 2018, and 15 countries in 2019. Unfortunately, upon looking at these numbers one has the feeling that there is a decreasing number of countries for which satisfaction has been expressed.[88]

As regards the collaboration between the Committee of Experts and the Conference Committee on the Application of Standards (CAS), it appears that it is rather based on mutual complementarity. At the beginning, the CAS discussed all the cases included in the CEACR reports. Nevertheless, from the mid-1950s, a division of labour was progressively established between both bodies and the CAS adopted the principle of selectivity. Thus, the CAS could focus only on cases in which the CEACR had drawn attention to clear discrepancies between the terms of ratified conventions and national law and practice.[89] However, sometimes it is pointed out that 'the selection of cases which reach the ILC tends to be haphazard'.[90]

Hepple argued that the procedures under Articles 22, 24 and 26 overlap to a substantial degree.[91] It should be noted, however, that the CEACR follows up on the effect given by governments to the recommendations made by tripartite committees (Article 24) and Commissions of Inquiry (Article 26). In this context, the governments in question shall indicate in their reports under Article 22 information on the measures taken on the basis of these recommendations. In this way, the information becomes part of the dialogue taking place between

---

87 Christopher McCrudden and Anne Davies, 'A Perspective on Trade and Labor Rights' (2000) 3(1) *Journal of International Economic Law* 43, 61 <https://doi.org/10.1093/jiel/3.1.43> accessed 18 November 2020. See also: Christopher McCrudden and Anne Davies, 'A Perspective on Trade and Labour Rights' in Francesco Francioni (ed), *Environment, Human Rights and International Trade* (Oxford, Portland OR: Hart Publishing 2001) 196–197.

88 ILO, *Monitoring Compliance with International Labour Standards: The Key Role of the ILO Committee of Experts on the Application of Conventions and Recommendations. Appendix III* (Geneva: International Labour Office 2019) 111–121.

89 ibid 30–31.

90 Bob Hepple, *Labour Laws and Global Trade* (Oxford: Hart Publishing 2005) 55.

91 ibid.

the government, the CEACR and the CAS. In a situation where a complaint or representation concerning a given case is made, the CEACR and the CAS may suspend their examination of that case. Once the Governing Body has decided on the outcome, a further CEACR's examination may embrace monitoring the follow-up to the recommendations of the body that examined the complaint or representation. Similarly, the Committee on Freedom of Association's (CFA) procedure involves the examination of measures taken by governments on its recommendations. In the light of the CFA rules of procedure, examination of the legislative aspects of the recommendations adopted by the Governing Body is often referred to the CEACR. The attention of the latter is particularly directed to possible discrepancies between the terms of the convention and national law and practice. In spite of a referral, the CFA does not refrain itself from examining the effect given to its recommendations.[92] All this leads to voices about the need to make the supervisory procedures more transparent[93] for they are relatively complicated.[94]

Still and all, steps taken by the ILO in recent years to strengthen the supervisory system require a positive assessment. This comment refers, among others, to 'The Standards Initiative: Implementing the workplan for strengthening the supervisory system'. Besides, it is only right that a new practice of 'urgent appeals' was established by the CEACR during its 88th and 89th sessions with a view to enhancing supervision of ratified ILO conventions. Similar considerations shall be made in relation to the measures approved by the Governing Body in 2018 and concerning the operation of the representations procedure under Article 24 of the ILO Constitution. Certainly, it is correct to support the adopted direction of change that consists of strengthening the ILO's enforcement machinery and to promote it in the future.

4.3 Evaluation of the ILO's effectiveness

As it was mentioned in Chapter 1, the Treaty of Versailles in its Article 419 (Article 33 of the ILO Constitution before 1946) read as follows:

> In the event of any Member failing to carry out within the time specified the recommendations, if any, contained in the report of the Commission of Enquiry, or in the decision of the Permanent Court of International Justice, as the case may be, any other Member may take against that Member the measures of an economic character indicated in the report of the Commission or in the decision of the Court as appropriate to the case.

92 ILO (n 88) 32.
93 Hepple (n 90) 55.
94 Weiss (n 62) 52.

This provision had never been used and, in 1946, the reference to economic sanctions was deleted. The clause was replaced with the current Article 33,[95] according to which:

> In the event of any Member failing to carry out within the time specified the recommendations, if any, contained in the report of the Commission of Inquiry, or in the decision of the International Court of Justice, as the case may be, the Governing Body may recommend to the Conference such action as it may deem wise and expedient to secure compliance therewith.

The aforementioned Myanmar case, in which Article 33 was invoked, showed poor effectiveness of the ILO mechanism since the Government of Myanmar did not cease to violate the Forced Labour Convention. For this reason, in March 2005, the Governing Body decided that measures imposed under Article 33 'clearly remain in force'.[96] In 2007, the Supplementary Understanding was concluded between the Government of the Union of Myanmar and the ILO. It provided a mechanism for Myanmar citizens to lodge complaints of forced labour through the ILO liaison officer.[97]

In view of this, it is argued that the ILO has, in general, the ability to define, evaluate and monitor international labour rights, but it lacks effective enforcement mechanisms to ensure that these rights are respected in practice.[98] In other words, the ILO has no effective mechanism to impose sanctions against countries that fail to comply with its agreements. It is emphasised that the ILO has never had the requisite jurisdiction to enforce compliance with its agreements and that it lacks an enforcement history.[99] Moreover, the ILO is often alleged to have 'no

---

95 Baatlhodi Molatlhegi, *Trade-Labour Debate: The State of Affairs* (Jaipur: CUTS Centre for International Trade, Economics & Environment 2004) 26.

96 Governing Body, *Developments Concerning the Question of the Observance by the Government of Myanmar of the Forced Labour Convention, 1930 (No. 29)* (GB292-Conclusions-2005-03-0364-1.doc/v2, 292nd Session, Geneva, March 2005) <www.ilo.org/public/english/standards/relm/gb/docs/gb292/pdf/gb-7-conc.pdf> accessed 18 November 2020.

97 <www.ilo.org/wcmsp5/groups/public/-asia/-ro-bangkok/-ilo-yangon/documents/legaldocument/wcms_106131.pdf> accessed 18 November 2020.

98 Joshua M Kagan, 'Making Free Trade Fair: How the WTO Could Incorporate Labor Rights and Why It Should' (2011–2012) 43 *Georgetown Journal of International Law* 195, 201, 223; Brittany Cohan Baclawski, 'Re-Thinking the WTO's Relationship to International Labor Standards: Is It Finally Time for a Global Approach' (2016–2017) 48 *Georgetown Journal of International Law* 235, 243; Tapan R Mohanty, Adil Hasan Khan and Gaurav Kamal, 'Law, Labour, and Legitimacy: The Complexion of WTO' (2004) 29(4) *Vikalpa* 83, 86.

99 Yasmin Moorman, 'Integration of ILO Core Rights Labor Standards into the WTO' (2001) 39 *Columbia Journal of Transnational Law* 555, 569.

teeth'.[100] The most severe critics of the ILO even claim that it is 'an institution that has proven woefully incapable of enforcing labor standards'.[101]

In fact, the instruments currently available to the ILO to achieve member compliance are limited to dialogue, publicity, moral persuasion, diplomacy, technical assistance and naming and shaming.[102] As regards the latter, following an analysis of the Committee of Expert's report, the Conference Committee on Application of Conventions and Recommendations chooses the most flagrant cases of non-compliance and calls governments before it in hearings with the aim of explaining the reasons for non-compliance. Subsequently, the Conference Committee issues a report and a special list of countries which fail to fulfil their obligations. There is also 'the special paragraph' containing the names of countries that have repeatedly failed to comply with ratified Conventions.[103]

However, a fundamental question arises as to whether shaming produces results. Is it not rather the case that the worst violators of labour standards do not feel ashamed of failing to comply with conventions they have ratified? China's example is again a good illustration of this. Maybe the wording of Article 33 of the ILO Constitution in its original version (Article 419 of the Treaty of Versailles) was better than the current one? Maybe such a provision would be defensible under current circumstances? If one finds such a solution questionable, another alternative could be to fully trust the ILO for, as pointed out by Maupain:

> While the organisation's greatest merit is that it already exists, . . . thanks to an ingenious constitutional framework it also has the capacity to reinvent itself from the inside to meet the expectations of its founders and become a more effective social regulator of the global economy.[104]

100 E.g. William A Douglas, John-Paul Ferguson and Erin Klett, 'An Effective Confluence of Forces in Support of Workers' Rights: ILO Standards, US Trade Laws, Unions, and NGOs' (May 2004) 26(2) *Human Rights Quarterly* 273, 276.
101 Baclawski (n 98) 247.
102 S Ehrenberg, 'From Intention to Action: An ILO-GATT/WTO Enforcement Regime for International Labor Rights' in Lance A Compa and Stephen F Diamond (eds), *Human Rights, Labor Rights, and International Trade* (Philadelphia: University of Pennsylvania Press 1996) 164.
103 US Government Printing Office, *U.S. Policy Toward the 1992 United Nations Conference on Environment and Development: Hearings Before the Subcommittee on Human Rights and International Organizations of the Committee on Foreign Affairs, House of Representatives, One Hundred Second Congress, First Session, April 17, July 24, and October 3, 1991* (vol 4, Washington DC: US Government Printing Office 1992) 253; Thomann (n 59) 16.
104 Maupain, *The Future* (n 27) 243.

Bibliography

Adalberto Perulli and Vania Brino, *Manuale di diritto internazionale del lavoro* (Turin: Giappichelli 2015).

Alessandra Zanobetti, *Diritto internazionale del lavoro: Norme universali, regionali e dell'Unione europea* (Milan: Giuffrè 2011).

André Raynauld and Jean-Pierre Vidal, *Labour Standards and International Competitiveness: A Comparative Analysis of Developing and Industrialized Countries* (Cheltenham, Northampton: Edward Elgar Publishing 1998).

Anil Verma, 'Global Labour Standards: Can We Get from Here to There?' (2003) 19(4) *The International Journal of Comparative Labour Law and Industrial Relations* 515.

Anne CL Davies, *Perspectives on Labour Law* (Cambridge, New York, Melbourne, Madrid, Capetown, Singapore, São Paulo, New Delhi: Cambridge University Press 2009).

Anthony Woodiwiss, *Making Human Rights Work Globally* (London, Sydney, Portland OR: Routledge-Cavendish 2003).

Anthony Woodiwiss, 'Globalization and Labour: Putting the ILO in Its Places' in Bryan S Turner and Robert J Holton (eds), *The Routledge International Handbook of Globalization Studies* (2nd edn, London: Routledge 2016).

Antonio Ojeda-Avilés, *Transnational Labour Law* (Alphen aan den Rijn: Wolters Kluwer 2015).

Arturo Bronstein, *International and Comparative Labour Law: Current Challenges* (Geneva: Palgrave Macmillan, International Labour Office 2009).

Baatlhodi Molatlhegi, *Trade-Labour Debate: The State of Affairs* (Jaipur: CUTS Centre for International Trade, Economics & Environment 2004).

Bob Hepple, *Labour Laws and Global Trade* (Oxford: Hart Publishing 2005).

Breen Creighton, 'The Future of Labour Law: Is There a Role for International Labour Standards?' in Catherine Barnard, Simon Deakin and Gillian S Morris (eds), *The Future of Labour Law: Liber Amicorum Bob Hepple QC* (Oxford, Portland OR: Hart Publishing 2004).

Brian A Langille, 'Core Labour Rights – The True Story' in Virginia A Leary and Daniel Warner (eds), *Social Issues, Globalisation and International Institutions: Labour Rights and the EU, ILO, OECD and WTO* (Leiden, Boston: Martinus Nijhoff Publishers 2005).

Brittany Cohan Baclawski, 'Re-Thinking the WTO's Relationship to International Labor Standards: Is It Finally Time for a Global Approach' (2016–2017) 48 *Georgetown Journal of International Law* 235.

Christine Kaufmann, *Globalisation and Labour Rights: The Conflict Between Core Labour Rights and International Economic Law* (Oxford, Portland OR: Hart Publishing 2007).

Christopher McCrudden and Anne Davies, 'A Perspective on Trade and Labour Rights' in Francesco Francioni (ed), *Environment, Human Rights and International Trade* (Oxford, Portland OR: Hart Publishing 2001).

Christopher McCrudden and Anne Davies, 'A Perspective on Trade and Labor Rights' (2000) 3(1) *Journal of International Economic Law* 43 <https://doi.org/10.1093/jiel/3.1.43> accessed 18 November 2020.

Committee of Experts on the Application of Conventions and Recommendations, Application of International Labour Standards 2020 (Report, ILC.109/III(A), 109th Session of the International Labour Conference, Geneva 2020).

Committee on the Application of Standards, Work of the Committee (Document C.App./D.1 Reproduced in Annex 1 of the Report of the Conference Committee on the Application of Standards, 107th Session of the International Labour Conference, Geneva, May–June 2018).

Daniel Maul, *The International Labour Organization: 100 Years of Global Social Policy* (Berlin, Geneva: De Gruyter Oldenbourg in Association with International Labour Office 2019).

Daniel S Ehrenberg, 'From Intention to Action: An ILO-GATT/WTO Enforcement Regime for International Labor Rights' in Lance A Compa and Stephen F Diamond (eds), *Human Rights, Labor Rights, and International Trade* (Philadelphia: University of Pennsylvania Press 1996).

David G Collings, Jonathan Lavelle and Patrick Gunnigle, 'The Role of MNEs' in Michael Barry and Adrian Wilkinson (eds), *Research Handbook of Comparative Employment Relations* (Cheltenham, Northampton: Edward Elgar Publishing 2011).

Francis Maupain, *The Future of the International Labour Organization in the Global Economy* (Oxford, Portland OR: Hart Publishing 2013).

Francis Maupain, 'ILO Normative Action in Its Second Century: Escaping the Double Bind?' in Adelle Blackett and Anne Trebilcock (eds), *Research Handbook on Transnational Labour Law* (Cheltenham, Northampton: Edward Elgar Publishing 2015).

Giuseppe Casale, 'International Labour Standards and EU Labour Law' in Nicola Countouris and Mark Freedland (eds), *Resocialising Europe in a Time of Crisis* (Cambridge: Cambridge University Press 2013).

Governing Body, *Developments Concerning the Question of the Observance by the Government of Myanmar of the Forced Labour Convention, 1930* (No. 29) (GB292-Conclusions-2005-03-0364-1.doc/v2, 292nd Session, Geneva, March 2005) <www.ilo.org/public/english/standards/relm/gb/docs/gb292/pdf/gb-7-conc.pdf> accessed 18 November 2020.

Governing Body, *Institutional Section* (Document GB.334/INS/PV, 334th Session, Geneva, 25 October–8 November 2018).

Guy Fiti Sinclair, *To Reform the World: International Organizations and the Making of Modern States* (Oxford: Oxford University Press 2017).

Harry C Katz, Thomas A Kochan and Alexander JS Colvin, *Labor Relations in a Globalizing World* (Ithaca, London: Cornell University Press 2015).

ILO, *Rules of the Game: A Brief Introduction to International Labour Standards* (3rd revised edn, Geneva: International Labour Office 2014) 19 <www.ilo.org/wcmsp5/groups/public/-ed_norm/-normes/documents/publication/wcms_318141.pdf> accessed 17 November 2020.

ILO, *Handbook of Procedures Relating to International Labour Conventions and Recommendations* (Centenary edn, Geneva: ILO 2019) <www.ilo.org/wcmsp5/groups/public/-ed_norm/-normes/documents/publication/wcms_697949.pdf> accessed 18 November 2020.

ILO, *Integrated Strategy on Fundamental Principles and Rights at Work 2017–2023* (Geneva: International Labour Office 2019).

ILO, *Monitoring Compliance with International Labour Standards: The Key Role of the ILO Committee of Experts on the Application of Conventions and Recommendations* (Appendix III, Geneva: International Labour Office 2019).

Janice R Bellace, 'Who Defines the Meaning of Human Rights at Work?' in Edoardo Ales and Iacopo Senatori (eds), *The Transnational Dimension of Labour Relations: A New Order in the Making?* (Turin: Giappichelli 2013).

Jean-Michel Servais, 'A New Declaration at the ILO: What for?' (2010) 1(2) *European Labour Law Journal* 286 <https://doi.org/10.1177/201395251000100210> accessed 17 November 2020.

Jean-Michel Servais, *International Labour Law* (4th edn, Alphen aan den Rijn: Kluwer Law International 2014).

Jen Kirby, 'Concentration Camps and Forced Labor: China's Repression of the Uighurs, Explained' *Vox Media* (25 September 2020) <www.vox.com/2020/7/28/21333345/uighurs-china-internment-camps-forced-labor-xinjiang> accessed 18 November 2020.

Jill Murray, *Transnational Labour Regulation: The ILO and EC Compared* (The Hague: Kluwer Law International 2001).

Joshua M Kagan, 'Making Free Trade Fair: How the WTO Could Incorporate Labor Rights and Why It Should' (2011–2012) 43 *Georgetown Journal of International Law* 195.

Justyna Sobeyko, 'Konwencje i zalecenia Międzynarodowej Organizacji Pracy dotyczące postępowania w miejscu pracy wobec osób żyjących z HIV/AIDS' in Andrzej Kijowski (ed), *HIV/AIDS: Prawa człowieka w miejscu pracy* (Warsaw: UNDP Poland 2003).

Kari Tapiola, 'Global Standards: The Policy of the ILO' in Ulrich Becker, Frans Pennings and Tineke Dijkhoff (eds), *International Standard-Setting and Innovations in Social Security* (Alphen aan den Rijn: Wolters Kluwer 2013).

Keith D Ewing, 'International Regulation: The ILO and Other Agencies' in Carola Frege and John Kelly (eds), *Comparative Employment Relations in the Global Economy* (Oxon: Routledge 2013).

Kimberly A Elliott and Richard B Freeman, *Can Labour Standards Improve Under Globalization?* (Washington DC: Peterson Institute for International Economics 2003).

Kofi Addo, *Core Labour Standards and International Trade: Lessons from the Regional Context* (Heidelberg, New York, Dordrecht, London: Springer 2015).

Lars Thomann, *Steps to Compliance with International Labour Standards: The International Labour Organization (ILO) and the Abolition of Forced Labour* (Wiesbaden: Springer 2011).

Lee Swepston, 'International Labour Law' in Roger Blanpain (ed), *Comparative Labour Law and Industrial Relations in Industrialized Market Economies* (11th edn, Alphen aan den Rijn: Wolters Kluwer 2014).

Lucio Baccaro and Valentina Mele, 'Pathology of Path Dependency? The ILO and the Challenge of New Governance' (2012) 65(2) *Industrial & Labor Relations Review* 195.

Manfred Weiss, 'Re-Inventing Labour Law?' in Guy Davidov and Brian Langille (eds), *The Idea of Labour Law* (Oxford: Oxford University Press 2011).

Manfred Weiss, 'International Labour Standards: A Complex Public-Private Policy Mix' (2013) 29(1) *The International Journal of Comparative Labour Law and Industrial Relations* 7.

Marilyn J Pittard and Stuart Butterworth, 'The Rich Panoply of Sources of Labor Law: National, Regional and International' in Matthew W Finkin and Guy Mundlak (eds), *Comparative Labor Law* (Cheltenham, Northampton: Edward Elgar Publishing 2015).

Martine Humblet and Monique Zarka-Martres, 'ILO Standards Policy' in Jean-Claude Javillier and Alberto Odero (eds), *International Labour Standards: A Global Approach: 75th Anniversary of the Committee of Experts on the Application of Conventions and Recommendations* (Preliminary version, Geneva: International Labour Office 2001).

Michael W Toffel, Jodi L Short and Melissa Ouellet, 'Codes in Context: How States, Markets, and Civil Society Shape Adherence to Global Labor Standards' (2015) 9(3) *Regulation & Governance* 205 <https://doi.org/10.1111/rego.12076> accessed 17 November 2020.

Neville Rubin, *Code of International Labour Law: Law, Practice and Jurisprudence: Vol I, Essentials of International Labour Law* (Consultation with Evance Kalula and Bob Hepple, Cambridge: Cambridge University Press 2005).

Nicolas Valticos, *International Labour Law* (Dordrecht: Springer 1979).

Nicolas Valticos, 'Fifty Years of Standard-Setting Activities by the International Labour Organisation' (1996) 135(3–4) *International Labour Review* 393.

Nicolas Valticos, 'The ILO: A Retrospective and Future View' (1996) 135(3–4) *International Labour Review* 473.

Philip Alston, ' "Core Labour Standards" and the Transformation of the International Labour Rights Regime' in Virginia A Leary and Daniel Warner (eds), *Social Issues, Globalisation and International Institutions: Labour Rights and the EU, ILO, OECD and WTO* (Leiden, Boston: Martinus Nijhoff Publishers 2005).

Raquel Vela Díaz, 'El trabajo decente como prioridad para la OIT y para la Agenda 2030 de desarrollo sostenible: ¿una realidad para el futuro del trabajo?' in Martha E Monsalve Cuéllar (ed), *El futuro del trabajo: Análisis jurídico y socioeconómico* (Cuenca: Alderabán 2017).

Richard Locke, Thomas Kochan, Monica Romis and Fei Qin, 'Beyond Corporate Codes of Conduct: Work Organization and Labour Standards at Nike's Suppliers' (2007) 146(1–2) *International Labour Review* 21.

Tapan R Mohanty, Adil Hasan Khan and Gaurav Kamal, 'Law, Labour, and Legitimacy: The Complexion of WTO' (2004) 29(4) *Vikalpa* 83.

Thomas Payne, 'Retooling the ILO: How a New Enforcement Wing Can Help the ILO Reach Its Goal Through Regional Free Trade Agreements' (2017) 24(2) *Indiana Journal of Global Legal Studies* 597.

US Government Printing Office, *U.S. Policy Toward the 1992 United Nations Conference on Environment and Development: Hearings Before the Subcommittee on Human Rights and International Organizations of the Committee on Foreign Affairs, House of Representatives, One Hundred Second Congress, First Session, April 17, July 24, and October 3, 1991* (vol 4, Washington DC: US Government Printing Office 1992).

Virginia A Leary, 'The Paradox of Workers' Rights as Human Rights' in Lance A Compa and Stephen F Diamond (eds), *Human Rights, Labor Rights, and International Trade* (Philadelphia: University of Pennsylvania Press 1996).

Werner Sengenberger, 'International Labour Standards in a Globalized Economy: The Issues' in Werner Sengenberger and Duncan Campbell (eds), *International Labour Standards and Economic Interdependence: Essays in Commemoration of the 75th Anniversary of the International Labour Organization and the 50th Anniversary of the Declaration of Philadelphia* (Geneva: International Institute for Labour Studies 1994).

William A Douglas, John-Paul Ferguson and Erin Klett, 'An Effective Confluence of Forces in Support of Workers' Rights: ILO Standards, US Trade Laws, Unions, and NGOs' (May 2004) 26(2) *Human Rights Quarterly* 273.

Yasmin Moorman, 'Integration of ILO Core Rights Labor Standards into the WTO' (2001) 39 *Columbia Journal of Transnational Law* 555.

3 The WTO needs reforms

Is there space for labour rights?

1 Introduction

As demonstrated in Chapter 2, it is unavoidable to pose questions about the effectiveness of the ILO's enforcement mechanisms. Although the ILO is quite successful in defining, evaluating and monitoring international labour standards, it lacks an enforcement history, the necessary jurisdiction to enforce compliance with ILO agreements and binding authority to impose sanctions against countries that fail to comply with its agreements.[1] Many authors draw attention to the potential of the WTO in this regard. There are opinions claiming that the WTO dispute resolution system is 'the jewel in the crown of the WTO',[2] and that thanks to the use of this system, the WTO would have the potential of being successful where the ILO has failed in holding member states responsible for labour violations.[3] However, it is not a secret that currently the WTO is facing a deep crisis. The stalemate in the Dispute Settlement Body (DSB) over the

---

1 Joshua M Kagan, 'Making Free Trade Fair: How the WTO Could Incorporate Labor Rights and Why It Should' (2011–2012) 43 *Georgetown Journal of International Law* 195, 201, 223; Yasmin Moorman, 'Integration of ILO Core Rights Labor Standards into the WTO' (2001) 39 *Columbia Journal of Transnational Law* 555, 569; Brittany Cohan Baclawski, 'Re-Thinking the WTO's Relationship to International Labor Standards: Is It Finally Time for a Global Approach' (2016–2017) 48 *Georgetown Journal of International Law* 235, 243, 247; William H Meyer, 'Testing Theories of Labor Rights and Development' (2015) 37(2) *Human Rights Quarterly* 414, 418 <https://doi.org/10.1353/hrq.2015.0036> accessed 1 December 2020; Tapan R Mohanty, Adil Hasan Khan and Gaurav Kamal, 'Law, Labour, and Legitimacy: The Complexion of WTO' (2004) 29(4) *Vikalpa* 83, 86; Marilyn J Pittard and Stuart Butterworth, 'The Rich Panoply of Sources of Labor Law: National, Regional and International' in Matthew W Finkin and Guy Mundlak (eds), *Comparative Labor Law* (Cheltenham, Northampton: Edward Elgar Publishing 2015) 50; Manfred Weiss, 'International Labour Standards: A Complex Public-Private Policy Mix' (2013) 29(1) *The International Journal of Comparative Labour Law and Industrial Relations* 7, 9, 19; Lars Thomann, *Steps to Compliance with International Labour Standards. The International Labour Organization (ILO) and the Abolition of Forced Labour* (Wiesbaden: Springer 2011) 179.
2 Kagan (n 1) 223; Cohan Baclawski (n 1) 260.
3 Cohan Baclawski (n 1) 260.

appointment of new members of the Appellate Body was just one of its symptoms.[4] As confirmed by G20 leaders at the Buenos Aires summit (30 November – 1 December 2018): 'The system is currently falling short of its objectives and there is room for improvement. We therefore support the necessary reform of the WTO to improve its functioning'.[5] Moreover, according to the G20 Osaka Leaders' Declaration (G20 summit in Japan, 28–29 June 2019): 'We reaffirm our support for the necessary reform of the World Trade Organization (WTO) to improve its functions'.[6]

On 27 March 2020, 'a stop-gap measure', that is, a temporary mechanism to resolve trade disputes, was agreed. Under the mechanism, there are ten arbitrators, three of whom hear any given appeal. The WTO's two-step dispute system is planned to be preserved until the WTO's Appellate Body becomes fully reinstated.[7] Could the forthcoming reforms turn out to be a now-or-never moment for a new emphasis on labour rights? Or maybe just the opposite? One should also take into account that, unfortunately, the international trade crisis is further deepened by the pandemic which has led to disruption of global supply chains. The WTO expects trade to fall by between 13% and 32% in 2020 because of COVID-19.[8] The forthcoming wave of reforms aiming at strengthening the WTO may turn out to be crucial in many ways.

Here comes the question of how could the potential of the WTO be used in order to help the ILO. It is important to note that a fundamental principle of the General Agreement on Tariffs and Trade (GATT) aims at national treatment, that is, non-discrimination between imported and domestic products. Article III of the GATT introduces a requirement that imported products are subject to the same treatment as domestic goods in regard to internal charges and other internal regulations connected to the marketing of products. Thus, we can talk of a gap between international labour standards and the rules of multilateral trading system, which is caused by the ILO principle of 'no sanctions' and the GATT principle of 'non-discrimination'.[9] The WTO and the ILO lack provisions creating a nexus between both organisations. Moreover, there is no other provision

4 Robert McDougall, 'Crisis in the WTO: Restoring the WTO Dispute Settlement Function' (October 2018) *CIGI Papers* No. 194, 1 <www.cigionline.org/publications/crisis-wto-restoring-dispute-settlement-function> accessed 18 November 2020.

5 G20 Leaders' Declaration: Building Consensus for Fair and Sustainable Development <www.consilium.europa.eu/media/37247/buenos_aires_leaders_declaration.pdf> accessed 18 November 2020.

6 <www.consilium.europa.eu/en/meetings/international-summit/2019/06/28-29/> accessed 18 November 2020.

7 Philip Blenkinsop, 'EU, China and 14 Others Agree Stop-Gap Fix for WTO Crisis' *Reuters* (27 March 2020) <www.reuters.com/article/us-trade-wto-idUSKBN21E2I0> accessed 18 November 2020.

8 <www.wto.org/english/news_e/pres20_e/pr855_e.htm> accessed 18 November 2020.

9 Wolfgang Plasa, *Reconciling International Trade and Labor Protection: Why We Need to Bridge the Gap Between ILO Standards and WTO Rules* (Lanham, Boulder, New York, London: Lexington Books 2015) 15.

established within the international law that could bridge this gap. The question is if the interpretation of WTO exceptions can fill it[10] and, if so, how flexible should it be? If such a solution fails, what are the other possibilities of creating a linkage between trade and labour standards understood as 'a provision of international law authorizing countries to regulate the access to their market by adopting discriminatory trade measures in accordance with the level of compliance with core labor standards in the country of origin'?[11] Drawing on historical and current concepts, it should be considered whether labour standards should be left to the ILO, encompassed by the WTO agenda or both forces should be combined. The chapter also attempts to answer the question as to whether or not the GATT could be amended to allow countries to impose sanctions on a particular sector of a country that has infringed core labour standards, if the ILO has detected a violation.

The chapter proceeds in ten subsections, including an introduction. Subsection 2 outlines the multilateral trading system, subsection 3 the Trade Policy Review Mechanismand subsection 4 the WTO dispute settlement system. Interpretation of the WTO exceptions is the subject of subsection 5. Subsection 6 details whether labour standards should remain within the ILO, could be absorbed by the WTO or could be administered by both organisations. Subsection 7 focuses on the scenario of the integrated legislative approach (the integration of core labour standards into the WTO through changes to law) and subsection 8 on the scenario of the institutional approach (proposals based on stronger cooperation or even the combination of the ILO and the WTO). Subsection 9 highlights some limitations to the trade and labour linkage and subsection 10 presents the conclusion.

2 The multilateral trading system

Among the milestones of the multilateral trading system after the Second World War, one ought to mention the following: the Bretton Woods Conference (July 1944) that created the International Monetary Fund (IMF), and the International Bank for Reconstruction and Development (the World Bank) and the United Nations Conference on Trade and Employment, held in Havana, Cuba (November 1947–March 1948) that established the Havana Charter for an International Trade Organization (ITO).[12] However, when it turned out that the US would not ratify the Havana Charter, it was agreed to temporarily apply its fundamental rules and principles, provided by the GATT. Actually, GATT 1947 became an international organisation and established the institutional framework of the multilateral trading system for almost 50 years.[13]

---

10 ibid 20.
11 ibid 35, 147.
12 Craig VanGrasstek, *The History and Future of the World Trade Organization* (Geneva: World Trade Organization 2013) 43.
13 Plasa (n 9) 9.

The revised GATT (1994) contains the former GATT as amended in the past (GATT 1947), the Marrakesh Protocol to the GATT 1994 and the new understanding on various GATT provisions.[14] The Preamble of the GATT sets out the objectives and purposes as well as the principles of the GATT. It states that the Parties to the Agreement recognise that their relations in the field of trade and economic endeavour should be conducted with a view to raising standards of living, ensuring full employment and a large and steadily growing volume of real income and effective demand, developing the full use of the resources of the world and expanding the production and exchange of goods. The Parties are desirous of contributing to these objectives by entering into reciprocal and mutually advantageous arrangements directed to the substantial reduction of tariffs and other barriers to trade and to the elimination of discriminatory treatment in international trade relations. Thus, the overriding goal of the multilateral trading system is not that of achieving complete liberalisation of trade but that of facilitating international trade between countries in order to promote economic growth and development.[15]

The multilateral trading system involves a number of fundamental rules and principles. As indicated here, a basic principle of the GATT is related to national treatment, that is non-discrimination between imported and domestic products. Another important element of the GATT system is the most-favoured-nation treatment. According to Article I:1 of the GATT 'any advantage, favor, privilege or immunity granted by any contracting party to any product originating in or destined for any other country shall be accorded immediately and unconditionally to the like product originating in or destined for the territories of all other contracting parties'. It means that trade advantages granted to one contracting party must be granted to all other parties. Both de jure and de facto discriminations are prohibited here.[16] Importantly, the most-favoured-nation treatment only applies to 'like' products. However, it turns out that the meaning of the notion of 'like products' depends on the context. According to the Appellate Body:

> there can be no one precise and absolute definition of what is 'like'. The concept of 'likeness' is a relative one that evokes the image of an accordion. The accordion of 'likeness' stretches and squeezes in different places as different provisions of the WTO Agreement are applied. The width of the accordion in any one of those places must be determined by the particular provision in which the term 'like' is encountered as well as by the context and the circumstances that prevail in any given case to which that provision may apply.[17]

---

14 Matthias Herdegen, *Principles of International Economic Law* (Oxford: Oxford University Press 2016) 197. See more: <www.wto.org/english/docs_e/legal_e/06-gatt_e.htm> accessed 18 November 2020.

15 Plasa (n 9) 9–10.

16 Herdegen (n 14) 213.

17 *Japan – Taxes on Alcoholic Beverages: Report of the Appellate Body* (4 October 1996) WT/DS8/AB/R, WT/DS10/AB/R and WT/DS11/AB/R.

In the context that interests us, 'like products' are defined by GATT panels as products whose crucial physical characteristics are the same.[18] Plasa highlights that discrimination is not permitted on the basis of production and processing methods (PPMs) where these methods remain without any influence on the consumption of the products concerned. The author points out that the labour conditions under which goods are produced do not determine the physical characteristics and do not affect consumption of the products concerned. Therefore, importing countries cannot implement import restrictions on the basis that the goods concerned were produced under conditions violating labour standards.[19] Although PPMs are not able to render products 'unlike', they may be subject to the exception clauses on public morality and environmental concerns, provided that the conditions of the chapeau are met. Such exemptions are important from the point of view of addressing labour standards and human rights issues in the chain of production of goods and services.[20]

Reciprocity/fairness is another crucial principle of the GATT. The principle refers to a balance of mutual benefits (in terms of trade concessions) and obligations between the contracting parties. It consists in giving trade concessions (e.g. market access or tariff reduction) by one country to another in order to receive similar benefits from it. In other words, if one country wants to gain an additional access to the markets of another country, it should in exchange provide to that country the same additional access to its own markets. Besides, the aforementioned principle also governs sanctions for non-compliance, that is, suspension of concessions. According to Article XXIII, if one country believes that another country's policies nullified or impaired its trade benefits, the GATT agreements provide for compensation, even in the event of absence of violations of any particular rule. Other GATT rules aim at making international trade predictable and transparent, thereby contributing to ensuring fairness.[21]

Additionally, we should give attention to the GATT Article XI, which requires that WTO Members not generally use quantitative import restrictions, and to the GATT Article II which states that the parties shall not apply tariffs in excess to the bound tariffs (in other words prohibits the application of tariffs above bound levels).

---

18 See more: Arthur E Appleton, 'The Agreement on Technical Barriers to Trade' in Patrick FJ Macrory, Arthur E Appleton and Michael G Plummer (eds), *The World Trade Organization: Legal, Economic and Political Analysis* (vol I, New York: Springer 2005) 389 et seq.

19 Plasa (n 9) 11. Otherwise: Robert Howse, 'The World Trade Organization and the Protection of Workers' Rights' (1999) 3 *Journal of Small and Emerging Business Law* 131, 142–145. Howse points out that: 'the distinction between products and PPMs has no basis in the text or the travaux (documented negotiating history) of GATT'.

20 Kateryna Holzer, 'Process and Production Methods (PPMs)' in Thomas Cottier and Krista Nadakavukaren Schefer (eds), *Elgar Encyclopedia of International Economic Law* (Cheltenham: Edward Elgar Publishing 2017) 190.

21 Plasa (n 9) 11. See also: Herdegen (n 14) 212.

The WTO's activities can be divided into two groups, with the first including regular activities of the main bodies of the WTO, which concern all members. As a general rule, decisions in these bodies are taken by consensus, but if consensus cannot be reached, a vote may be called. Qualified majorities are required for important decisions.[22] The second group of activities comprises eight rounds of trade negotiations held under the aegis of the GATT, and organised with a view to amending and supplementing trade rules and to further liberalising world trade.[23] The completed rounds are the following: Geneva 1947, Annecy 1949, Torquay 1950, Geneva 1956, Dillon 1960–1961, Kennedy 1962–1967, Tokyo 1973–1979 and Uruguay 1986–1994. The latest round started in 2001 in Doha.[24]

Taking into account the institutional aspect, the WTO is based on three pillars: for trade in goods, for trade in services and for intellectual property rights. Therefore, three bodies report directly to the General Council and the Ministerial Conference: the Council for Trade in Goods, the Council for Trade in Services and the Council for Trade-Related Aspects of Intellectual Property Rights (the TRIPS Council).[25]

3 The Trade Policy Review Mechanism

WTO members are supposed to inform the organisation of all measures, policies and laws that exert an influence over international trade. Besides, through the 'Trade Policy Review Mechanism' (TPRM) all members' trade policies are subject to periodic review in order to ensure their adherence to the obligations of the organisation.[26] According to Annex 3 of the WTO Agreement, the purpose of the TPRM is 'to contribute to improved adherence by all Members to rules, disciplines and commitments made under the Multilateral Trade Agreements and, where applicable, the Plurilateral Trade Agreements, and hence to the smoother functioning of the multilateral trading system, by achieving greater transparency in, and understanding of, the trade policies and practices of Members'.[27] To this end, the trade policies and practices of all WTO members are required to periodically review by the WTO Secretariat, more specifically, by a special unit called the Trade Policy Review Mechanism Division, entrusted with the responsibility to prepare the reports.[28]

---

22 Mitsuo Matsushita, Thomas Schoenbaum, Petros C Mavroidis and Michael Hahn, *The World Trade Organization: Law, Practice, and Policy* (Oxford: Oxford University Press 2015) 14; Plasa (n 9) 12.

23 Plasa (n 9) 12.

24 Matsushita, Schoenbaum, Mavroidis and Hahn (n 22) 9.

25 Plasa (n 9) 13.

26 Matsushita, Schoenbaum, Mavroidis and Hahn (n 22) 19.

27 <www.wto.org/english/docs_e/legal_e/29-tprm_e.htm> accessed 18 November 2020.

28 Petros C Mavroidis, *Trade in Goods* (Oxford: Oxford University Press 2012) 836.

WTO Members are reviewed with different frequency. As stated in Annex 3 of the WTO Agreement:

> The impact of individual Members on the functioning of the multilateral trading system, defined in terms of their share of world trade in a recent representative period, will be the determining factor in deciding on the frequency of reviews. The first four trading entities so identified (counting the European Communities as one) shall be subject to review every two years. The next 16 shall be reviewed every four years. Other Members shall be reviewed every six years, except that a longer period may be fixed for least-developed country Members.[29]

4 The WTO dispute settlement system

The creation of the WTO dispute settlement system, set forth in the Dispute Settlement Understanding (DSU), has been perceived as one of the most important achievements of the Marrakesh Agreement (1994). It has not gone as far as full judicialisation. It involves diplomatic means, i.e. the initial consultations, arbitral and judicial organs (the panels and the Appellate Body) and the DSB.[30] The WTO DSB comprises of all WTO members, and is responsible for the administration of the adjudicative dispute settlement system.[31] It is authorised to establish panels, adopt reports of panels and the Appellate Body, and monitor the implementation of rulings and recommendations. The adoption of a ruling cannot be blocked by a country losing a case[32] as automatic adoption of panel rulings is one of the main characteristics of the WTO DSU. It can be avoided only through a unanimous vote of the WTO DSB.[33]

The WTO DSB is also authorised to impose retaliatory measures in case of lack of implementation of rulings of a panel or the Appellate Body. First, the complaining party can seek compensation pending full implementation. Second, if no

---

29   <www.wto.org/english/docs_e/legal_e/29-tprm_e.htm> accessed 18 November 2020.
30   See: Giorgio Sacerdoti, 'The Nature of WTO Arbitrations on Retaliation' in Chad P Bown and Joost Pauwelyn (eds), *The Law, Economics and Politics of Retaliation in WTO Dispute Settlement* (Cambridge: Cambridge University Press 2010) 23; Han Liyu and Henry Gao, 'China's Experience in Utilizing the WTO Dispute Settlement Mechanism' in Gregory C Shaffer and Ricardo Meléndez-Ortiz (eds), *Dispute Settlement at the WTO. The Developing Country Experience* (Cambridge: Cambridge University Press 2010) 137.
31   Qianlan Wu, *Competition Laws, Globalization and Legal Pluralism: China's Experience* (Oxford, Portland OR: Hart Publishing 2013) 61.
32   Plasa (n 9) 14.
33   Wilhelm Kohler, 'The WTO Dispute Settlement Mechanism: Battlefield or Cooperation? A Commentary on Fritz Breuss' (2004) 4(4) *Journal of Industry, Competition and Trade* 317 <https://doi.org/10.1023/B:JICT.0000048719.06536.b7> accessed 21 November 2020.

agreement on compensation is reached, the WTO DSB may authorise retaliation. According to Article 22.3 of the DSU:

> In considering what concessions or other obligations to suspend, the complaining party shall apply the following principles and procedures:
>
> (a) the general principle is that the complaining party should first seek to suspend concessions or other obligations with respect to the same sector(s) as that in which the panel or Appellate Body has found a violation or other nullification or impairment;
>
> (b) if that party considers that it is not practicable or effective to suspend concessions or other obligations with respect to the same sector(s), it may seek to suspend concessions or other obligations in other sectors under the same agreement;
>
> (c) if that party considers that it is not practicable or effective to suspend concessions or other obligations with respect to other sectors under the same agreement, and that the circumstances are serious enough, it may seek to suspend concessions or other obligations under another covered agreement.[34]

It means that, in general, sanctions are imposed in the sector where the dispute arose. If this is considered not to be practicable or effective, sanctions may be used in other sectors under the same agreement or under another agreement. The mechanism is known as 'cross-retaliation'.[35]

5 Interpretation of the WTO exceptions: the possibility of the authorisation of trade sanctions for reasons related to violations of workers' rights

WTO principles are subject to exceptions not only for trade-related but also for non-trade-related reasons. This subsection responds to this observation by examining some of these exceptions and answering the question whether they may be interpreted in a way allowing trade sanctions for reasons related to violations of workers' rights.

Starting from GATT Article VI, it should be clearly stated that the notion of 'dumping' has many meanings. One of them is 'social dumping', that is, exporting a product from a country where wages are extremely low and, therefore, where the export price is low, or where substandard working conditions prevail. Is this meaning adequate in a context in which – in order to counteract

---

34 <www.wto.org/english/tratop_e/dispu_e/dsu_e.htm#22> accessed 21 November 2020.
35 More: Elimma C Ezeani, *The WTO and Its Development Obligation: Prospects for Global Trade* (London, New York, New Delhi: Anthem Press 2011) 128 et seq.

dumping – countries can impose 'antidumping' duties on imports of the products that are being dumped?[36] It is necessary to determine whether GATT Article VI and the 'Agreement on Implementation of Article VI of the General Agreement on Tariffs and Trade 1994' could be applied here.

In order to ascertain whether a product is dumped, the antidumping authority of the importing country has to determine whether there is a difference between the export price and the normal value (mainly domestic price) of the product.[37] Besides, GATT Article VI characterises the normal value by referring to the price for the like products for export to other countries or to the costs of production. Since savings from substandard working conditions lower the price of the product on any market (including domestic one), the normal value of the products would include these savings. For this reason, social dumping cannot be treated as dumping. In other words, if the price of the products represents the cost of production in the domestic and in the foreign market, we cannot speak about dumping.[38] In contrast, some scholars claim that: 'Anti-dumping measures are supposed to counteract the unfair nature of dumping. By analogy, social dumping also constitutes unfair trade, which should therefore justify analogous countermeasures'.[39]

Can GATT Article XVI and the Agreement on Subsidies and Countervailing Measures be interpreted as a nexus between labour and trade? On closer analysis, such a possibility should also be excluded.

WTO law does not prohibit subsidies, but rather disciplines their use.[40] It limits itself to the legal obligation not to harm, or, more specifically, not to use subsidies that exert adverse effects on fellow WTO members.[41] In terms of economics, the state which allows national companies to employ substandard labour conditions grants them a subsidy. However, substandard labour conditions do not correspond with a legal definition of subsidies. 'The definition contains three basic elements: (i) a financial contribution (ii) by a government or any public body within the territory of a Member (iii) which confers a benefit. All three of these elements must be satisfied in order for a subsidy to exist'.[42] Even though the governments of some countries seem to exacerbate a 'race to the bottom' in labour standards, for example, appear to be involved in the reduction of wages, this cannot be perceived as a subsidy.[43]

36 Matsushita, Schoenbaum, Mavroidis and Hahn (n 22) 375, 378.
37 ibid 383. More: Ross Becroft, *The Standard of Review in WTO Dispute Settlement: Critique and Development* (Cheltenham, Northampton: Edward Elgar Publishing 2012) 160.
38 Adalberto Perulli, 'Globalisation and Social Rights' in Wolfgang Benedek, Koen De Feyter and Fabrizio Marrella (eds), *Economic Globalisation and Human Rights* (Cambridge: Cambridge University Press 2007) 109; Plasa (n 9) 16–17.
39 Sarah Joseph, *Blame It on the WTO? A Human Rights Critique* (Oxford: Oxford University Press 2011) 130. See also the cited literature.
40 <www.wto.org/english/tratop_e/scm_e/scm_e.htm> accessed 21 November 2020.
41 Matsushita, Schoenbaum, Mavroidis and Hahn (n 22) 300.
42 <www.wto.org/english/tratop_e/scm_e/subs_e.htm> accessed 21 November 2020. See also: Becroft (n 37) 170.
43 Perulli (n 38) 110; Matsushita, Schoenbaum, Mavroidis and Hahn (n 22) 304 et seq.; Plasa (n 9) 17.

Turning to GATT Article XIX and safeguard measures, it should be clearly indicated that in the broadest terms, safeguards and safeguard measures concern the right of a WTO member to impose temporary tariffs, quotas, tariff rate quotas or other measures in order to avoid serious harm (in its economy or domestic industries) from imports and trade concessions. GATT Article XIX is the so-called 'escape clause' as it lets WTO members free themselves from their WTO obligations.[44]

Safeguard remedies allow for the imposition of restrictions on fairly-traded imports. Contrary to the rights to impose import restrictions with the purpose of counteracting dumping and subsidies, safeguard remedies do not rest 'on any concept of unfair trade or remedy for distortions by exporters'. It is also worth stressing that there are three prerequisites to be fulfilled for the imposition of safeguard measures by WTO members. First, there must be an increase of imports of the product concerned. Second, the increase of imports must be the result of developments that were not foreseen and must stem from obligations that the country using the safeguard measure is bound to respect under the GATT. Third, the increase of imports causes or threatens to cause 'serious injury' to a domestic industry that produces a 'like' or 'directly competitive' product.[45]

Of course, low wages, labour rights violations and poor working conditions in the exporting country may contribute to such an increase in imports. If so, GATT Article XIX would authorise the importing country to apply trade restrictions for reasons related to labour conditions. However, given that safeguard remedies do not respond to a situation in which trade is regarded as unfair, and taking into account that safeguard measures can only be applied erga omnes (i.e. to all countries supplying the same products), GATT Article XIX should be excluded as a potential tool for building the bridge between labour and trade.[46]

As it seems, GATT Article XX (General Exceptions) could be treated as the key point about the trade and labour linkage. Since, according to this Article:

> Subject to the requirement that such measures are not applied in a manner which would constitute a means of arbitrary or unjustifiable discrimination between countries where the same conditions prevail, or a disguised restriction on international trade, nothing in this Agreement [the GATT] shall be construed to prevent the adoption or enforcement by any contracting party of measures:
>
> (a) necessary to protect public morals;
> (b) necessary to protect human, animal or plant life or health;
> (d) necessary to secure compliance with laws or regulations which are not inconsistent with the provisions of this Agreement, including those relating to customs enforcement, the enforcement of monopolies

---

44 Matsushita, Schoenbaum, Mavroidis and Hahn (n 22) 409–410. More: Becroft (n 37) 174.
45 Matsushita, Schoenbaum, Mavroidis and Hahn (n 22) 409–411; Becroft (n 37) 175.
46 Plasa (n 9) 17.

operated under paragraph 4 of Article II and Article XVII, the protection of patents, trade marks and copyrights, and the prevention of
deceptive practices;

(e) relating to the products of prison labour;

(h) undertaken in pursuance of obligations under any intergovernmental
commodity agreement which conforms to criteria submitted to the
contracting parties and not disapproved by them or which is itself so
submitted and not so disapproved.[47]

Article XX (a) and (b) permit exceptions from GATT rules and disciplines
where such exceptions are necessary in order to protect public morals, human,
animal or plant life or health.[48] Exceptions could be built in a way allowing the
application of trade measures against countries where, for example, child labour
or forced labour occur, and – as a consequence – labour conditions are incompatible with public morals or present a threat to health. In fact, the EC – Seals
decision[49] demonstrates that the notion of 'public morals' has a broad scope
extending far beyond issues such as gambling or animal welfare.[50] As pointed
out by Williams, there is no clear academic argument that logically precludes
connecting trade with labour standards and human rights on the aforementioned
basis.[51]

Howse was the first scholar to address the exception of public morals in the
context in which it could be used in order to enforce core labour standards. As
pointed out by the author: 'Article XX(a), which permits otherwise GATT-incon-
sistent measures "necessary to protect public morals", might be invoked to justify

47 <www.wto.org/english/res_e/booksp_e/gatt_ai_e/art20_e.pdf> accessed 21 November 2020.
48 More: Marion Jansen, 'Internal Measures in the Multilateral Trading System: Where Are
the Borders of the WTO Agenda?' in Thomas Cottier and Manfred Elsig (eds), *Governing the World Trade Organization: Past, Present and Beyond Doha* (Cambridge, New York,
Melbourne, Madrid, Cape Town, Singapore, São Paulo, New Delhi, Tokyo, Mexico City:
Cambridge University Press 2011) 58–59.
49 European Communities – Measures Prohibiting the Importation and Marketing of Seal
Products: Reports of the Appellate Body (22 May 2014) WT/DS400/AB/R and WT/
DS401/AB/R [5.199].
50 'The Panel accepted the definition of "public morals" developed by the panel in US – Gambling, according to which "the term 'public morals' denotes 'standards of right and wrong
conduct maintained by or on behalf of a community or nation' ". The Panel also referred to
the reasoning developed by the panel in US – Gambling that the content of public morals
can be characterized by a degree of variation, and that, for this reason, Members should be
given some scope to define and apply for themselves the concept of public morals according
to their own systems and scales of values'.
51 Jessica Williams, 'Addressing Child Labour: Reflections on the WTO's Role' (2015) 14(1)
Journal of International Trade Law and Policy 4, 19 <https://doi.org/10.1108/JITLP-05-
2015-0011> accessed 21 November 2020.

trade sanctions against products that involve the use of child labor or the denial of workers' basic rights'.[52] On the one hand, Howse discerns that

> the reference to prison labor in Article XX(e), as well as the fact that explicit language on labor rights was in the failed Havana Charter, suggests that if GATT Article XX had been designed to encompass sanctions with respect to labor rights, explicit language would have been used to articulate such an exception.

As 'exceptiones non sunt extendendae', it means that if GATT Article XX (e) expressis verbis deals with prison labour, it is not possible to conclude that other labour conditions fall within the scope of other exceptions indicated in GATT Article XX without being explicitly laid down. On the other hand, Howse justifies his theory by stating that

> the interpretation of public morals should not be frozen in time and that with the evolution of human rights as a core element in public morality in many post-war societies, the content of public morals extends to include disapprobation of labor practices that violate universal human rights. This argument now has much added strength after the approval of the ILO Declaration by the vast majority of the ILO membership.[53]

Entering into this way of thinking, some authors add:

> The meaning of "public moral" . . . needs to be examined not only in the regime of international law but also from common parlance of human sensitivity that allows a minimum degree of duty of care and compassion necessary for a meaningful survival of less privileged population.[54]

The possibility of using the exception of public morals in order to enforce core labour standards has been also admitted by other authors, for example, Joseph, who claims that: 'labour rights measures might feasibly be permitted under the "public morals" exceptions in Articles XX(a) GATT'.[55] Similarly, as pointed out

---

52 Howse (n 19) 142–45. See also: 'Article XX(a) is potentially important for a number of "linkage" issues, including the relations between the trade regime and human rights, labor rights, animal rights and environmental protection. Each can be understood in moral terms, and so might fall under Article XX(a)', Oisin Suttle, 'What Sorts of Things Are Public Morals? A Liberal Cosmopolitan Approach to Article XX GATT' (2017) 80(4) *Modern Law Review* 569, 571.
53 Howse (n 19) 142.
54 Mohanty, Khan and Kamal (n 1) 87.
55 Joseph (n 39) 136.

by Humbert, who conducted research on child labour, trade measures on child labour may possibly fall within the scope of the term 'public morals'.[56]

The Appellate Body has adopted a two-fold test in order to find out if a trade measure can be justified in the light of GATT Article XX. The first stage of the test is to determine whether the disputed measure contributes to the promotion of the underlying policy objective pursued, for example, protection of public morals. The second stage of the test is to discover if the measure is applied in good faith and if the use of the exception does not amount to an abuse or misuse of treaty rights. In particular, the application of the measure must not mean unjustifiable or arbitrary discrimination, or tantamount to disguised protectionism.[57] WTO jurisprudence clarifies:

> the assessment of a claim of justification under Article XX involves a two-tiered analysis in which a measure must first be provisionally justified under one of the subparagraphs of Article XX, before it is subsequently appraised under the chapeau of Article XX. As the Appellate Body has stated, provisional justification under one of the subparagraphs requires that a challenged measure 'address the particular interest specified in that paragraph' and that 'there be a sufficient nexus between the measure and the interest protected'. In the context of Article XX(a), this means that a Member wishing to justify its measure must demonstrate that it has adopted or enforced a measure 'to protect public morals', and that the measure is 'necessary' to protect such public morals. As the Appellate Body has explained, a necessity analysis involves a process of 'weighing and balancing' a series of factors, including the importance of the objective, the contribution of the measure to that objective, and the trade-restrictiveness of the measure. The Appellate Body has further explained that, in most cases, a comparison between the challenged measure and possible alternatives should then be undertaken. The burden of proving that a measure is 'necessary to protect public morals' within the meaning of Article XX(a) resides with the responding party, although a complaining party must identify any alternative measures that, in its view, the responding party should have taken.[58]

56 Franziska Humbert, 'The WTO and Child Labour: Implications for the Debate on International Constitutionalism' in Henner Gött (ed), *Labour Standards in International Economic Law* (Cham: Springer 2018) 102. See also: Thomas Cottier, 'The Implications of *EC – Seal Products* for the Protection of Core Labour Standards in WTO Law' in Henner Gött (ed), *Labour Standards in International Economic Law* (Cham: Springer 2018) 69 et seq.

57 More: Gabrielle Marceau, 'Trade and Labour' in Daniel Bethlehem, Donald McRae, Rodney Neufeld and Isabelle Van Damme (eds), *The Oxford Handbook of International Trade Law* (Oxford: Oxford University Press 2009) 549–550; Cottier (n 56) 76.

58 European Communities – Measures Prohibiting the Importation and Marketing of Seal Products: Reports of the Appellate Body (22 May 2014) WT/DS400/AB/R and WT/DS401/AB/R [5.169].

The idea of using Article XX(d) – on measures necessary to secure compliance with laws or regulations not inconsistent with the GATT – in regard to labour standards was considered and finally abandoned during the negotiations on the Havana Charter.[59]

The only distinct reference to labour standards can be found in Article XX(e). Under this provision, countries may bar imports of products made by prison labour. Prima facie Article XX(e) seems to create a link with the international labour standard prohibiting forced or compulsory labour. However, as rightly pointed out by Plasa, prison labour is not banned by the relevant ILO conventions in general, but only under certain specific circumstances. Therefore, a common denominator between GATT Article XX(e) and ILO labour standards is limited to a narrow area.[60]

Under GATT Article XX(h) members are allowed to adopt measures 'undertaken in pursuance of obligations under any intergovernmental commodity agreement which conforms to criteria submitted to the contracting parties and not disapproved by them or which is itself so submitted and not so disapproved'. In fact, a number of international commodity agreements contain provisions on 'fair labour standards', but they are more of a declaratory nature rather than of a binding character. They make only general references to fair working conditions without quoting any concrete provisions referring to existing international agreements and without imposing an obligation on the parties to apply trade measures against countries where labour standards are not fair. Besides, these documents lack special sanctions or control mechanisms, and 'their effects in practice depend largely on the leverage which concerned countries can exert in securing compliance with such clauses'.[61] Examples of typical wordings can be found in the International Rubber Agreement of 1979 ('Members declare that they will endeavor to maintain labor standards designed to improve the levels of living of labor'), the International Tin Agreement of 1975 (member states 'will seek to ensure fair labour standards')[62] or the International Sugar Agreement of 1977 ('members shall ensure that fair labour standards are maintained in their respective sugar industries and, as far as possible, shall endeavor to improve the standard of living of agricultural and industrial workers in the various branches of sugar production, and of growers of sugar cane and sugar beet').[63]

According to GATT Article XXI (Security Exceptions): 'Nothing in this Agreement shall be construed. . . (c) to prevent any contracting party from

---

59 OECD, *Trade, Employment and Labour Standards: A Study of Core Workers' Rights and International Trade* (Paris: OECD Publishing 1996) 173 <https://doi.org/10.1787/9789264104884-en> accessed 16 November 2020.

60 Plasa (n 9) 18.

61 OECD (n 59) 173–174.

62 Sebastian Krebber, 'The Search for Core Labor Standards in Liberalized Trade' in Eyal Benvenisti and Georg Nolte (eds), *The Welfare State, Globalization, and International Law* (Berlin, Heidelberg: Springer 2004) 194. See also the cited literature.

63 Plasa (n 9) 19.

taking any action in pursuance of its obligations under the United Nations Charter for the maintenance of international peace and security'. This provision would allow trade sanctions authorised by the UN Security Council under Chapter VII of the UN Charter in order to maintain international peace and security. Nevertheless, caution is required as regards this form of reasoning. It would be rather difficult to prove that infringements of labour rights threaten the maintenance of international peace and security. For this reason, GATT Article XXI (c) does not seem to be an effective tool for establishing the linkage between trade and labour.

Under Article XXIII (Nullification or Impairment), in order to successfully rely on the WTO dispute settlement, a party has to prove that

> benefit accruing to it directly or indirectly under this Agreement is being nullified or impaired or that the attainment of any objective of the Agreement is being impeded as the result of
>
> (a) the failure of another contracting party to carry out its obligations under this Agreement, or
> (b) the application by another contracting party of any measure, whether or not it conflicts with the provisions of this Agreement, or
> (c) the existence of any other situation.[64]

It is not hard to imagine that infringements of labour standards nullify or impair the benefit accrued to importing country. Cassimatis has examined the possibility of linking violations of labour rights with trade measures based on GATT Article XXIII. The author mentions three main obstacles to this kind of approach. One of them is the drafting history and the practice of GATT parties. The second limitation is connected with the interpretation given to Article XXIII by GATT and WTO panels and the WTO Appellate Body. Third, Cassimatis highlights that reliance on Article XXIII as a means to justify trade measures seems to be further restricted by the DSU.[65]

Referring to GATT/WTO practice, notwithstanding the US view expressed in 1953,[66] no state appears to have formally relied on Article XXIII in an attempt to eradicate unfair labour practices. Moreover, looking closely at the drafting history of the GATT, the document did not include any specific labour related obligations

---

64 <www.wto.org/english/docs_e/legal_e/gatt47_02_e.htm#articleXXIII> accessed 21 November 2020.

65 Anthony E Cassimatis, *Human Rights Related Trade Measures Under International Law: The Legality of Trade Measures Imposed in Response to Violations of Human Rights Obligations Under General International Law* (Leiden, Boston: Martinus Nijhoff Publishers 2007) 305.

66 The US was arguing in favour of the possibility of bringing complaints under GATT XXIII in the case of a trade problem caused by competition on the basis of 'unfair' labour standards. See more: Cassimatis (n 65) 304.

in Article XXIII:1(a). Thus, this provision is not adequate to justify trade measures related to labour rights. Among the possibilities given by Article XXIII, it is Article XXIII:1(b) on the basis of which efforts to justify trade measures could be grounded.[67] Nevertheless, the panel reports in the Japan – Film Case that Article XXIII:1(b) 'should be approached with caution and should remain an exceptional remedy'.[68] The Appellate Body in the Asbestos Case repeated the same position.[69] In addition, a very difficult burden of proof has been placed on the complaining party (the Japan – Film Case). The panel concluded that the requirements of Article XXIII:1(b) are as follows:

> The text of Article XXIII:1(b) establishes three elements that a complaining party must demonstrate in order to make out a cognizable claim under Article XXIII:1(b): (1) application of a measure by a WTO Member; (2) a benefit accruing under the relevant agreement; and (3) nullification or impairment of the benefit as the result of the application of the measure.

Besides, it is not irrelevant that non-violation complaints do not have the consequence that the measure complained of should be withdrawn. This constitutes a further argument for not linking violations of labour rights with trade measures on the basis of GATT Article XXIII.[70]

Turning now to the third obstacle for such a nexus, trade measures appear to be further restricted by the DSU. Article XXIII:1(c) was successfully transformed into a dead letter of law by Article 26.2 of the DSU[71] since a finding based on Article XXIII:1(c) can be blocked by the losing party. Moreover, according to Article 26.1(a) of the DSU: 'the complaining party shall present a detailed justification in support of any complaint relating to a measure which does not conflict with the relevant covered agreement'. Labour-related claims can hardly be regarded as suitable for this kind of detailed justification. In addition, no counter-complaints can be made under the DSU (Article 3.10 of the DSU in fine).[72]

Under GATT Article XXIII, there is another extremely important element on which non-violation complaint is based, that is, 'reasonable expectations' of a 'benefit'. The panel considered this factor an additional element that is added to the other three elements mentioned in this provision:

> To [the three elements included in Article XXIII:1(b)] we would add the notion that has been developed in all these cases that the nullification or

67 ibid 306, 308.
68 *Japan – Measures Affecting Consumer Photographic Film and Paper: Report of the Panel* (31 March 1998) WT/DS44/R [10.37].
69 *European Communities – Measures Affecting Asbestos and Asbestos-Containing Products: Report of the Appellate Body* (12 March 2001) WT/DS135/AB/R [36].
70 More: Cassimatis (n 65) 312.
71 <www.wto.org/english/tratop_e/dispu_e/dsu_e.htm> accessed 21 November 2020.
72 For a detailed explanation see: Cassimatis (n 65) 312–319.

impairment of the benefit as a result of the measure must be contrary to the reasonable expectations of the complaining party at the time of the agreement.[73]

As it has been determined, adopting a measure which lowers a standard could be a basis for a non-violation complaint. But how should the panel and the Appellate Body determine the reasonable expectation? What are the criteria for distinction between a standard that is reasonably expected at the time of negotiation and a standard which is not reasonably expected? Razavi has sought to explain how to fill this gap. He has proposed taking into consideration both the textual interpretation of the WTO Agreement and the principles of justice.[74]

Justice requires parallel processes of social and economic development. This ambition has been reflected in the WTO Agreement. According to GATT Article XXXVI (a), the basic objectives of the Agreement include the raising of standards of living and the progressive development of the economies of all contracting parties. Besides, in the light of Article XXXVI(e), international trade has been recognised as a means of achieving economic and social advancement. It follows that violation of labour standards as a barrier hindering competitiveness, could constitute a basis for a non-violation complaint if it has been proved that standards have not been enhanced parallel to economic development. The theoretical context requires also a reference to the International Difference Principle (not to treat in a similar way with unlike conditions and situations). It means that a similar group of countries can be treated similarly and can be required a similar level of standards. Nevertheless, expecting from these countries the same level of standards if they represent a different level of economic and social development would not be a just treatment. In other words, a low standard should not be expected from a high-income country and a high standard from a low-income one.[75]

With the aim of clarifying the notion of reasonable expectations, Razavi has presented the idea of an 'Interpretive Guideline' that should be further developed by a group of economic and social experts. In this regard, the author has proposed the creation of a classification based on diverse economic indicators pertinent to the development process of the WTO Members. Thus, on the one hand, the countries would be classified into classes, for example, 10, 15 or 20 categories and, on the other hand, international labour standards would be graded according to different categories of Members. The 'Interpretive Guideline' should not be binding for WTO's judicial organs but could help them identify what kind of

---

73 *Korea – Measures Affecting Government Procurement: Report of the Panel* (1 May 2000) WT/DS163/R [7.85]. See also: Abd El-Rehim Mohamed Al-Kashif, 'GATS's Non-Violation Complaint: Its Elements and Scope Comparing to GATT 1994' in Kern Alexander and Mads Andenas (eds), *The World Trade Organization and Trade in Services* (Leiden, Boston: Martinus Nijhoff Publishers 2008) 538.
74 Seyed Mohamad Hassan Razavi, 'Labour Standards and WTO – Dilemma of Legitimacy and Efficacy' (2010) 11(5) *The Journal of World Investment & Trade* 879, 892–893.
75 ibid 892–893.

standards should be expected from the respondent member and would encourage countries to raise social standards parallel to economic development. Razavi has highlighted that both developing and developed countries would benefit from the 'Interpretive Guideline' since it would not only establish a basis for the use of sanctions by developed countries against those who have not improved their standards parallel to their economic development, but also it would relieve the developing countries of excessive demand for higher standards. Moreover, the new perspective would facilitate the burden of proof in non-violation complaints by establishing a presumption in favour of complaining party.[76]

GATT Article XXXV (Non-application of the Agreement between Particular Contracting Parties) establishes an opt-out clause, under which the WTO member state, upon its own accession to WTO or upon the accession of a new member state, can declare that it will not apply the GATT in its trade relations with another member state.[77] This provision has been used by several dozen states for different reasons, such as commercial reasons in the case of Japan in 1955 (the refusal of e.g. Austria, the Benelux countries, France and the UK to apply GATT rules to imports originating from Japan) or political reasons, for example, as an opposition of Pakistan and India to trade relations with apartheid South Africa.[78] An opt-out clause could potentially be used for reasons related to labour standards; however, in reality it would be rather problematic due to its limited scope.

The purpose of this subsection was to reflect upon the interpretation of the WTO exceptions and to answer the question whether there is a possibility of the authorisation of trade sanctions for reasons related to violations of workers' rights. The current legal framework appears to preclude such an interpretation. What we need is a different way to think about the issue. By means of analysis and detailed criticism, a novel conceptual framework created to deal with the potential relevance of the WTO in the protection of labour rights, addresses both – what the author calls – 'the institutional approach' and 'the integrated legislative approach'.

6 Labour standards: within the ILO, the WTO or both?

As held in previous sections, the ILO does not have the capacity to directly enforce the standards it adopts. It is in position to detect and reveal cases of

---

76 ibid 893–894.
77 <www.wto.org/english/docs_e/legal_e/gatt47_02_e.htm#articleXXXV> accessed 21 November 2020.
78 Vaughan Lowe, *International Law* (Oxford: Oxford University Press 2007) 219; Sabina Nüesch, *Voluntary Export Restraints in WTO and EU Law: Consumers, Trade Regulation and Competition Policy* (Bern: Peter Lang 2010) 40; John Howard Jackson, *The World Trading System: Law and Policy of International Economic Relations* (Cambridge MA, London: The MIT Press 1997) 60–61; Bob Hepple, *Labour Laws and Global Trade* (Oxford: Hart Publishing 2005) 145; Andreas F Lowenfeld, *International Economic Law* (Oxford, New York: Oxford University Press 2008) 36.

non-compliance, but it is not able to react to such cases, particularly the more grave the infringements are.[79] When we look at the Myanmar case and observe how the ILO legal system really works, we realise that it is not a system ensuring enforcement, whatsoever.[80] According to Maupain, 'a massive project lays before the organisation, but only so long as it does more than survive'.[81] Although Hepple argued that the WTO is appropriate neither in terms of institutional design nor in terms of democratic legitimacy as a body for labour regulation,[82] the desperation over the lack of international enforcement mechanisms for worker rights provokes proposals to link labour rights with WTO trade rules.[83] As it has been stated, the WTO dispute resolution system is often perceived as 'the jewel in the crown of the WTO'.[84] The WTO could contribute to making free trade fair trade through opening this system to labour complaints that exert impact on trade among state parties.[85] The WTO is seen as the best and the only venue where the labour-trade linkage could be realised.[86]

However, the task that consists in linking labour rights with WTO trade rules is very demanding. With regard to the current situation, the WTO is required to reconcile free trade with intellectual property rights, issues relating to public health, environment and labour. Surprisingly, the degree of legalisation of non-trade concerns in the WTO is different across subject matters. While intellectual property rights enjoy strong legalisation, moderate legalisation can be proved in the case of public health and environmental matters, labour issues remain weakly legalised.[87] In fact, it is strange that, for example, intellectual property (which emerged later in the trade debate) has found its place within the WTO framework,

79 Thomann (n 1) 339–340.
80 Brian Langille, 'The Curious Incident of the ILO, Myanmar and Forced Labour' in Adelle Blackett and Anne Trebilcock (eds), *Research Handbook on Transnational Labour Law* (Cheltenham, Northampton: Edward Elgar Publishing 2015) 522.
81 Francis Maupain, *The Future of the International Labour Organization in the Global Economy* (Oxford, Portland OR: Hart Publishing 2013) 258.
82 Bob Hepple, 'The WTO as a Mechanism for Labour Regulation' in Brian Bercusson and Cynthia Estlund (eds), *Regulating Labour in the Wake of Globalisation: New Challenges, New Institutions* (Oxford, Portland OR: Hart Publishing 2008) 161 et seq.
83 See: Gary Vause, 'Labor Issues in International Trade' (2000) 51(3) *Labor Law Journal* 86, 92.
84 Kagan (n 1) 223; Cohan Baclawski (n 1) 260.
85 Kagan (n 1) 223.
86 ibid 224.
87 Sieglinde Gstöhl, 'Blurring Regime Boundaries: Uneven Legalization of Non-Trade Concerns in the WTO' (2010) 9(3) *Journal of International Trade Law and Policy* 275, 275–276, 285, 287, 289 <https://doi.org/10.1108/14770021011075518> accessed 21 November 2020. See also: Montserrat González-Garibay, 'The Trade-Labour and Trade-Environment Linkages: Together or Apart?' (2011) 10(2) *Journal of International Trade Law and Policy* 165 <https://doi.org/10.1108/14770021111140334> accessed 21 November 2020.

whereas labour remains marginalised.[88] More and more voices appear willing to challenge the status quo. As pointed out by McCrudden and Davies:

> It seems increasingly anomalous . . . that the WTO should not even have a committee considering labour issues and trying to assess more systematically than has yet been attempted the parameters of the problem, in the way that trade-environment issues are now regularly considered within the WTO.[89]

Cohan Baclawski discusses three crucial arguments as to why the WTO should adopt and has the power to adopt labour standards. The lack of an effective enforcement mechanism is only one of these arguments. The second point is that the WTO is saddled with the obligation of adopting and enforcing labour standards because they protect basic human rights. Third, the WTO is competent to include labour in its regulation of international trade since labour is an essential aspect of trade.[90] Wolffgang and Feuerhake are also among supporters of the incorporation of core labour standards in the WTO – an international organisation endowed with its own personality under international law and having the possibility of triggering both positive and negative sanctions with the aim of ensuring compliance. Incentives and sanctions are important for an organisation which is expected to administer the core labour standards effectively since the impact of the core labour standards is principally of an economic character, and violations are mainly caused by economic factors. Therefore, the WTO 'is not only the most appropriate organization to make a serious effort to help achieve international recognition for the core labour standards, but is in fact ideally suited for this purpose. Incorporation of the core labour standards in the WTO regulations is the only appropriate way of doing justice to their claims to validity under international law'.[91]

88 Joseph (n 39) 131.
89 Christopher McCrudden and Anne Davies, 'A Perspective on Trade and Labor Rights' (2000) 3(1) *Journal of International Economic Law* 43, 61; Christopher McCrudden and Anne Davies, 'A Perspective on Trade and Labour Rights' in Francesco Francioni (ed), *Environment, Human Rights and International Trade* (Oxford, Portland OR: Hart Publishing 2001) 196. On how the trade-environment jurisprudence established by the WTO dispute settlement system may be used to guide debates relating to the trade-labour linkage proposals see: Tapiwa V Warikandwa and Patrick C Osode, 'Exploring the World Trade Organisation's Trade and Environment/Public Health Jurisprudence as a Model for Incorporating a Trade-Labour Linkage into the Organisation's Multilateral Trade Regime: Should African Countries Accept a Policy Shift?' (2017) 25(1) *African Journal of International and Comparative Law* 47, 54–62.
90 Cohan Baclawski (n 1) 239–240.
91 Hans-Michael Wolffgang and Wolfram Feuerhake, 'Core Labour Standards in World Trade Law: The Necessity for Incorporation of Core Labour Standards in the World Trade Organization' (2002) 36(5) *Journal of World Trade* 883, 900–901.

7 The scenario of the integrated legislative approach

The integration of core labour standards into the WTO could be carried out in different ways; however, all of them would require changes to law. In my opinion, such an approach may be termed 'the integrated legislative approach'.

Of course, it could be suggested that the WTO may establish an entirely new clause dealing with labour standards. It would mean the adoption by the WTO of a social clause ensuring that its members not only implement minimum workers' rights but also establish enforcement mechanisms incorporating trade sanctions. It should be realised, however, how difficult it is to find a just equilibrium between drafting standards with the necessary precision to be effective and those that are flexible and broad enough so that member states will be willing to agree on them.[92] As pointed out by Williams, the inclusion of a social clause in the WTO framework 'is incredibly unlikely within the current climate of the WTO'.[93]

In this connection, it seems that the simplest solution would be to incorporate labour standards into the existing structure of GATT Article XX. Cohan Baclawski highlights that protecting public morals or protecting human life through the imposition of labour standards in line with the core standards undoubtedly falls under GATT Article XX(a) or (b), but she rather suggests that the WTO amends GATT Article XX(e)[94] and adopts the following language:

> relating to the products of forced or compulsory labor, child labor, products produced under conditions preventing freedom of association and collective bargaining, and products produced under parties who employ discriminatory practices, and products produced under unacceptable conditions of work with respect to minimum wages, hours of work, and occupational safety and health.

This formulation of the provision should provide explicit guidelines on the types of labour practices that are forbidden and should bring the core labour standards within the dispute settlement mechanism under the framework of the WTO. Besides, the author proposes to introduce transitional periods in order to soothe developing countries' concerns that they will be deprived of the opportunity to realise their competitive and comparative economic and trade advantages. Moreover, she suggests the creation of an incentive-based rewards system, which would provide the necessary impetus for countries that fear that excessively burdensome labour protection rules will curb their economic growth. The author adds that some developed countries, for example, the US might help developing

---

92 Cohan Baclawski (n 1) 240, 246.

93 Williams (n 51) 18.

94 About such a possibility see also: Susan A Aaronson, 'Seeping in Slowly: How Human Rights Concerns Are Penetrating the WTO' (2007) 6(3) *World Trade Review* 413, 430 <https://doi.org/10.1017/S147474560700345X> accessed 21 November 2020. See the cited literature.

countries by providing them with trade advantages for demonstrated progress in labour standards.[95]

Similarly, Elliott and Freeman see the involvement of the WTO in labour standards in the traded goods sector through the prism of the adaptation of the GATT Article XX (on the contrary, the authors claim that in the non-traded goods, informal, and subsistence agricultural sectors the ILO should remain the primary organisation responsible for promoting and enforcing labour standards). It should be noted that they emphasise the usefulness of GATT Article XX(h) stating that it could be adapted to permit trade measures authorised by the ILO under its supervisory procedures. However, the authors stress more on Article XX(e) arguing that the WTO should build on it by adding a provision that permits countries to sanction the particular sector of a country that has violated core labour standards, if the ILO has detected that there is an infringement. While determining violations suitable for Article XX action, one should obviously consider forced labour, the worst forms of child labour, and de jure national policies that discriminate on one of the prohibited grounds that employers can exploit in order to promote exports. Elliott and Freeman realise, however, that the identification of actionable violations of collective bargaining rights and freedom of association would be a far greater challenge. Hence, guidelines should concentrate not only on the degree of violation but also on its relation to trade. Moreover, evidence that union organisers are actually deprived of the possibility of entering export processing zones, are dismissed or arrested for making attempts to organise an exporting firm could be considered actionable (in addition to the examples of legal restrictions on unions in such zones). Another helpful guideline would refer to the assessment whether or not the country is cooperating with the ILO with the purpose of solving problems. Importantly, countries relying on GATT Article XX(e) should be required to submit evidence from the ILO's supervisory process before taking any action.[96]

Not all authors agree, however, that expanding the scope of GATT Article XX(e) to include all core labour standards would be the best option. Plasa concludes that GATT Article XX(e) would allow trade restrictions even in the case of the lack of material injury to the domestic industries of importing countries. Therefore, an amendment to Article XX incorporating core labour standards would have to state that trade restrictions could be applied only if they were necessary in order to avoid such injury. This would not be in line with the architecture of GATT Article XX. Therefore, one of the links proposed by the author is based on antidumping rules. According to this view, the following conditions must be met to permit trade restrictions:

1   Certain imported goods are produced under conditions in which core labour standards are not respected.

---

95 Cohan Baclawski (n 1) 245, 261–262.
96 Kimberly A Elliott and Richard B Freeman, *Can Labour Standards Improve Under Globalization?* (Washington DC: Peterson Institute for International Economics 2003) 90–91.

2   The cost of labour entailed in producing these goods is lower than it would be if core labour standards were met (the savings from non-compliance).
3   There is material injury to the domestic industry producing the like products.
4   A causal link between the aforementioned elements (between non-compliance with core labour standards and material injury) can be identified.

Of course, checking prerequisite number 3 and prerequisite number 4 should not pose any problems to authorities entrusted with carrying out antidumping investigations. However, the situation may be different in the case of prerequisite number 1 and prerequisite number 2. Because of the lack of experience of these authorities in such matters, the ILO should be competent to conduct such assessment. Moreover, Plasa highlights that a special agreement like the one on antidumping would be required in order to satisfy the complexity of these rules. As regards the types of trade measures, the rules establishing such a link should ensure that variable duties equivalent to the savings from non-compliance or the extent of injury to the domestic industry producing the like products, could be imposed.[97]

The second link proposed by Plasa consists in the establishment of the new WTO rule meant as an addition to the general exceptions enumerated in GATT Article XX.[98] At the margin, proposals similar to this has already existed in the literature. According to Kagan, it would be sufficient to add to the GATT Article XX a clause allowing for 'measures necessary to promote labor rights and designated labor standards' or to adopt a suitable interpretation of the existing exceptions.[99] However, Plasa's proposal goes further and envisages the creation of an agreement including detailed specifications. Furthermore, the author explains that trade restrictions would be permitted if the following conditions were satisfied:

1   Goods had been imported, over a period of time, from a country in which core labour standards are not respected.
2   Over the same period of time, a steady increase in imports from that country (at a considerable rate, that is, a rate considerably above the average of world trade growth) was recorded.

Of course, placing this link in the framework of GATT Article XX would mean that all the conditions mentioned in the chapeau of this provision should be met. Besides, we should bear in mind that, in the rhetoric of general exceptions, trade restrictions are permitted if they are necessary. With regard to the types of trade measures, Plasa allows for using quantitative restrictions or quotas above which additional duties would be applied. Last but not least, with a view to monitoring

97 Plasa (n 9) 153, 155.
98 ibid 156.
99 Kagan (n 1) 223.

compliance, the information provided by the ILO should constitute the basis for any action, whereas the WTO, in the framework of its TPRM, could ask its members to submit information concerning compliance with core labour standards.[100]

The debate on how to create the link between labour rights and WTO trade rules is extensive and wide ranging, and it is cast in terms of GATT Article XXIII. De Wet argued that cooperation with the ILO and the effectiveness of a social clause would be guaranteed by placing this clause in the framework of the aforementioned provision. A new norm that should be inserted should state that the WTO membership ipso jure subjects the party to the obligations arising from specific ILO conventions. Any disclosure of a violation of these conventions would enable the measures directed at solving such a problem. In addition, the author draws attention to the reference in this provision to consultations with, inter alia, intergovernmental organisations, that would assure the link for cooperation with the ILO. In the proposed approach, a two-step enforcement process is assumed. The first consists in moral suasion in accordance with ILO procedures, and the second envisages economic sanctions applied by the contracting parties of the GATT/WTO (as the result of multilateral negotiations). Given this, two reservations should be mentioned. The first point is that a social clause would require cooperation between the ILO and the GATT/WTO. When determining whether certain labour standards have been violated, the latter should take into consideration information provided by the ILO. This is important because the lack of cooperation between the two organisations could lead to the situation in which different organisations deal with the same issues but come to divergent conclusions. The second reservation is that such a system could work only if the membership of the ILO and the GATT/WTO remains (almost) identical.[101]

8 The scenario of the institutional approach

Given the need to ensure the effective enforcement of labour standards, some proposals to combine the institutions, that is, the ILO with the WTO, have appeared in the literature. To my mind, such an approach may be termed 'the institutional approach'. From a broader perspective of the shape of transnational labour law, for example, Trubek and Compa have suggested that this law should be formed in a way that would both articulate global standards and provide means for enforcement. According to the authors, the WTO and the ILO could, indeed, jointly establish such a system.[102] The WTO could adopt labour standards

---

100 Plasa (n 9) 156–158.
101 Erika de Wet, 'Labor Standards in the Globalized Economy: The Inclusion of a Social Clause in the General Agreement on Tariff and Trade/World Trade Organization' (1995) 17(3) *Human Rights Quarterly* 443, 456, 458. See also: <www.ilo.org/public/english/standards/relm/country.htm> accessed 21 November 2020; <www.wto.org/English/thewto_e/whatis_e/tif_e/org6_e.htm> accessed 21 November 2020.
102 David M Trubek and Lance Compa, 'Trade Law, Labor, and Global Inequality' in Paul Carrington and Trina Jones (eds), *Law and Class in America: Trends Since the Cold War*

and labour rights into its trade disciplines and could base any trade-related sanctions on the ILO's conclusive findings. However, the authors have conceded that there is a lack of consensus that empowering the WTO in labour matters is a welcome move. They have highlighted that further debate is indispensable before agreement is reached on the best way to connect universal standards and effective enforcement.[103]

8.1 The joint ILO-GATT/WTO enforcement regime

Ehrenberg has proposed 'the synergistic linkage', namely the establishment of an enforcement regime jointly administered by the ILO and the WTO and based on each international organisation's expertise. The author has declared that linking the ILO with the WTO would establish the most effective enforcement system as regards assuring compliance with international labour standards with respect to goods that enter the international trading system. This would be because the WTO and the ILO are the most competent organisations in the field of international trade and in the area of international labour standards, respectively.[104]

Importantly, access to the enforcement mechanism would be granted not only to states but also to employers' and workers' associations because, as highlighted by Ehrenberg, allowing only states to initiate complaints would not be sufficient to eliminate violations of labour rights. By filing a complaint, the enforcement regime process would begin. Screening the complaint for admissibility by a permanent 'Admissibility Committee' would be the first stage of the process. Next, in the author's view, the joint ILO-GATT/WTO enforcement regime should operate in a two-step procedure with first the determination phase and then the remedial phase. The determination phase would be launched with the aim of detecting any gross and persistent violations of labour rights that take place in the production of goods. On the contrary, the choice of adequate measures to be established to weed out bad practices and the construction of a timetable under which compliance can be achieved would be among the objectives of the remedial phase.[105]

The determination phase would involve the establishment of a joint ILO-GATT/WTO Dispute Panel. It would be its responsibility to consider fully the

---

(New York: New York University Press 2006) 239. Similarly: Thomas Cottier, 'The Common Law of International Trade and the Future of the World Trade Organization' (2015) 18(1) *Journal of International Economic Law* 3, 17–18 <https://doi.org/10.1093/jiel/jgv005> accessed 21 November 2020. According to this author: 'Addressing labour standards calls for close cooperation between the WTO and the ILO'.
103 Trubek and Compa (n 102) 239.
104 Daniel S Ehrenberg, 'From Intention to Action: An ILO-GATT/WTO Enforcement Regime for International Labor Rights' in Lance A Compa and Stephen F Diamond (eds), *Human Rights, Labor Rights, and International Trade* (Philadelphia: University of Pennsylvania Press 1996) 164–165.
105 ibid 165–168.

complaint, make an objective assessment of the problem and prepare a report that would contain findings. The document would specify a timeframe for compliance, recommendations and programmes (i.e., technical cooperation programmes and certification procedures) to help achieve compliance, and possible countermeasures.

The state concerned would have up to three months to appeal to the International Court of Justice (ICJ), which would make a final determination. At the same time, taking advantage of the three-month period, the state should formulate and develop a technical cooperation programme with the ILO that could encompass a set of activities, for example, strengthening the labour inspectorate and state enforcement mechanisms, changing domestic legislation, imposing harsher penalties against domestic violators, establishing public education and compulsory education programmes, organising diverse campaigns, generating poverty eradication programmes and developing efficient production processes with a view to eliminating violations of labour standards during the process of production of goods. The technical cooperation programme would include a timeline for compliance of no longer than two years from the date of adoption of the Dispute Panel report. Notwithstanding the technical cooperation programme, the ILO Governing Body and the GATT Council would meet in order to decide on the actions that the violating state would need to take to adhere to the report. Overseeing compliance monitoring of the violating state would also be the purpose of the meeting.[106]

The joint ILO-GATT/WTO remediation committee (with five members from the ILO Governing Body and five from the GATT Council) would be another important body within the framework of the enforcement regime in question. It would be established within ten days after the adoption of the panel's report. The remediation committee would use the Dispute Panel report as the starting point for the development of the remediation plan, timeframe for compliance and a timetable for countermeasures and economic sanctions. The body would complete the work within two months from the date of its creation and would submit the remediation plan to the ILO Governing Body and the GATT Council for adoption.[107]

If the country did not achieve compliance in one year (and two years maximum) after the adoption of the Dispute Panel's report, countermeasures and/or sanctions would be applied. The ILO Governing Body and the GATT Council would consider compliance four months after the approval or implementation of the remediation plan. These bodies would also be required to review the report of the remediation committee every four months and to monitor its activities (until full compliance had been reached). A lack of positive effects would result in the meeting held between the chair of the remediation committee, the chairs of the ILO Governing Body and the GATT Council and the Directors-General

106 ibid 168–169, 171–172.
107 ibid 172.

of the ILO and the GATT/WTO. The construction of the revised monitoring strategy would be the result of the meeting. Finally, the remediation committee could decide, upon all the information received, that the state had fully complied with the rulings included in the report of the Dispute Panel or, eventually, the state could at any time declare that it had reached full compliance and could ask to be visited by a joint ILO-GATT/WTO inspection team (a body composed of International Labour Office and GATT/WTO Secretariat employees) that would verify compliance.[108]

Moreover, in his proposal, Ehrenberg has put pressure on a certification procedure that would be developed with the aim of certifying the products listed in the Dispute Panel report. In other words, scrutinising if the products were not made under conditions that violate labour rights would be the objective of the certification procedure, which could result in banning of all implicated products. The certification plan would imply periodic mandatory inspections conducted by a joint inspection team that, without warning, would be authorised to enter and inspect all facilities where the production process is carried out.[109]

8.2 The Agency for Trade and Labour Standards (ATLAS)

The proposal which involves the establishment of the Agency for Trade and Labour Standards (ATLAS) jointly governed by the WTO and the ILO also fits into the institutional approach. Barry and Reddy, the authors of this concept, have suggested that the ILO and the WTO should be substantially reformed with the aim of being able to play a legitimate role in the system of trade and labour linkage. Focusing on the agency's activities, Barry and Reddy have highlighted its developmental and adjudicative roles, both of the same significance attached to the promotion of labour standards. The first one consists in helping countries to identify and execute measures that promote compliance with labour standards, and the second one is connected with the detection of serious neglect of labour standards, and if need be, with identifying the steps that should be taken by the country to remedy this neglect.[110]

Clearly, the Agency for Trade and Labour Standards (ATLAS) would have its specialised instruments. Interestingly, the authors propose the secretariat, the peer-and-partner review committee, the advocate's office and the adjudicative tribunal. With a view to the secretariat (selected under the conditions of open competition, using criteria based on merit), it would be responsible for administrative support activities. Each country would be obliged to share the costs that arose as a result of promoting labour standards abroad and promoting good practices by firms owned by the country's citizens or registered or managed in

---

108 ibid 173–175.
109 ibid 173–174.
110 Christian Barry and Sanjay Reddy, *International Trade & Labor Standards: A Proposal for Linkage* (New York: Columbia University Press 2008) 81.

the country. Accordingly, the secretariat would collect 'labor standards progress reports' periodically prepared by all member countries. These documents would indicate whether the state in question has failed to fulfil its obligations since a country's repeated failures would incur censure or withdrawal of preferences. Besides, the secretariat would be endowed with the power not only to make the reports publicly available but also to provide information to the worldwide public relating to countries' current obligations and the procedures for expressing concern or initiating an investigation. It would also manage a multilateral burden-sharing fund, collect contributions from countries and grant them to countries that need support for their action plans.[111]

Given the need to assess each country's labour standards progress report, the governing council of the agency would periodically constitute the peer-and-partner review committee with representatives of states and nonstate organisations, including workers' organisations as its members. The committee would also be authorised to conduct its own research on practices of a country's firms and conditions that exist in the country and to recommend actions that the country could take in order to raise its level of compliance. A country's action plan including explicit goals, time-bound schedules and verifiable targets would be the answer for such recommendations. The committee would be then able to recommend modifications to the action plan and, finally, to inform the advocate's office if a country would still be in serious breach of its obligations.[112]

Interestingly, the advocate's office would undertake investigatory activities not only at the request of the peer-and-partner review committee but also on its own initiative or because of a notice brought to it by a member of the public, or a country. The advocate's office would be of assistance and would furnish potential complainants wishing to submit grievances to the adjudicative tribunal with information. As regards investigatory activities, they would obviously concern potentially serious negligence in the area of labour standards. On the basis thereof, the advocate's office would decide whether to initiate a complaint before the adjudicative tribunal.[113]

Barry and Reddy have well understood the importance of the adjudicative body's rulings. They have contributed to discussions by developing the concept of the adjudicative tribunal that would decide which concerns should be taken into consideration and would determine adequate activities that should be undertaken by the countries. The adjudicative tribunal could commission research and studies which it considers to be useful from the point of view of the investigation of concerns brought to its attention. The analysis of the research and studies and the completion of the investigation could lead to different results. First, the adjudicative tribunal could rule that there is no merit in the matter and, therefore, prescribe no action. Second, it could determine that the concern is substantiated

111 ibid 81–82.
112 ibid 83.
113 ibid 83–84.

and request further action. Here would be a set of possibilities. One of them would be a recommendation to grant the country not only technical assistance but also financial aid from the burden-sharing fund. Moreover, the country could be required to create an action plan for promotion of agreed labour standards and to report on the actions that it has taken. Ultimately, the adjudicative tribunal could recommend that (all) other countries withdraw trade preferences or other supports accorded to the country.[114]

The authors of the discussed proposal have developed a unique approach to the participation in the system of linkage. However, caution is required as regards their claim that such a system would have a voluntary character and would not bind all WTO members. To put it differently, there is no evidence that the system would be joined by the least developed and developing countries. Anyway, the authors have believed that: 'At least some countries are likely to find benefits in joining a linkage system. . . . Over time, as confidence in the system of linkage increase, it is possible that it will develop into a system all countries enter'.[115]

8.3 *The Global Labour and Trade Framework Agreement (GLTFA)*

Another extremely interesting concept is that of a GLTFA. This is Addo's proposal based on international framework agreements and the ILO tripartite system. It is projected that the GLTFA would be accommodated to suit regional trade agreements, thus creating a regional labour and trade framework agreement (RLTFA) as part of future RTAs. The joint ILO/WTO enforcement mechanism should not only fill the gap between adherence to the core labour standards and international trade, but also should have a positive impact on economic growth and social justice.[116]

As the author has rightly noted, the ILO and the WTO are not prepared to handle the linkage problem individually without encroaching on each other's area of expertise. Additionally, there is a plethora of competing issues. For this reason, the foundation of a multilateral enforcement mechanism built on a new governance structure is required. On the one hand, it should create conditions for wider participation in the formulation of policy at the national, regional, and multilateral levels, in a way that would allow making balanced decisions. On the other hand, an enforcement regime could be accomplished with the participation of all the ILO's and WTO's member states, and the employers' and workers' groups, too. The participation of member states both in the standards creation process and in the enforcement mechanisms would guarantee that no single state gains an unfair advantage by weakening its labour standards. Thus, the fear

114 ibid 84.
115 ibid 84–85.
116 Kofi Addo, *Core Labour Standards and International Trade: Lessons from the Regional Context* (Heidelberg, New York, Dordrecht, London: Springer 2015) 320–321, 329.

of protectionism would be reduced and the 'race to the bottom' phenomenon would be avoided. The proposal consists of a joint mechanism agreed by the ILO's and the WTO's Members, and signed by governments, employers' associations and global unions on behalf of all workers and in the operations of all multinational corporations (MNCs) involved across their operations worldwide. It should connect the respect for the core labour standards with international trade. Addo's intention is not to set up a new mechanism but to take advantage of what already exists: for the ILO, the Committee of Experts and their technical cooperation programmes and for the WTO, the Trade Policy Review Mechanism and panel procedures. The ILO/WTO labour and trade commission should deal with the issues that result from the linkage, depending on the particular core labour standard under challenge. In case of a complaint filed against the ILO's or the WTO's member state, and activities of an MNC within a member state, the work of the commission, formed on an ad hoc basis, should split the procedure for: first, determination phase and second, remedy the alleged offence. During the initial determination phase, the commission would need to estimate whether the state or MNC has demonstrated a consistent pattern of gross and reliably attested violations of the core labour standards and determine the extent of the practice, too. The ILO should use similar procedures under its complaint procedure but in conjunction with the WTO. When a complaint is made, the ILO Governing Body and the WTO General Council should form an Inquiry Commission. It would consist of five independent members: two of them selected by the ILO Governing Body, two by the WTO General Council and the fifth – Chairperson – shall be chosen by both the Director-Generals of the ILO and the WTO. The crucial aim of the Inquiry Commission would be to determine whether a consistent breach of the core labour standards has taken place and how it influences trade relations. The Inquiry Commission would initiate the second phase if it reveals that there have been infringements and there has been an impact on trade relations. It would focus on how to remedy the situation, on the appropriate measures to apply and on the timeline for eventual resolution. The second stage should be devoted to implementing the recommendations of the Inquiry Commission. On the one hand, the ILO would verify whether the infringements have terminated and would decide what assistance to provide through its technical cooperation programmes. On the other hand, the WTO would state how the practices have influenced trade flows and provide an evaluation. Then, both organisations would supervise the compliance programme put in place and make a decision to apply sanctions. The activities of both organisations in the area of cooperation should follow the ILO reporting procedures and the WTO Trade Policy Review Mechanism, whereas the work of the Inquiry Commission should be based on the GLTFA developed by both organisations.[117]

---

117 ibid 321–323. See the cited literature.

8.4 *The 'cross-cutting linkage model'*

Arnold, another author who has contributed to the discourse on trade-labour nexus, has proposed a 'cross-cutting linkage model'. The starting point for this path is the intention to show how the discussion can proceed without endless references to the traditional conceptual differentiations, such as 'trade/non-trade; north/south; liberalisation/protectionism; economic development/poverty; consumption/production; universalist/relativist; WTO/ILO; and sanctions/welfare'.[118]

The model does not fuse the ILO and the WTO but assumes operation of both organisations. According to the author's view, the so-called 'comply or explain-and-enforce' mechanism which would function in export sectors would concern only the four 'core rights', that is, freedom of association, freedom from forced labour, freedom from child labour and freedom from discrimination. This mechanism would give countries the right to choose between a 'comply' or an 'explain-and-enforce' schemes. The selection of the former would involve the application of sanctions in the case of a lack of enforcement of the aforementioned rights in the country's export sector, for reasons other than institutional incapacity. The selection of the latter scheme would result in two obligations imposed on the country. First, it would be required to submit explanations to the WTO Secretariat for the failure to opt in to the 'comply' scheme. Second, the country would be required to establish and enforce its own laws concerning the core labour rights within its export sector. Choosing an 'explain-and-enforce' scheme would lead to shifting the enforcement of these rights beyond the WTO's jurisdiction. It is worth stressing that it was the 'enforce your own laws' provision included in the North American Agreement on Labor Cooperation (NAALC) that inspired the author to create an 'explain-and-enforce' scheme.[119]

9 Limitations

In relation to limitations to the trade-labour nexus, the Singapore Ministerial Declaration adopted at the first WTO Ministerial Conference on 13 December 1996 appears to be one of the key points. It clearly reflected the anti-linkage approach using the following wording:

> We renew our commitment to the observance of internationally recognized core labour standards. The International Labour Organization (ILO) is the competent body to set and deal with these standards, and we affirm our support for its work in promoting them. We believe that economic growth and development fostered by increased trade and further trade liberalization

---

118 Luke L Arnold, 'Labour and the World Trade Organization: Towards a Reconstruction of the Linkage Discourse' (2005) 10(1) *Deakin Law Review* 83, 109.
119 ibid 110, 117.

contribute to the promotion of these standards. We reject the use of labour standards for protectionist purposes, and agree that the comparative advantage of countries, particularly low-wage developing countries, must in no way be put into question. In this regard, we note that the WTO and ILO Secretariats will continue their existing collaboration.

At the Seattle Ministerial in 1999, the Clinton administration proposed to establish a Working Group within the WTO to examine the linkage issue. President Clinton's suggestion that the WTO should use sanctions to enforce core labour rights met with tough criticism. The Egyptian trade minister, Youssef Boutros-Ghali, argued: 'If you start using trade as a lever to implement non-trade related issues that will be the end of the multilateral trading system'. He said that the Clinton proposal on trade sanctions 'derailed any hope of a compromise agreement'. The trade minister from Pakistan added: 'We will block consensus on every issue if the United States proposal goes ahead. . . . We will explode the meeting'.[120]

The Singapore Ministerial Declaration was reiterated at the Doha Ministerial Meeting in 2001.[121] Most developing countries stood categorically against the linkage. It was reflected, for example, by India's statement to the Doha Ministerial: 'We should firmly resist negotiations in this area. . . . We consider [core labour standards] Trojan horses of protectionism'.[122] Such resistance has resulted mainly from economic arguments based on the view that the linkage is motivated by protectionism. It should be noted, however, that this opposition has also been the consequence of other arguments, including concerns about neocolonialism and political sovereignty, about the proper institutional capacities of the ILO and the WTO, about the roles of both organisations, about the manner in which respective actors would be involved in the implementation of a workers' rights clause, and about sanctions as an appropriate and effective tool for enforcing labour rights.[123]

The lack of willingness to employ the scenario of the linkage, including the institutional approach appears to be a problem. The WTO and the ILO seem to be satisfied with the existing collaboration between them, that is, 'participation by the WTO in meetings of ILO bodies, the exchange of documentation and

120 Steven Greenhouse and Joseph Kahn, 'U.S. Efforts to Add Labor Standards to Agenda Fails' *The New York Times* (3 December 1999) in Michael Veseth (ed), *The New York Times, 20th Century in Review: The Rise of the Global Economy* (Chicago, London: Fitzroy Dearborn Publishers 2002) 558.

121 See: Arnold (118) 85.

122 Simon Pahle, 'Bringing Workers' Rights Back In? Propositions Towards a Labour-Trade Linkage for the Global South' (2014) 46(1) *Development and Change* 121, 122 <https://doi.org/10.1111/dech.12145> accessed 21 November 2020.

123 Kevin Kolben, 'The New Politics of Linkage: India's Opposition to the Workers' Rights Clause' (2006) 13(1) *Indiana Journal of Global Legal Studies* 225, 227, 244–256.

informal cooperation between the ILO and WTO Secretariats'.[124] According to
the information which can be found on the WTO's Web site: 'The WTO Secretariat maintains technical exchanges with the International Labour Organization with a view to helping members' global economic policies. Activities range
from compiling statistics, research and technical assistance and training'.[125] It is
very unlikely that these organisations would be interested in further deepening
their cooperation, especially in the times of the crisis caused by the COVID-19
pandemic.

Moreover, the ILO and the WTO regimes differ from one another. The ILO
members can freely choose which conventions they commit to whereas the WTO
members commit to all agreements or forfeit membership altogether according
to the single undertaking principle.[126] Besides, what is extremely troublesome,
the ILO and the WTO memberships do not fully overlap.

The next source of doubt arises from the application of trade sanctions. The
construction of the WTO implies that in most cases trade sanctions do not constitute a proper safeguard of compliance with labour standards. As pointed out
by Kaufmann, generally speaking, international agencies do not sponsor actions
that are contrary to their own aims, and the WTO would be doing exactly that
by applying trade sanctions. According to the author, the increasing pressure to
reduce labour standards is a result of a lack of compensation for the higher costs
involved in observing higher labour standards and the subsequent loss of competitive advantage.[127]

As indicated in the literature, decisions about imposing sanctions for labour
rights infringements would be virtually impossible to achieve within the WTO.
This is because the WTO normally acts by consensus, effectively giving every
Member a veto. This does not coincide with the ILO's system where conventions can be adopted by a two-thirds majority of delegates but should be ratified
before they are binding on a member state. However, acting by a majority in case
of the International Labour Conference comes into question for the securing
compliance with the recommendations of a Commission of Inquiry under Article
33 of the ILO Constitution, such as in the case of Myanmar. Hepple expressed
his doubts on whether WTO-authorised sanctions would be more effective than
action under Article 33.[128] However, the author's scepticism is not synonymous
with the need to displace the sanctions from the system of transnational labour

124 <www.wto.org/english/thewto_e/minist_e/min99_e/english/about_e/18lab_e.htm>
    accessed 21 November 2020.
125 <www.wto.org/english/thewto_e/coher_e/wto_ilo_e.htm> accessed 21 November 2020.
126 See: Pahle (n 122) 130.
127 Christine Kaufmann, *Globalisation and Labour Rights: The Conflict Between Core Labour
    Rights and International Economic Law* (Oxford, Portland OR: Hart Publishing 2007)
    239–240.
128 Hepple (n 78) 150.

regulation. Quite the contrary, persuasion and conciliation will not function unless there is ultimately a sanction which can be invoked.[129]

Some authors point out that the employment of sanctions may have counter-productive effects. The experience of Bangladesh in 1993 is given as an example. The owners of garment factories in Dhaka dismissed all children below the age of 16 due to the threat of US sanctions under the 1992 Child Labour Deterrence Act. As a result, many of these children ended up as prostitutes and street vendors or in factories and workshops not producing for export. As Addo correctly argues:

> The emphasis on sanctions should not only be in terms of trade and the after-effects considered as social and left to governments of the targeted countries to deal with, but rather the so-called social effects should be considered in the light of whether sanctions are appropriate in correcting what may be regarded as a 'social ill'.[130]

10 Concluding remarks

The chapter has presented different ideas on how the trade and labour linkage could be framed. It has made three contributions. First, it has shown that the current interpretation of the WTO exceptions rather precludes imposing trade sanctions for reasons related to violations of labour rights. Second, the chapter has introduced the most important historical views and has detailed whether labour standards should be left to the ILO (e.g. Hepple), encompassed by the WTO agenda (e.g. Cohan Baclawski; Wolffgang and Feuerhake) or both forces should be combined (the institutional approach). The latter could take the form of, for example, the Agency for Trade and Labour Standards (ATLAS) jointly governed by the WTO and the ILO (Barry and Reddy) or joint ILO-GATT/WTO Enforcement Regime (Ehrenberg). Particular attention should also be paid to the concept of a GLTFA developed by Addo. It assumes that the foundation of a multilateral enforcement mechanism would rest on the principle of participation and would be agreed by the ILO's and the WTO's members, and signed by governments, employers' associations and global unions. From the point of view of labour scholars, the concept is beautiful but idealistic at the same time. It would be rather unrealistic to reach consensus between so many actors presenting divergent interests. In any case, it seems clear that the shape of the project would require development. Third, the chapter has focused on the integrated legislative approach which consists in the integration of core labour standards into the WTO through changes to law, for example, the view according to which the WTO should build on Article XX(e) of GATT by adding a provision that allows

129 ibid 274.
130 Addo (n 116) 36–37.

countries to sanction the specific sector of a country that has violated core labour standards, if the ILO has determined that there is a violation (e.g. Elliott and Freeman; Plasa). Indeed, it seems that the incorporation of labour standards into the existing structure of GATT Article XX would constitute the simplest solution but currently there is no political will to support such an approach.

Finally, this chapter makes it clear that a variety of perspectives conveyed by diverse authors generally assumes the application of trade sanctions. By contrast, for example, Pahle has systematically discussed and analysed the linkage premised on positive trade measures, which would entail rewarding compliance, however determined, with tariff rebates.[131] Nevertheless, there is always the apprehension that in such a situation, that is, relying only on positive measures, the worst violators would continue infringing labour rights thereby undermining the efforts of the others. However, it should be stated that maybe in favourable times beyond the crisis nothing would stand in the way to combine positive and negative sanctions basing them on the carrot-and-stick principle.

Today, it should be the task of international organisations to regain their role and significance that are currently being questioned. Only then will it be possible to think about equipping the ILO and the WTO with new mechanisms consisting in strengthening their cooperation. It seems that the crucial problem we are facing is how to reinstate the Appellate Body. This may, however, prove problematic. High hopes to resolve the WTO crisis have been placed on the Twelfth WTO Ministerial Conference, originally planned for June 2020, but it has been postponed because of the pandemic.[132] In the meantime, when looking at the pandemic situation and the rising unemployment, the question is whether we should rather focus on the potential of trade agreements for improving the situation of workers (these will be discussed in Chapter 5). Actually, that assessment is consistent with the G20 Osaka Leaders' Declaration, according to which:

> We agree that action is necessary regarding the functioning of the dispute settlement system consistent with the rules as negotiated by WTO members. Furthermore, we recognize the complementary roles of bilateral and

131 The author has argued that such linkage must form part of a broader North-South labour consensus since the linkage might help workers' rights at the expense of the right to work, what constitutes workers' main concern. Moreover, a linkage must be constructed so as to superimpose ILO rulings onto the WTO, and not the other way around. In this context, the ILO-WTO linkage would not entail any ' "operation" of labour standards by the WTO'. Finally, the linkage must reinforce the trade union rights of unprotected or unorganised workers. The author has highlighted that a linkage would require a new single WTO undertaking. See Pahle (n 122) 124, 127, 129, 133. Positive measures are supported by many authors, for example, Kolben. He has pointed out that there should be a move away from a sanctions model toward an incentives model. This would mean that tariff reductions would be the carrot in return for verified compliance with international labour standards. See: Kolben (n 123) 258.

132 <www.wto.org/english/thewto_e/minist_e/mc12_e/mc12_e.htm> accessed 21 November 2020.

regional free trade agreements that are WTO-consistent. We will work to ensure a level playing field to foster an enabling business environment.

One can only hope that the G20 leaders would go beyond lofty words and seriously address these problems. In the era of intensification of trade and geopolitical tensions, they need to try to establish a consensus in favour of the reforms, maybe even taking into consideration a comprehensive renewal of the global trade governance system.

Bibliography

Abd El-Rehim Mohamed Al-Kashif, 'GATS's Non-Violation Complaint: Its Elements and Scope Comparing to GATT 1994' in Kern Alexander and Mads Andenas (eds), *The World Trade Organization and Trade in Services* (Leiden, Boston: Martinus Nijhoff Publishers 2008).

Adalberto Perulli, 'Globalisation and Social Rights' in Wolfgang Benedek, Koen De Feyter and Fabrizio Marrella (eds), *Economic Globalisation and Human Rights* (Cambridge: Cambridge University Press 2007).

Andreas F Lowenfeld, *International Economic Law* (Oxford, New York: Oxford University Press 2008).

Anthony E Cassimatis, *Human Rights Related Trade Measures Under International Law: The Legality of Trade Measures Imposed in Response to Violations of Human Rights Obligations Under General International Law* (Leiden, Boston: Martinus Nijhoff Publishers 2007).

Arthur E Appleton, 'The Agreement on Technical Barriers to Trade' in Patrick FJ Macrory, Arthur E Appleton and Michael G Plummer (eds), *The World Trade Organization: Legal, Economic and Political Analysis* (vol I, New York: Springer 2005).

Bob Hepple, *Labour Laws and Global Trade* (Oxford: Hart Publishing 2005).

Bob Hepple, 'The WTO as a Mechanism for Labour Regulation' in Brian Bercusson and Cynthia Estlund (eds), *Regulating Labour in the Wake of Globalisation: New Challenges, New Institutions* (Oxford, Portland OR: Hart Publishing 2008).

Brian Langille, 'The Curious Incident of the ILO, Myanmar and Forced Labour' in Adelle Blackett and Anne Trebilcock (eds), *Research Handbook on Transnational Labour Law* (Cheltenham, Northampton: Edward Elgar Publishing 2015).

Brittany Cohan Baclawski, 'Re-Thinking the WTO's Relationship to International Labor Standards: Is It Finally Time for a Global Approach' (2016–2017) 48 *Georgetown Journal of International Law* 235.

Christian Barry and Sanjay Reddy, *International Trade & Labor Standards: A Proposal for Linkage* (New York: Columbia University Press 2008).

Christine Kaufmann, *Globalisation and Labour Rights: The Conflict Between Core Labour Rights and International Economic Law* (Oxford, Portland OR: Hart Publishing 2007).

Christopher McCrudden and Anne Davies, 'A Perspective on Trade and Labor Rights' (2000) 3(1) *Journal of International Economic Law* 43.

Christopher McCrudden and Anne Davies, 'A Perspective on Trade and Labour Rights' in Francesco Francioni (ed), *Environment, Human Rights and International Trade* (Oxford, Portland OR: Hart Publishing 2001).

Craig VanGrasstek, *The History and Future of the World Trade Organization* (Geneva: World Trade Organization 2013).

Daniel S Ehrenberg, 'From Intention to Action: An ILO-GATT/WTO Enforcement Regime for International Labor Rights' in Lance A Compa and Stephen F Diamond (eds), *Human Rights, Labor Rights, and International Trade* (Philadelphia: University of Pennsylvania Press 1996).

David M Trubek and Lance Compa, 'Trade Law, Labor, and Global Inequality' in Paul Carrington and Trina Jones (eds), *Law and Class in America: Trends Since the Cold War* (New York: New York University Press 2006).

Elimma C Ezeani, *The WTO and Its Development Obligation: Prospects for Global Trade* (London, New York, New Delhi: Anthem Press 2011).

Erika De Wet, 'Labor Standards in the Globalized Economy: The Inclusion of a Social Clause in the General Agreement on Tariff and Trade/World Trade Organization' (1995) 17(3) *Human Rights Quarterly* 443.

European Communities – *Measures Affecting Asbestos and Asbestos-Containing Products: Report of the Appellate Body* (12 March 2001) WT/DS135/AB/R.

European Communities – *Measures Prohibiting the Importation and Marketing of Seal Products: Reports of the Appellate Body* (22 May 2014) WT/DS400/AB/R and WT/DS401/AB/R.

Francis Maupain, *The Future of the International Labour Organization in the Global Economy* (Oxford, Portland OR: Hart Publishing 2013).

Franziska Humbert, 'The WTO and Child Labour: Implications for the Debate on International Constitutionalism' in Henner Gött (ed), *Labour Standards in International Economic Law* (Cham: Springer 2018).

Gabrielle Marceau, 'Trade and Labour' in Daniel Bethlehem, Donald McRae, Rodney Neufeld and Isabelle Van Damme (eds), *The Oxford Handbook of International Trade Law* (Oxford: Oxford University Press 2009).

Gary Vause, 'Labor Issues in International Trade' (2000) 51(3) *Labor Law Journal* 86.

Giorgio Sacerdoti, 'The Nature of WTO Arbitrations on Retaliation' in Chad P Bown and Joost Pauwelyn (eds), *The Law, Economics and Politics of Retaliation in WTO Dispute Settlement* (Cambridge: Cambridge University Press 2010).

G20 Leaders' Declaration: Building Consensus for Fair and Sustainable Development <www.consilium.europa.eu/media/37247/buenos_aires_leaders_declaration. pdf> accessed 18 November 2020.

Han Liyu and Henry Gao, 'China's Experience in Utilizing the WTO Dispute Settlement Mechanism' in Gregory C Shaffer and Ricardo Meléndez-Ortiz (eds), *Dispute Settlement at the WTO: The Developing Country Experience* (Cambridge: Cambridge University Press 2010).

Hans-Michael Wolffgang and Wolfram Feuerhake, 'Core Labour Standards in World Trade Law: The Necessity for Incorporation of Core Labour Standards in the World Trade Organization' (2002) 36(5) *Journal of World Trade* 883.

Japan – *Taxes on Alcoholic Beverages: Report of the Appellate Body* (4 October 1996) WT/DS8/AB/R, WT/DS10/AB/R and WT/DS11/AB/R.

Japan – *Measures Affecting Consumer Photographic Film and Paper: Report of the Panel* (31 March 1998) WT/DS44/R.

Jessica Williams, 'Addressing Child Labour: Reflections on the WTO's Role' (2015) 14(1) *Journal of International Trade Law and Policy* 4 <https://doi.org/10.1108/JITLP-05-2015-0011> accessed 21 November 2020.

John Howard Jackson, *The World Trading System: Law and Policy of International Economic Relations* (Cambridge MA, London: The MIT Press 1997).

Joshua M Kagan, 'Making Free Trade Fair: How the WTO Could Incorporate Labor Rights and Why It Should' (2011–2012) 43 *Georgetown Journal of International Law* 195.

Kateryna Holzer, 'Process and Production Methods (PPMs)' in Thomas Cottier and Krista Nadakavukaren Schefer (eds), *Elgar Encyclopedia of International Economic Law* (Cheltenham, Northampton: Edward Elgar Publishing 2017).

Kevin Kolben, 'The New Politics of Linkage: India's Opposition to the Workers' Rights Clause' (2006) 13(1) *Indiana Journal of Global Legal Studies* 225.

Kimberly A Elliott and Richard B Freeman, *Can Labour Standards Improve Under Globalization?* (Washington DC: Peterson Institute for International Economics 2003).

Kofi Addo, *Core Labour Standards and International Trade: Lessons from the Regional Context* (Heidelberg, New York, Dordrecht, London: Springer 2015).

Korea – *Measures Affecting Government Procurement: Report of the Panel* (1 May 2000) WT/DS163/R.

Lars Thomann, *Steps to Compliance with International Labour Standards: The International Labour Organization (ILO) and the Abolition of Forced Labour* (Wiesbaden: Springer 2011).

Luke L Arnold, 'Labour and the World Trade Organization: Towards a Reconstruction of the Linkage Discourse' (2005) 10(1) *Deakin Law Review* 83.

Manfred Weiss, 'International Labour Standards: A Complex Public-Private Policy Mix' (2013) 29(1) *The International Journal of Comparative Labour Law and Industrial Relations* 7.

Marilyn J Pittard and Stuart Butterworth, 'The Rich Panoply of Sources of Labor Law: National, Regional and International' in Matthew W Finkin and Guy Mundlak (eds), *Comparative Labor Law* (Cheltenham, Northampton: Edward Elgar Publishing 2015).

Marion Jansen, 'Internal Measures in the Multilateral Trading System: Where Are the Borders of the WTO Agenda?' in Thomas Cottier and Manfred Elsig (eds), *Governing the World Trade Organization: Past, Present and Beyond Doha* (Cambridge, New York, Melbourne, Madrid, Cape Town, Singapore, São Paulo, New Delhi, Tokyo, Mexico City: Cambridge University Press 2011).

Matthias Herdegen, *Principles of International Economic Law* (Oxford: Oxford University Press 2016).

Mitsuo Matsushita, Thomas Schoenbaum, Petros C Mavroidis and Michael Hahn, *The World Trade Organization: Law, Practice, and Policy* (Oxford: Oxford University Press 2015).

Montserrat González-Garibay, 'The Trade-Labour and Trade-Environment Linkages: Together or Apart?' (2011) 10(2) *Journal of International Trade Law and Policy* 165 <https://doi.org/10.1108/14770021111140334> accessed 21 November 2020.

OECD, *Trade, Employment and Labour Standards: A Study of Core Workers' Rights and International Trade* (Paris: OECD Publishing 1996) <https://doi.org/10.1787/9789264104884-en> accessed 16 November 2020.

Oisin Suttle, 'What Sorts of Things are Public Morals? A Liberal Cosmopolitan Approach to Article XX GATT' (2017) 80(4) *Modern Law Review* 569.

Petros C Mavroidis, *Trade in Goods* (Oxford: Oxford University Press 2012).

108 *The WTO needs reforms*

Philip Blenkinsop, 'EU, China and 14 Others Agree Stop-Gap Fix for WTO Crisis' *Reuters* (27 March 2020) <www.reuters.com/article/us-trade-wto-idUSKB-N21E2I0> accessed 18 November 2020.

Qianlan Wu, *Competition Laws, Globalization and Legal Pluralism: China's Experience* (Oxford, Portland OR: Hart Publishing 2013).

Robert Howse, 'The World Trade Organization and the Protection of Workers' Rights' (1999) 3 *Journal of Small and Emerging Business Law* 131.

Robert McDougall, 'Crisis in the WTO. Restoring the WTO Dispute Settlement Function' (October 2018) *CIGI Papers* No. 194 <www.cigionline.org/publications/crisis-wto-restoring-dispute-settlement-function> accessed 18 November 2020.

Ross Becroft, *The Standard of Review in WTO Dispute Settlement: Critique and Development* (Cheltenham, Northampton: Edward Elgar Publishing 2012).

Sabina Nüesch, *Voluntary Export Restraints in WTO and EU Law: Consumers, Trade Regulation and Competition Policy* (Bern: Peter Lang 2010).

Sarah Joseph, *Blame It on the WTO? A Human Rights Critique* (Oxford: Oxford University Press 2011).

Sebastian Krebber, 'The Search for Core Labor Standards in Liberalized Trade' in Eyal Benvenisti and Georg Nolte (eds), *The Welfare State, Globalization, and International Law* (Berlin, Heidelberg: Springer 2004).

Seyed Mohamad Hassan Razavi, 'Labour Standards and WTO – Dilemma of Legitimacy and Efficacy' (2010) 11(5) *The Journal of World Investment & Trade* 879.

Sieglinde Gstöhl, 'Blurring Regime Boundaries: Uneven Legalization of Non-Trade Concerns in the WTO' (2010) 9(3) *Journal of International Trade Law and Policy* 275 <https://doi.org/10.1108/14770021011075518> accessed 21 November 2020.

Simon Pahle, 'Bringing Workers' Rights Back in? Propositions Towards a Labour-Trade Linkage for the Global South' (2014) 46(1) *Development and Change* 121 <https://doi.org/10.1111/dech.12145> accessed 21 November 2020.

Steven Greenhouse and Joseph Kahn, 'U.S. Efforts to Add Labor Standards to Agenda Fails' *The New York Times* (3 December 1999) in Michael Veseth (ed), *The New York Times, 20th Century in Review: The Rise of the Global Economy* (Chicago, London: Fitzroy Dearborn Publishers 2002).

Susan A Aaronson, 'Seeping in Slowly: How Human Rights Concerns Are Penetrating the WTO' (2007) 6(3) *World Trade Review* 413 <https://doi.org/10.1017/S147474560700345X> accessed 21 November 2020.

Tapan R Mohanty, Adil Hasan Khan and Gaurav Kamal, 'Law, Labour, and Legitimacy: The Complexion of WTO' (2004) 29(4) *Vikalpa* 83.

Tapiwa V Warikandwa and Patrick C Osode, 'Exploring the World Trade Organisation's Trade and Environment/Public Health Jurisprudence as a Model for Incorporating a Trade-Labour Linkage into the Organisation's Multilateral Trade Regime: Should African Countries Accept a Policy Shift?' (2017) 25(1) *African Journal of International and Comparative Law* 47.

Thomas Cottier, 'The Common Law of International Trade and the Future of the World Trade Organization' (2015) 18(1) *Journal of International Economic Law* 3 <https://doi.org/10.1093/jiel/jgv005> accessed 21 November 2020.

Thomas Cottier, 'The Implications of EC – Seal Products for the Protection of Core Labour Standards in WTO Law' in Henner Gött (ed), *Labour Standards in International Economic Law* (Cham: Springer 2018).

Vaughan Lowe, *International Law* (Oxford: Oxford University Press 2007).

Wilhelm Kohler, 'The WTO Dispute Settlement Mechanism: Battlefield or Cooperation? A Commentary on Fritz Breuss' (2004) 4(4) *Journal of Industry, Competition and Trade* 317 <https://doi.org/10.1023/B:JICT.0000048719.06536.b7> accessed 21 November 2020.

William H Meyer, 'Testing Theories of Labor Rights and Development' (2015) 37(2) *Human Rights Quarterly* 414 <https://doi.org/10.1353/hrq.2015.0036> accessed 1 December 2020.

Wolfgang Plasa, *Reconciling International Trade and Labor Protection: Why We Need to Bridge the Gap Between ILO Standards and WTO Rules* (Lanham, Boulder, New York, London: Lexington Books 2015).

Yasmin Moorman, 'Integration of ILO Core Rights Labor Standards into the WTO' (2001) 39 *Columbia Journal of Transnational Law* 555.

4 Generalised System of Preferences

The US and the EU compared

1 Introduction

As mentioned in the previous chapter, the social clause can have a unilateral source. In this case, it is included by a state in its national law on foreign trade.[1] A recognised exception to part IV of the General Agreement on Tariffs and Trade and the so-called 'Enabling Clause' allow for a Generalised System of Preferences (GSP) beneficial to developing countries, which otherwise breaches the most-favoured-nation (MFN) principle. The GSP, in other words, is an exception to the WTO's MFN principle,[2] to which I refer in the previous chapter. Under a GSP scheme, certain products from developing countries may enter free of duties if the exporting country agrees to some conditions. The first country in the world to institute its own GSP scheme was Australia, which applied for and received a waiver of the MFN principle in 1966.[3] GSP is also operated, inter alia, by Canada, New Zealand, Japan, Norway and Switzerland.[4] It is a matter of discretion on the part of importing countries, whether to establish a GSP scheme and, on what conditions. The EU and the US make much use of GSP schemes as regards labour rights.[5] Thus, there is plenty to be explored in this chapter, not

---

1 Arturo Bronstein, *International and Comparative Labour Law: Current Challenges* (Geneva: Palgrave Macmillan, International Labour Office 2009) 95. Some parts of this chapter were published previously in Poland: Aneta Tyc, 'The US's and the EU's Generalised System of Preferences: A Comparison in the Context of Workers' Rights' 2020 (2) *Studia z Zakresu Prawa Pracy i Polityki Społecznej* 115.
2 James Yap, 'One Step Forward: The European Union Generalised System of Preferences and Labour Rights in the Garment Industry in Bangladesh' in Jan Wouters, Axel Marx, Dylan Geraets and Bregt Natens (eds), *Global Governance Through Trade: EU Policies and Approaches* (Cheltenham, Northampton: Edward Elgar Publishing 2015) 216; Peter S Liapis, *Preferential Trade Agreements: How Much Do They Benefit Developing Economies?* (Paris: OECD Publishing 2007) 15 <https://doi.org/10.1787/9789264033696-en> accessed 21 November 2020.
3 Anthony N Cole, 'Labor Standards and the Generalized System of Preferences: The European Labor Incentives' 2003 (25)1 *Michigan Journal of International Law* 179, 189.
4 Kofi Addo, *Core Labour Standards and International Trade: Lessons from the Regional Context* (Heidelberg, New York, Dordrecht, London: Springer 2015) 149.
5 Alan Hyde, 'A Game-Theory Account and Defence of Transnational Labour Standards – a Preliminary Look at the Problem' in John DR Craig and Michael Lynk (eds), *Globalization and the Future of Labour Law* (Cambridge, New York, Melbourne, Madrid, Cape Town,

only from the point of view of the EU but also in the context of recent Trump administration steps. For example, on 25 October 2019, USTR announced that the US suspended duty-free treatment of certain Thai products for failure to 'adequately provide internationally-recognised worker rights'. As a consequence, as from 25 April 2020, 573 US Harmonized Tariff Schedule line items from Thailand, including all seafood, are no longer subject to duty-free GSP treatment. According to data presented by USTR, the removal of benefits for these imports affects approximately one-third of Thailand's GSP trade, which totalled $4.4 billion in 2018.[6] The example illustrates pressure that is exerted by one country on another with the use of GSP. In this chapter, we will find out, inter alia, what procedures apply before the suspension of GSP benefits. In this particular Thai case, the suspension was actually a consequence of an eligibility review commenced with a petition (2015) from the AFL-CIO, and the US engagement with Thailand on labour issues (even before the AFL-CIO petition).[7] The topic related to GSP schemes is particularly important from the point of view of the trade-labour debate given that the opponents of the trade-labour linkage often support the concept of GSP as a means of the improvement of standards.[8]

2 The US Generalised System of Preferences (GSP)

2.1 Legal basis

The US GSP is a programme aimed at promoting economic growth in the developing world. It provides preferential duty-free treatment for over 3,500 products from many designated beneficiary countries, including some least developed beneficiary developing countries.[9] Another 1,500 products are eligible for GSP preferences only when imported from least developed beneficiary developing countries. The US GSP programme was implemented on 1 January 1976, and authorised under the Trade Act of 1974 (19 USC 2461 et seq.),[10] according to

Singapore, São Paulo: Cambridge University Press 2006) 166; Christine Kaufmann, *Globalisation and Labour Rights: The Conflict Between Core Labour Rights and International Economic Law* (Oxford, Portland OR: Hart Publishing 2007) 136.

6 Brooke Ringel, 'President Trump Suspends Preferential Trade Treatment for Thailand' *Trade and Manufacturing Monitor* (28 October 2019) <www.ustrademonitor. com/2019/10/president-trump-suspends-preferential-trade-treatment-for-thailand/> accessed 21 November 2020.

7 ibid; <https://asia.nikkei.com/Economy/Trade-war/Trump-suspends-duty-free-trade-for-some-Thai-goods> accessed 21 November 2020.

8 Seyed Mohamad Hassan Razavi, 'Labour Standards and WTO – Dilemma of Legitimacy and Efficacy' (2010) 11(5) The Journal of World Investment & Trade 879, 888.

9 The International Corporate Accountability Roundtable, *Tools of Trade: The Use of U.S. Generalized System of Preferences to Promote Labor Rights for All* (2018) 2, 7 <https:// static1.squarespace.com/static/583f3fca725e25fcd45aa446/t/5a723fflec212d3d5866 35d9/1517436916673/ICAR+GSP+Report+FINAL.pdf> accessed 21 November 2020.

10 Office of the United States Trade Representative, Executive Office of the President, *U.S. Generalized System of Preferences Guidebook* (Washington DC 2019) <https://

which the GSP beneficiary status could not be accorded to any country that, inter alia, was communist, was uncooperative in international drug control efforts or was terrorist-abetting.[11] However, as it soon turned out, these grounds were not enough. Frightening events in the 1970s and 1980s, including Pinochet's military dictatorship in Chile (1973–1990), the civil war in El Salvador (1979–1992), labour rights violations in the banana plantations in Honduras and trade union suppression in the maquiladora factories in Guatemala, led to the establishment of a coalition of trade unions and civil society organisations. It was aimed at finding a trade-related solution on how to hold companies and governments accountable for human and labour rights violations.[12] Thus, under the GSP Renewal Act of 1984 other relevant grounds for exclusion from the programme were added. One of the most important prohibited the president from designating as a GSP privileged trading partner any country that 'has not taken or is not taking steps to afford internationally recognised worker rights' to its own workers.[13] There are, nevertheless, some major ambiguities in this formulation, especially vague expressions, that is, 'taking steps', 'afford' or unclear criteria for withdrawal of GSP benefits.[14] 'Internationally recognised worker rights' – as defined by the statute – meant that the US GSP scheme required privileged countries to uphold the right of association, the right to organise and bargain collectively, a prohibition on forced labour, a minimum age for employed children, and acceptable conditions relating to

ustr.gov/sites/default/files/IssueAreas/gsp/GSP_Guidebook-December_2019. pdf?utm_source=google&utm_medium=google&utm_term=(not%20provided)&utm_content=undefined&utm_campaign=(not%20set)&gclid=undefined&dclid=undefined&GAID=false> accessed 21 November 2020.

11 George Tsogas, 'Labour Standards in the Generalized Systems of Preferences of the European Union and the United States' (2000) 6(3) *European Journal of Industrial Relations* 349, 352.

12 Paula Church Albertson and Lance Compa, 'Labour Rights and Trade Agreements in the Americas' in Adelle Blackett and Anne Trebilcock (eds), *Research Handbook on Transnational Labour Law* (Cheltenham, Northampton: Edward Elgar Publishing 2015) 475.

13 Philip Alston, 'Labor Rights Provisions in U.S. Trade Law: "Aggressive Unilateralism"?' in Lance A Compa and Stephen F Diamond (eds), *Human Rights, Labor Rights, and International Trade* (Philadelphia: University of Pennsylvania Press 1996) 72; Adalberto Perulli and Vania Brino, *Manuale di diritto internazionale del lavoro* (Turin: Giappichelli 2015) 102; Paul Alois, 'Better Work and Global Governance' (A dissertation submitted to the Graduate faculty in Political Science in partial fulfillment of the requirements for the degree of Doctor of Philosophy, The City University of New York 2016) 52–53; William A Douglas, John P Ferguson and Erin Klett, 'An Effective Confluence of Forces in Support of Workers' Rights: ILO Standards, US Trade Laws, Unions, and NGOs' (May 2004) 26(2) *Human Rights Quarterly* 273, 276; Angel Torres, 'A Wishful Thought: Enforceability and Avoidance of Labor Provisions in Foreign Trade Agreements' (2014) 20(4) *Law and Business Review of the Americas* 617, 621; Steve Charnovitz, 'International Trade and Worker Rights' (1987) 7(1) *Steve SAIS Review* 185, 185; Kevin Kolben, 'A Development Approach to Trade and Labor Regimes' (2010) 45(2) *Wake Forest Law Review* 355, 359.

14 Church Albertson and Compa (n 12) 475.

minimum wages, work hours and safety and health.[15] It is worth stressing that the GSP Act of 1984 has been the most frequently used legal mechanism.[16]

Congressional authorisation of the GSP programme expired end of December 2017.[17] Further, on 23 March 2018, the president signed into law H.R. 1625 (Public Law 115–141), the 'Consolidated Appropriations Act, 2018',[18] which provided full-year federal appropriations through 30 September 2018 and included the renewal for the GSP through 31 December 2020. Interestingly, the Act extended GSP with retroactive effect, for goods entered or withdrawn from warehouse for consumption from 1 January 2018 through 31 December 2020.[19] What is important, the aforementioned Act states that none of the funds appropriated or otherwise made available under its titles III through VI may be obligated or expended to provide assistance for any programme, project, or activity that contributes to the violation of internationally recognised workers' rights, as

15 Thomas R Donahue, 'Workers' Rights in the Global Village: Observations of an American Trade Unionist' in Werner Sengenberger and Duncan Campbell (eds), *International Labour Standards and Economic Interdependence: Essays in Commemoration of the 75th Anniversary of the International Labour Organization and the 50th Anniversary of the Declaration of Philadelphia* (Geneva: International Institute for Labour Studies 1994) 202; André Raynauld and Jean-Pierre Vidal, *Labour Standards and International Competitiveness: A Comparative Analysis of Developing and Industrialized Countries* (Cheltenham, Northampton: Edward Elgar Publishing 1998) 11; Jane A Winzer, 'Expanding the Scope of Multilateral Regimes: The Uruguay Round of GATT Negotiations' (A dissertation or thesis submitted to the Faculty of the Graduate School of Emory University in partial ulfillment of the requirements for the degree of Doctor of Philosophy, Department of Political Science 2006) 161; Tsogas (n 11) 352; Lance Compa and Jeffrey S Vogt, 'Labor Rights in the Generalized System of Preferences: A 20-Year Review' (2001) 22 (2–3) *Comparative Labor Law & Policy Journal* 199, 202; Charnovitz (n 13) 191; Clotilde Granger and Jean-Marc Siroën, 'Core Labour Standards in Trade Agreements: From Multilateralism to Bilateralism' (2006) 40(5) *Journal of World Trade* 813, 834; Stephen Herzenberg, 'In from the Margins: Morality, Economics, and International Labor Rights' in Lance A Compa and Steven F Diamond (eds), *Human Rights, Labor Rights, and International Trade* (Philadelphia: University of Pennsylvania Press 1996) 104–105; Alston (n 13) 74; Michael Gadbaw and Michael T Medwig, 'Multinational Enterprises and International Labor Standards: Which Way for Development and Jobs?' in Lance A Compa and Steven F Diamond (eds), *Human Rights, Labor Rights, and International Trade* (Philadelphia: University of Pennsylvania Press 1996) 148.
16 Antonio Ojeda-Avilés, *Transnational Labour Law* (Alphen aan den Rijn: Wolters Kluwer Law & Business 2015) 111. Apart from the US GSP there are also three regional preference programmes: The Caribbean Basin Initiative (CBI), the Andean Trade Preference Act (ATPA) and the African Growth and Opportunity Act (AGOA) – all with a similar workers' rights conditionality clause. See: Marley S Weiss, 'International Labor and Employment Law: From Periphery to Core' (2010) 25 ABA *Journal of Labor & Employment Law* 487, 499.
17 Office of the United States Trade Representative, Executive Office of the President (n 10).
18 <www.congress.gov/115/bills/hr1625/BILLS-115hr1625enr.pdf> accessed 22 November 2020.
19 <www.cbp.gov/trade/priority-issues/trade-agreements/special-trade-legislation/generalized-system-preferences> accessed 22 November 2020.

defined in section 507(4) of the Trade Act of 1974, of workers in the recipient country, including any designated zone or area in that country (sec. 7079).[20]

2.2 Pros and cons

The GSP programme is equal to only about 3–4% of total dutiable US imports over the last decade. From the point of view of the US, therefore, it does not seem to play a decisive role. GSP is, however, extremely important for developing countries that rely on preferential market access to the US. In fact, according to Kofi Annan, a former UN Secretary General: 'the main losers in today's very unequal world are not those who are too much exposed to globalisation. They are those who have been left out'.[21] In this context, from the US perspective, its GSP gains in importance. The key point about the scheme is that it gives the US government the possibility of withdrawing custom duties exemptions to imports coming from countries that do not comply with internationally recognised workers' rights. Sometimes such a solution is perceived to have better effectiveness than multilateral social clause.[22] Donahue even claims that: 'In the US, the most successful linkage has been made in the GSP programme'.[23]

Moreover, GSP supporters point out its considerable influence on the US labour movement. It is highlighted that long before NAFTA the GSP helped to increase the labour movement's awareness of international issues. Furthermore, the GSP labour rights review process is appreciated for its contribution to broader information and precious experience on monitoring labour rights infringements and enforcement of labour laws for all over the world. Supporters also claim that this knowledge has, then, had a great positive effect on research, on issues connected to social labelling programmes, corporate codes of conduct, child labour and many other forms of international standard setting, monitoring and enforcement of labour regulation. Finally, they put emphasis on the fact that the GSP review mechanism has given rise to, inter alia, a number of lobbying groups, a global network of unions, human rights organisations, labour think tanks, networking organisations, NGOs and development agencies. In this way, the scope of international labour solidarity was augmented through GSP petitions.[24]

---

20 At the margin, in practice, GSP implementation falls under the umbrella of the USTR and its cross-agency GSP Subcommittee, which typically includes representatives from the departments of commerce, labour, agriculture, state and customs and immigration; the US International Trade Commission performs an advisory role. See: Emily Blanchard and Shushanik Hakobyan, 'The US Generalised System of Preferences in Principle and Practice' (2015) 38(3) *The World Economy* 399, 401 <https://doi.org/10.1111/twec.12216> accessed 22 November 2020.

21 ibid 400; <www.un.org/press/en/2000/20000211.sgsm7298.doc.html> accessed 22 November 2020.

22 Bronstein (n 1) 108.

23 Donahue (n 15) 201.

24 Tsogas (n 11) 360. However, some authors have pointed out that the GSP labour clause sets North American unions against each other instead of encouraging them to file complaints

For example, banana workers in Guatemala built an international campaign in order to deal with illegal dismissal of union members by Del Monte in 1999. The union named SITRABI (Sindicato de Trabajadores de Bananeros de Izabal) cooperated with USLEAP (US Labor Education in the Americas Project, a US-based NGO) with the aim of exerting direct pressure on Del Monte through a corporate campaign and indirect pressure through threatening the Guatemalan government with US sanctions under the GSP, which were used as an instrument for organising. Finally, the problem was successfully resolved – most of the workers and the union leaders were reinstated.[25]

In the historical context, in many cases the only threat of blocking imports to the US was enough to reform legislation in a country that violated fundamental employment rights.[26] For example, in 1974 the United Mine Workers of America pressured the US government to ban the import of South African coal produced by indentured labour under penal sanctions. This delivered results in terms of reforming South African legislation by the government.[27]

Going further, in 1985 labour unions and human rights groups filed petitions against Nicaragua, Korea, Guatemala, Chile, Haiti, Paraguay, the Philippines, Romania, Suriname, Taiwan and Zaire. In consequence, at the beginning of 1987 President Reagan removed Nicaragua and Romania from the list of GSP-eligible developing countries. On the contrary, Paraguay was suspended for one year.[28] Subsequently, Chile was suspended in 1988, and Burma and the Central African Republic in 1989. Liberia was removed in 1990. Mauritania was suspended in 1993, and continuing review period of six months was provided for some other countries, for example, Guatemala, El Salvador, Indonesia, Malawi, Thailand and Oman.[29] All of this – and especially the eventuality of having GSP privileges withdrawn – contributed to not only changing labour laws in many of these countries,

together. Unions bring complaints unilaterally against other governments and expect the US to withdraw trade preferences from countries that violate labour laws. It is not conducive to building collective power among unions. See: Tamara Kay, *NAFTA and the Politics of Labor Transnationalism* (New York: Cambridge University Press 2011) 23.

25 Stephanie Luce, 'The Case for International Labour Standards: A "Northern" Perspective' (2005) *Institute of Development Studies Working Paper* 250, 22–24 <www.ids.ac.uk/files/Wp250.pdf> accessed 22 November 2020. See also: Edmé Domínguez, Rosalba Icaza, Cirila Quintero, Silvia López and Åsa Stenman, 'Women Workers in the Maquiladoras and the Debate on Global Labor Standards' (2010) 16(4) *Feminist Economics* 185, 197 <http://dx.doi.org/10.1080/13545701.2010.530603> accessed 22 November 2020. See the cited literature.

26 Ojeda-Avilés (n 16) 111.

27 ibid.

28 Winzer (n 15) 234; Tsogas (n 11) 356; Jennifer L Tobin and Marc L Busch, 'The Disadvantage of Membership: How Joining the GATT/WTO Undermines GSP' (2019) 18(1) *World Trade Review* 133, 138 <https://doi.org/10.1017/S1474745618000034> accessed 22 November 2020.

29 Gadbaw and Medwig (n 15) 148; Tsogas (n 11) 355–356; Compa and Vogt (n 15) 209.

inter alia, Indonesia, Guatemala[30] and El Salvador[31] but also countries like the Dominican Republic,[32] Costa Rica, India, Pakistan and Sri Lanka. The authorities of these countries significantly improved labour legislation and increased inspection according to the American recommendations.[33]

On the other hand, the example of the suspension of GSP for Bangladesh in June 2013 is not so obvious in the context of elimination of violations of workers' rights. In this regard, it must be recalled that the suspension followed the collapse of the Rana Plaza complex in Dacca in April 2013, which killed over 1,100 textile workers.[34] Indeed, this was due to substandard working conditions, and terrible state of the factory buildings, which jeopardised the safety of workers. There was no trade union representation to prevent disaster when workers were intimidated into continuing to work despite a clear order from the government inspectorate concerning the abandonment of the building. The tragedy was a culmination of years of being mistreated, and years of severe labour violations, including child labour, and violations of the right to freedom of association and to bargain collectively. As a result of the suspension of GSP, a national tripartite plan of actions was developed in Bangladesh and some attempts were made to reform the law. However, it did not lead to any important changes. Contrary to the EU, Bangladesh's garment exports did not benefit much under the US GSP programme. For this reason, the suspension of the US GSP was neither turning point nor catalysts for change. Labour rights violations did not stop after the tragedy.[35] If the EU's GSP had been suspended, the effect would have been more significant.[36]

---

30 Bronstein (n 1) 95, 108–109. More: Douglas, Ferguson and Klett (n 13) 288–291; Tsogas (n 11) 359; Compa and Vogt (n 15) 212–222.
31 More: Douglas, Ferguson and Klett (n 13) 281–284; Tsogas (n 11) 359–360.
32 More: Douglas, Ferguson and Klett (n 13) 277–281.
33 Ojeda-Avilés (n 16) 111.
34 We should also keep in mind the November 2012 Tazreen Fashion factory fire with tragic outcome for many people (at least 117 dead). See: Scott Cooper, 'Global Supply Chain Governance: ILO, ISO & Worker Safety' (October 2018) 63(10) *Professional Safety* 70, 70.
35 In November 2013, the US and Bangladesh signed a Trade and Investment Cooperation Forum Agreement (TICFA). The parties to the agreement agreed to work together on a regular basis in order to solve issues of concern regarding the trade and investment relationship. The last meeting of the TICFA Council took place in September 2018, and during that meeting officials from both states pledged to deepen their engagement with these matters. It should be noted, however, that US officials expressed concerns as regards overall labour reforms and highlighted the need for Bangladesh to continue to collaborate with the private sector in the field of worker safety. Moreover, the US, the EU, Canada and the ILO are engaged in the Bangladesh Sustainability Compact, namely 'Compact for Continuous Improvements in Labour Rights and Factory Safety in the Ready-Made Garment and Knitwear Industry in Bangladesh'. The last review of the Sustainability Compact took place in July 2018, and its members noted that more work needed to be done as regards aligning Bangladesh's labour legislation with international labour conventions and implementation. See: Congressional Research Service, *Generalized System of Preferences (GSP): Overview and Issues for Congress* (Report RL33663, 2019, 26–27) <https://fas.org/sgp/crs/misc/RL33663.pdf> accessed 25 November 2020; <https://trade.ec.europa.eu/doclib/events/index.cfm?id=1853> accessed 25 November 2020.
36 See: Martin Myant, *The Impact of Trade and Investment Agreements on Decent Work and Sustainable Development* (Brussels: European Trade Union Institute 2017) 48. More: The

It appears desirable to present here some remarks concerning further imperfections of the US GSP, including its effectiveness. As has been explained previously, the first doubts appear on the background of the formulation: 'has not taken or is not taking steps to afford internationally recognised worker rights'. It would seem more reasonable to use the terminology developed by the ILO. The category of 'international labour standards' or 'labour rights' could be adopted with the aim of giving substance to the currently existing vague expressions. Unfortunately, the US legislation effectively guards against any reference to the ILO standards.[37]

The trouble here is that the US is convinced about being exempted from attempting to bring all standards into line with those that exist in the US. As it has been highlighted in one report: 'It is clear that Congress did not intend to . . . match all of the rights prevailing in this country. For instance, nations do not have to pay the American minimum wage or meet our work-place safety standards to qualify'.[38]

Following on from this, unilateral imposition of transnational labour standards by one country, as in case of the US and its GSP programme, entails a risk that other countries will be concerned about the fact that the US will not comply with genuine international standards and thus that other countries would be 'foolish to do so'.[39]

Furthermore, it should be noted that in principle strong political interference has always been a characteristic of the administration of the US GSP scheme.[40] It is to a large degree political mainly because of three reasons. First, GSP beneficiary countries become ineligible for the programme after reaching a certain level of wealth. Second, as said earlier, GSP is characterised by the fact that it is non-reciprocal. It means that beneficiary countries do not grant preferential market access to rich countries. Third, as conditionality is inscribed in the GSP, a violation of workers' rights can mean discretionary or even mandatory suspension from the GSP programme. From the point of view of exporters in poor countries, the GSP is unpredictable since it is highly vulnerable to the political whims of the

International Corporate Accountability Roundtable (n 9) 14–15; Jeffrey S Vogt, 'The Bangladesh Sustainability Compact: An Effective Tool for Promoting Workers' Rights?' in Gerda Van Roozendaal and Jan Orbie (eds), *Labour Standards in a Global Environment* (2017) 5(4) Politics and Governance 80, 86 <http://dx.doi.org/10.17645/pag.v5i4.1093> accessed 25 November 2020; Sabrina Zajak, *Transnational Activism, Global Labor Governance, and China* (Basingstoke: Palgrave Macmillan 2017) 103; Layna Mosley and Lindsay Tello, 'Labor Rights, Material Interests, and Moral Entrepreneurship' (2015) 37(1) *Human Rights Quarterly* 53, 54; Robert JS Ross, 'Bringing Labor Rights to Bangladesh' *The American Prospect* (12 July 2015) <https://prospect.org/labor/bringing-labor-rights-back-bangladesh/> accessed 25 November 2020; Yap (n 2) 214 et seq.
37 Alston (n 13) 74.
38 Jeremy B Grace, 'Environment and Labor Standards in World Trade: Cognitive Approaches to Changes in Regime Scope' (A dissertation submitted to the Faculty of the School of International Service of the American University in partial fulfillment of the requirements for the degree of Master of Arts in International Affairs 1995) 48–49. See the cited literature.
39 Hyde (n 5) 154.
40 ibid 166.

granting country. It is therefore less enticing to said exporters, what equals to the probability of underutilisation of the preferences.[41] It should be also noted that the GSP political nature is firmly confirmed by the most recent studies which indicate that while the US's political friends are equally likely to be investigated, they are much less likely to have their benefits suspended.[42]

A matter of enforcement of the labour rights eligibility criteria is another problem.[43] GSP critics pay attention to undermining its effectiveness and credibility due to the fact that countries in which labour rights violations occur have been provided privileged access to US markets, and have gained an unfair advantage over other countries, not excluding the US. A few implementation gaps for which the enforcement is so weak can be identified. First, there is considerable discretion in deciding on the GSP eligibility without much taking into account, for example, the national economic-interest waiver (according to the Trade Act) or the lack of minimum standards of compliance in the beneficiary country. Second, the review of country compliance petitions remains plagued by very poor transparency. Third, there are neither clear standards nor timeline for determining non-compliance. Moreover, the abuse of the continuing review process makes itself felt. It comes down to placing countries on an indefinite probation while they continue to benefit from preferential treatment. Fourth, the reinstatement criteria applied after the revocation of GSP eligibility may require to be emphasised as they are subject to political assessment and remain largely ineffective.[44]

The question that we must tackle is the question of how to remedy the problems uncovered in the previous four points. From the US point of view, solutions can be sought, of course, in the activity of the USTR and Congress. The latter could improve the effectiveness of the GSP scheme by amending the Trade Act with the aim of reinforcing the labour rights criteria and by employing more stringent monitoring on the USTR's implementation of the GSP. On the other hand, the Office of the USTR could enhance transparency of the eligibility determination process, ensure further clarification of timelines and standards for determining non-compliance, and 'ensure adequate follow through of benchmarks and targets set forth by the agency itself'.[45]

41 Tobin and Busch (n 28) 136.

42 Martin Gassebner and Arevik Gnutzmann-Mkrtchyan, 'Politicized Trade: What Drives Withdrawal of Trade Preferences?' (2018) 167(C) *Economics Letters 10–13* <https://doi.org/10.1016/j.econlet.2017.12.005> accessed 25 November 2020.

43 Furthermore, see a number of examples given by Collingsworth who has highlighted the failure of US administrations to enforce the GSP worker rights provisions: Terry Collingsworth, 'International Worker Rights Enforcement: Proposals Following a Test Case' in Lance A Compa and Stephen F Diamond (eds), *Human Rights, Labor Rights, and International Trade* (Philadelphia: University of Pennsylvania Press 1996) 227 et seq.

44 See: The International Corporate Accountability Roundtable (n 9) 2.

45 ibid.

As demonstrated by Elliott and Freeman,[46] there are some circumstances under which GSP's leverage is more likely to contribute to the improvement of workers' rights. These are as follows: greater dependency of the 'target' country on the US market, greater political openness of the 'target', involvement of human rights group, greater political capacity of the 'target' country to implement promised changes, and more emphasis on less politically sensitive labour standards.

In the light of this, it should be stressed that in October 2017, USTR Robert Lighthizer announced new enforcement priorities for GSP, i.e. a new effort to ensure beneficiary countries are meeting the eligibility criteria of the GSP trade preference programme. A new, 'more proactive process' assumes an intensification of efforts to conclude outstanding country practices reviews, and a triennial assessment by USTR and other relevant agencies of each beneficiary's compliance with the statutory GSP eligibility criteria. If the assessment of a beneficiary country creates doubts as to whether the country complies with an eligibility criterion, the administration is authorised to self-initiate a full country practice review of that country's continued eligibility for GSP. It is noteworthy that this interagency process is of additional character and complements the current petition receipt and public input process for country practice reviews. Interestingly, the first assessment period concentrated on Asian Business Development Companies. The new country practice reviews of Indonesia, India and Turkey were, in part, self-initiated (in 2018) by the Trade Policy Staff Committee as a consequence of this compliance review strategy. On 15 October 2018, an additional hearing of GSP beneficiaries for ongoing reviews of specific country practices was announced by the USTR. Some countries (Bolivia, Georgia, Iraq, Thailand, Uzbekistan) were the targets in his crosshairs because of failure to respect labour rights.[47] On 25 October 2019, USTR announced the closing of reviews of GSP eligibility for Bolivia, Iraq, and Uzbekistan without changes to those programmes, and the initiation of GSP eligibility reviews for Azerbaijan (what also relates to workers' rights).[48] Having discussed new enforcement priorities for GSP, it is still doubtful whether these reforms will really contribute to overcoming all mentioned disadvantages.

46 Kimberly A Elliott and Richard B Freeman, *Can Labour Standards Improve Under Globalization?* (Washington DC: Peterson Institute for International Economics 2003) 158.
47 Congressional Research Service (n 35) 21; <https://ustr.gov/about-us/policy-offices/press-office/press-releases/2017/october/ustr-announces-new-enforcement> accessed 25 November 2020; <www.federalregister.gov/documents/2018/10/15/2018-22374/generalized-system-of-preferences-gsp-notice-regarding-a-hearing-for-ongoing-country-practice> accessed 25 November 2020.
48 Ringel (n 6).

3 The EU Generalised System of Preferences (GSP)

3.1 Legal basis

In the case of the EU, the Generalised System of Preferences (GSP) has been applied since 1971 and has entailed lower tariffs to developing countries on some or all the EU imports from them.[49] It followed a resolution of the United Nations Conference on Trade and Development (UNCTAD) to establish a system of preferences with the aim of supporting developing countries.[50] The first cycle of the EU GSP scheme covered the period from 1971 to 1981 with further renewal for an additional ten years (1981–1991). In 1991, the scheme went through major revision[51] and was extended until 1994, at which time it was transformed into the third cycle spanning the period 1995–2004. As regards individual years of this period, the following legislation was enacted by the Community: Council Regulation (EC) No 3281/94 of 19 December 1994 applying a four-year scheme of generalised tariff preferences (1995 to 1998) in respect of certain industrial products originating in developing countries; Council Regulation (EC) No 1256/96 of 20 June 1996 applying multiannual schemes of generalised tariff preferences from 1 July 1996 to 30 June 1999 in respect of certain agricultural products originating in developing countries; Council Regulation (EC) No 2820/98 of 21 December 1998 applying a multiannual scheme of generalised tariff preferences for the period 1 July 1999 to 31 December 2001;[52] Council Regulation (EC) No 2501/2001 of 10 December 2001 applying a scheme of generalised tariff preferences for the period from 1 January 2002 to 31 December 2004. The latter envisaged major changes in the GSP scheme, establishing, inter alia, five arrangements:

49 Ojeda-Avilés (n 16) 111; Peter-Tobias Stoll, 'International Economic and Social Dimensions: Divided or Connected?' in Henner Gött (ed), *Labour Standards in International Economic Law* (Cham: Springer 2018) 29.

50 European Commission, *Report from the Commission to the European Parliament and the Council on the Application of Regulation (EU) No 978/2012 Applying a Scheme of Generalised Tariff Preferences and Repealing Council Regulation (EC) No 732/2008* (COM(2018) 665 final, Brussels, 4 October 2018).

51 In 1991, political conditionality appeared. It took the form of a provision under which some Latin American countries were granted preferential market access as a reward for their efforts in the field of fighting drugs production and trafficking. On the other hand, negative political conditionality appeared only in the 1994 Regulation, initially permitting the temporary withdrawal of preferences in case of forced labour and prison labour. André Sapir, 'The Impact of Globalization on Employment in Europe' in Mathias Dewatripont, André Sapir and Khalid Sekkat (eds), *Trade and Jobs in Europe: Much Ado About Nothing?* (Oxford: Oxford University Press 1999) 186.

52 In 1998, a social incentive system was established which granted additional trade preferences to developing countries complying with the ILO Conventions Nos 87, 98 and 138. See also: Jan Orbie and Olufemi Babarinde, 'The Social Dimension of Globalization and EU Development Policy: Promoting Core Labour Standards and Corporate Social Responsibility' (2008) 30(3) *European Integration* 459, 462 <https://doi.org/10.1080/07036330802142178> accessed 25 November 2020.

general arrangements; special incentive arrangements for the protection of labour rights; special incentive arrangements for the protection of the environment; special arrangements to combat drug production and trafficking; and special arrangements for the least developed countries (LDCs), such as the Everything But Arms (EBA) initiative. As observed by Weiss, a 'carrot and stick' balancing strategy has been adopted by Council Regulation 2501/2001. The special incentive arrangement for the protection of labour rights was a carrot. A recipient country had to prove that the eight ILO core conventions were incorporated in national law and that their rules were effectively implemented. On the other hand, temporary withdrawal of preferences was a stick. It was possible to use it when core conventions were violated and when goods were produced by prison or slave labour.[53] Subsequently, Council Regulation (EC) No 980/2005 of 27 June 2005 applying a scheme of generalised tariff preferences was adopted and covered the period from 1 January 2006 to 31 December 2008.[54] This regulation reduced the number of arrangements to three, that is: general arrangements; special incentive arrangements for sustainable development and good governance – GSP Plus; and special arrangements for LDCs – EBA.[55] Next, Council Regulation (EC) No

---

53 In other words, in 2001, all eight ILO conventions became a point of reference for the incentive and the withdrawal mechanisms. See: Manfred Weiss, 'The EU Generalised Scheme of Preferences and the Special Incentive Arrangement for Sustainable Development and Good Governance' in Adalberto Perulli and Tiziano Treu (eds), *Sustainable Development, Global Trade and Social Rights* (Alphen aan den Rijn: Kluwer Law International 2018) 122. More: Clara Portela and Jan Orbie, 'Sanctions Under the EU Generalised System of Preferences and Foreign Policy: Coherence by Accident?' (2014) 20(1) *Contemporary Politics* 63, 65 <http://10.1080/13569775.2014.881605> accessed 25 November 2020; Anne CL Davies, 'Should the EU Have the Power to Set Minimum Standards for Collective Labour Rights in the Member States?' in Philip Alston (ed), *Labour Rights as Human Rights* (Oxford: Oxford University Press 2005) 187–189.

54 Cleopatra Doumbia-Henry and Eric Gravel, 'Free Trade Agreements and Labour Rights: Recent Developments' (2006) 145(3) *International Labour Review* 185, 190.

55 The 2005 reform was triggered by the case of India, which on December 9 2002, requested that a WTO Dispute Settlement Panel be formed in order to consider its allegations of discriminatory application of the EU's GSP programme, strictly speaking, its drugs incentive system (the argument was that the MFN principle stands in the way of the selective choice of countries that are granted preferential treatment) and its labour and environmental standards. The Dispute Settlement Panel upheld the complaint, and the WTO's Appellate Body assumed the GSP drugs incentive system discriminatory. The Appellate Body explained (para 99) that 'the Enabling Clause is an "exception" to Article I:1 of the GATT 1994' (an exception to the MFN principle). Moreover, it reversed the Panel's finding that 'the term "non-discriminatory" in footnote 3 [to paragraph 2(a) of the Enabling Clause] requires that identical tariff preferences under GSP schemes be provided to all developing countries without differentiation, except for the implementation of a priori limitations' (para 174), European Communities – Conditions for the Granting of Tariff Preferences to Developing Countries: Report of the Appellate Body (7 April 2004) WT/DS246/AB/R. The 2005 revision extended the list of conventions significant from the point of view of the GSP+ beyond the core ILO conventions. It included also those relating to sustainable development and human rights. The temporal withdrawal of the preferential arrangements was possible in respect of all or of certain

732/2008 of 22 July 2008 applying a scheme of generalised tariff preferences from 1 January 2009 and amending Regulations (EC) No 552/97, (EC) No 1933/2006 and Commission Regulations (EC) No 1100/2006 and (EC) No 964/2007 was introduced and was in force initially for a period of three years. Then, it was slightly amended and extended until 31 December 2013.[56]

Regulation (EU) No 978/2012 of the European Parliament and of the Council of 25 October 2012 applying a Scheme of Generalised Tariff Preferences and repealing Council Regulation (EC) No 732/2008 is now in force and the Treaty on the European Union (TEU) and the Treaty of the Functioning of the European Union (TFEU) are the legal basis for the current system. In more specific terms, the aforementioned Regulation has its basis in Article 207 TFEU,[57] but it is also set out in its Preamble that 'The Union's common commercial policy shall be guided by the principles and pursue the objectives set out in the general provisions on the Union's external action, laid down in Article 21 of the Treaty on European Union (TEU)' (second recital). Moreover, the Regulation states that

> The Union's common commercial policy is to be consistent with and to consolidate the objectives of the Union policy in the field of development cooperation, laid down in Article 208 of the Treaty on the Functioning of the European Union (TFEU), in particular the eradication of poverty and the promotion of sustainable development and good governance in the developing countries. It is to comply with WTO requirements, in particular with the Decision on Differential and More Favourable Treatment, Reciprocity and Fuller Participation of Developing Countries (the 'Enabling Clause'), adopted under the GATT in 1979, under which WTO Members may accord differential and more favourable treatment to developing countries (fourth recital).

This clearly shows us that, although the EU's GSP is covered by the Common Commercial Policy framework, it also pursues a broader agenda.[58]

---

products, originating in a beneficiary country, inter alia for the reason of 'serious and systematic violations of principles laid down in the conventions. . ., on the basis of the conclusion of the relevant monitoring bodies' (Article 16 paragraph 1). See also: Portela and Orbie (n 53) 65–66; Kaufmann (n 5) 136; Hyde (n 5) 166; Cole (n 3) 180, 196–209.

56 For more on the history, see: United Nations, *Generalized System of Preferences: Handbook on the Scheme of the European Union* (New York, Geneva: United Nations 2015) 2–3.

57 According to Article 207 paragraph 1 TFEU, 'The common commercial policy shall be based on uniform principles, particularly with regard to changes in tariff rates, the conclusion of tariff and trade agreements relating to trade in goods and services, and the commercial aspects of intellectual property, foreign direct investment, the achievement of uniformity in measures of liberalisation, export policy and measures to protect trade such as those to be taken in the event of dumping or subsidies. The common commercial policy shall be conducted in the context of the principles and objectives of the Union's external action'.

58 See more: Joris Larik, 'Good Global Governance Through Trade: Constitutional Moorings' in Jan Wouters, Axel Marx, Dylan Geraets and Bregt Natens (eds), *Global Governance*

According to Article 21 paragraph 1 TEU

> The Union's action on the international scene shall be guided by the principles which have inspired its own creation, development and enlargement, and which it seeks to advance in the wider world: democracy, the rule of law, the universality and indivisibility of human rights and fundamental freedoms, respect for human dignity, the principles of equality and solidarity, and respect for the principles of the United Nations Charter and international law,

and according to paragraph 2

> The Union shall define and pursue common policies and actions, and shall work for a high degree of cooperation in all fields of international relations, in order to: (a) safeguard its values, fundamental interests . . . (b) consolidate and support democracy, the rule of law, human rights and the principles of international law; (c) preserve peace, prevent conflicts and strengthen international security . . . (d) foster the sustainable economic, social and environmental development of developing countries, with the primary aim of eradicating poverty; (e) encourage the integration of all countries into the world economy, including through the progressive abolition of restrictions on international trade; (h) promote an international system based on stronger multilateral cooperation and good global governance.

Article 21 TEU should be analysed in conjunction with Article 3 TEU according to which

> The Union shall establish an internal market. It shall work for the sustainable development of Europe based on balanced economic growth and price stability, a highly competitive social market economy, aiming at full employment and social progress, and a high level of protection and improvement of the quality of the environment. It shall promote scientific and technological advance.
>
> It shall combat social exclusion and discrimination, and shall promote social justice and protection, equality between women and men, solidarity between generations and protection of the rights of the child.
>
> It shall promote economic, social and territorial cohesion, and solidarity among Member States' (paragraph 3).

Through Trade: EU Policies and Approaches (Cheltenham, Northampton: Edward Elgar Publishing 2015) 66; Laura Beke and Nicolas Hachez, 'The EU GSP: A Preference for Human Rights and Good Governance? The Case of Myanmar' in Jan Wouters, Axel Marx, Dylan Geraets and Bregt Natens (eds), *Global Governance Through Trade: EU Policies and Approaches* (Cheltenham, Northampton: Edward Elgar Publishing 2015) 185.

Moreover, according to paragraph 5,

> In its relations with the wider world, the Union shall uphold and promote its values and interests and contribute to the protection of its citizens. It shall contribute to peace, security, the sustainable development of the Earth, solidarity and mutual respect among peoples, free and fair trade, eradication of poverty and the protection of human rights, in particular the rights of the child, as well as to the strict observance and the development of international law, including respect for the principles of the United Nations Charter.

The legal basis provided for in the TEU should be taken into consideration together with the legal basis laid down in the TFEU where according to Article 208 TFEU 'Union policy in the field of development cooperation shall be conducted within the framework of the principles and objectives of the Union's external action'.

'Union development cooperation policy shall have as its primary objective the reduction and, in the long term, the eradication of poverty' (paragraph 1). According to paragraph 2 'The Union and the Member States shall comply with the commitments and take account of the objectives they have approved in the context of the United Nations and other competent international organisations'.

Furthermore, according to Article 209 TFEU 'The European Parliament and the Council, acting in accordance with the ordinary legislative procedure, shall adopt the measures necessary for the implementation of development cooperation policy, which may relate to multiannual cooperation programmes with developing countries or programmes with a thematic approach' (paragraph 1), and according to paragraph 2:

> The Union may conclude with third countries and competent international organisations any agreement helping to achieve the objectives referred to in Article 21 of the Treaty on European Union and in Article 208 of this Treaty.
>
> The first subparagraph shall be without prejudice to Member States' competence to negotiate in international bodies and to conclude agreements.

3.2 *The three different arrangements*

Regulation (EU) No 978/2012 of the European Parliament and of the Council of 25 October 2012 entered into force on 1 January 2014 (for a period of ten years) and consists of only three arrangements:

1   A general arrangement (Standard GSP) for developing countries that have not achieved high or upper middle-income status (18 beneficiaries);
2   A special incentive arrangement for sustainable development and good governance (GSP+) for Standard GSP beneficiaries that are also considered vulnerable (8 beneficiaries); and

3   A special arrangement for the least developed countries (LDCs) (Everything
     But Arms [EBA]) (49 beneficiaries).[59]

The list of beneficiary countries has been reduced according to the Regulation
(EU) No 978/2012, but those no more eligible do not remain without support.
Some of them, for example, have concluded free trade agreements; others have
achieved high or upper middle-income status.[60]

3.2.1 General arrangement

This scheme is contained in Chapter II of the Regulation (EU) No 978/2012,
more specifically in its Articles 4–8. It should be borne in mind that an eligible
country benefits from the tariff preferences provided under the general arrangement unless it has been classified by the World Bank as a high-income or an upper-
middle-income country during three consecutive years immediately preceding the
update of the list of beneficiary countries, or it benefits from a preferential market
access arrangement which provides the same tariff preferences as the scheme, or
better, for substantially all trade. These reservations, of course, do not apply to
least developed countries. It is notable that a full list of GSP beneficiary countries is
established in Annex II, which is subject to a review conducted by the Commission
by 1 January of each year. It is also noteworthy, as Weiss rightly reminds us, that the
beneficiary countries have to comply with the principles set out in the eight ILO
core conventions and seven UN conventions on human rights.[61]

3.2.2 Special incentive arrangement for sustainable development and good governance (GSP+)

This scheme is regulated by articles 9 to 16, inclusive. The GSP+ offers even broader
tariff cuts of the same tariff lines for vulnerable countries which ratify and implement
27 international conventions on human and labour rights, environment and good
governance,[62] and which cooperate with the Commission to monitor implementation of these conventions.[63] It is based on the integral concept of sustainable development, as recognised by, for example: the 1986 UN Declaration on the Right to

---

59 European Commission (n 50).
60 See: Weiss (n 53) 123; Alessandra Zanobetti, *Diritto internazionale del lavoro: Norme uni-
    versali, regionali e dell'Unione europea* (Milan: Giuffrè 2011) 299–300 <http://ec.europa.
    eu/trade/policy/countries-and-regions/development/generalised-scheme-of-prefer-
    ences/index_en.htm> accessed 26 November 2020.
61 Weiss (n 53) 124.
62 Annelien Gansemans, Deborah Martens, Marijke D'Haese and Jan Orbie, 'Do Labour Rights
    Matter for Export? A Qualitative Comparative Analysis of Pineapple Trade to the EU' in Gerda
    Van Roozendaal and Jan Orbie (eds), *Labour Standards in a Global Environment* (2017) 5(4)
    Politics and Governance 93, 95 <http://dx.doi.org/10.17645/pag.v5i4.1082> accessed 26
    November 2020; Weiss (n 53) 124; Stoll (n 49) 29; Myant (n 36) 54.
63 <https://ec.europa.eu/trade/policy/countries-and-regions/development/generalised-
    scheme-of-preferences/> accessed 26 November 2020.

Development, the 1992 Rio Declaration on Environment and Development, the 1998 ILO Declaration on Fundamental Principles and Rights at Work, the 2000 UN Millennium Declaration and the 2002 Johannesburg Declaration on Sustainable Development. In the light of the objectives of the Regulation, the additional tariff preferences provided under the GSP+ should be granted to those developing countries which, due to a lack of diversification and insufficient integration within the international trading system, are vulnerable, in order to help them assume the special burdens and responsibilities resulting from the ratification of core international conventions on human and labour rights, environmental protection and good governance, as well as from the effective implementation thereof (point 11 of the Preamble to the Regulation). According to the established criteria of eligibility, the following countries benefited from GSP+ preferences as of 1 January 2019: Armenia, Bolivia, Cape Verde, Kyrgyzstan, Mongolia, Pakistan, Philippines and Sri Lanka.[64] Having discussed the GSP+ framework, it seems clear that it is a model example of harnessing trade policy with the aim of realising a wider normative agenda.[65]

3.2.3 Special arrangement for the least developed countries

Articles 17–18 of the Regulation deal with Everything But Arms (EBA). It is a special arrangement for the least developed countries, which – under some conditions – grants full duty-free and quota free access to the EU Single Market for all products (except arms and armaments). In order to be granted EBA status, a country has to be listed as a Least Developed Country (LDC) by the UN Committee for Development Policy. Countries are not required to apply to benefit from EBA, because they are added to (or removed from) the list through a delegated regulation. In addition, as opposed to the Standard GSP, conclusion of a free trade agreement with the EU does not entail a loss of EBA status.[66]

3.3 Sanctions in case of violations

3.3.1 Temporary withdrawal (common to all arrangements)

Three preferential arrangements discussed earlier may be withdrawn temporarily, in respect of all or of certain products originating in a beneficiary country, for any of the reasons mentioned in the Regulation. Those reasons are as follows:

a)   serious and systematic violation of principles laid down in the core human and labour rights UN/ILO Conventions (Annex VIII, Part A);[67]

---

64   <https://trade.ec.europa.eu/doclib/docs/2019/may/tradoc_157889.pdf> accessed 26 November 2020.
65   See: Larik (n 58) 66; Beke and Hachez (n 58) 185.
66   <https://trade.ec.europa.eu/tradehelp/everything-arms> accessed 26 November 2020.
67   It is also essential to pay attention to point 24 of the Preamble to the Regulation, according to which tariff preferences under the special incentive arrangement for sustainable development

b)   export of goods made by prison labour;
c)   serious shortcomings in customs controls on the export or transit of drugs (illicit substances or precursors), or failure to comply with international conventions on anti-terrorism and money laundering;
d)   serious and systematic unfair trading practices which are prohibited or actionable under the WTO Agreements take place;
e)   serious and systematic infringement of the objectives adopted by Regional Fishery Organisations or any international arrangements to which the Union is a party concerning the conservation and management of fishery resources.

According to Article 21 of the Regulation, a beneficiary country should provide administrative cooperation as required for the implementation and policing of the preferential arrangements. The lack of such a cooperation may entail temporary withdrawal of the preferential arrangements provided for in the Regulation. According to Article 21 paragraph 2, the administrative cooperation requires, inter alia, that a beneficiary country:

a)   communicate to the Commission and update the information necessary for the implementation of the rules of origin and the policing thereof;
b)   assist the Union by carrying out, at the request of the customs authorities of the Member States, subsequent verification of the origin of the goods, and communicate its results in time to the Commission;
c)   assist the Union by allowing the Commission, in coordination and close cooperation with the competent authorities of the Member States, to conduct the Union administrative and investigative cooperation missions in that country, in order to verify the authenticity of documents or the accuracy of information relevant for granting the preferential arrangements referred to in Article 1(2);
d)   carry out or arrange for appropriate inquiries to identify and prevent contravention of the rules of origin;
e)   comply with or ensure compliance with the rules of origin in respect of regional cumulation, within the meaning of Regulation (EEC) No 2454/93, if the country benefits therefrom; and
f)   assist the Union in the verification of conduct where there is a presumption of origin-related fraud, whereby the existence of fraud may be presumed where imports of products under the preferential arrangements provided for in this Regulation massively exceed the usual levels of the beneficiary country's exports.

---

and good governance should be temporarily withdrawn if the beneficiary country does not respect its binding undertaking to maintain the ratification and effective implementation of certain international conventions concerning core human rights and labour rights or to comply with the reporting requirements imposed by the respective conventions, or if the beneficiary country does not cooperate with the Union's monitoring procedures as set out in the Regulation.

Before taking a decision about temporary withdrawal, the Commission shall first publish a notice in the Official Journal of the European Union, stating that there are grounds for reasonable doubt about compliance with aforementioned reasons, which may call into question the right of the beneficiary country to continue to enjoy the benefits granted by the Regulation. Importantly, the Commission shall inform the beneficiary country concerned of any decision about temporary withdrawal, before it becomes effective. The period of temporary withdrawal shall not exceed six months, however, the Commission is authorised to extend it. Member states shall communicate to the Commission all relevant information that may justify temporary withdrawal of the tariff preferences or its extension.

3.3.2 Monitoring mechanism for GSP+

In regard to GSP+, the regulation currently in force also stipulates that 'the Commission shall keep under review the status of ratification of the relevant conventions and shall monitor their effective implementation, as well as cooperation with the relevant monitoring bodies' (Article 13). It means that granting GSP+ benefits entails continuous monitoring of the GSP+ beneficiaries' obligations. Each GSP+ beneficiary receives a List of Issues – the so-called 'scorecard' – prepared by the Commission in order to measure the compliance with their commitments. The document identifies serious weaknesses which should be purged. Above all, it contains deficiencies referred to by the Commission in its assessment of the GSP+ entry applications. Moreover, the irregularities detected by the monitoring bodies of the relevant core international conventions are also included in said document. And over time, other information can be added to the List of Issues, delivered not only by the European Parliament and the Council but also by stakeholders, for example, business, civil society or social partners.[68]

The so-called 'GSP+ dialogue' is another tool in the framework of the monitoring mechanism for GSP+. It consists quite simply in the fact that the Commission and the European External Action Service (EEAS) establish a dialogue on GSP+ compliance with the beneficiary countries, trying to bring to their notice the areas indicated in the List of Issues.[69] As pointed out by Weiss, the aim of the GSP+ dialogue is 'to build a relationship based on trust and cooperation'.[70]

3.4 General safeguards (common to all arrangements)

The general safeguards are regulated under Articles 22–28 of the Regulation. By the letter of the law, where a product originating in a beneficiary country is

---

68 <https://trade.ec.europa.eu/doclib/docs/2017/january/tradoc_155235.pdf>   accessed 26 November 2020.
69 ibid.
70 Weiss (n 53) 124.

imported in volumes and/or at prices which cause, or threaten to cause, serious difficulties to EU producers of like or directly competing products, normal Common Customs Tariff duties on that product may be reintroduced (Article 22 paragraph 1).

Serious difficulties shall be considered to exist where EU producers suffer deterioration in their economic and/or financial situation. In examining whether such deterioration exists, the Commission shall take account of a number of factors concerning EU producers, where such information is available. These are market share, production, stocks, production capacity, bankruptcies, profitability, capacity utilisation, employment, imports and prices.

The Commission shall investigate whether the normal Common Customs Tariff duties should be reintroduced if there is sufficient prima facie evidence that the conditions of Article 22 paragraph 1 are met. An investigation shall be initiated upon request by a member state, by any legal person or any association not having legal personality, acting on behalf of EU producers, or on the Commission's own initiative. An investigation, including all the procedural steps referred to in the Regulation, shall be concluded within 12 months from its initiation.

3.5 Pros and cons

In the appraisal of the EU GSP, we should remember that it defines the level of aspiration of the EU as regards conventions that should be ratified and implemented by future Free Trade Agreement (FTA) partners. These provisions mirror the EU hopes to be achieved in the long run. This level of aspiration constitutes also a bottom line in sustainable development negotiations.[71] In other words, the GSP is perceived as a 'preliminary step', while the conclusion of FTA is the objective – a step forward as a result of the negotiation process[72].

According to the aforementioned Report from the Commission to the European Parliament and the Council on the Application of Regulation (EU) No 978/2012 applying a Scheme of Generalised Tariff Preferences and repealing Council Regulation (EC) No 732/2008,[73] an overall positive impact of the GSP on social development and human rights in the beneficiary countries is noticeable. In addition, it has been highlighted that the most recent version of GSP has contributed to the promotion of sustainable development and good governance, especially thanks to the EU's enhanced monitoring of the implementation of the international conventions relating to GSP+. Clear examples are given to illustrate these observations. First, in accordance with the commitment formulated in the Communication from the Commission to the European Parliament,

---

71 Ludo Cuyvers, 'The Sustainable Development Clauses in Free Trade Agreements of the EU with Asian Countries: Perspectives for ASEAN?' (2014) 22(4) *Journal of Contemporary European Studies* 427–428, 437 <https://doi.org/10.1080/14782804.2014.92375 2> accessed 26 November 2020.
72 See Weiss (n 53) 127.
73 European Commission (n 50).

the Council, the European Economic and Social Committee and the Committee of the Regions 'Trade for all: Towards a more responsible trade and investment policy', the Commission and the High Representative have increased their
involvement with certain EBA beneficiary countries with the aim of contributing
to EU efforts to ensure respect of fundamental human and labour rights. Second,
GSP has exerted a profound positive influence on the role of women in society.
For instance, in the textile and clothing sectors (in Bangladesh and Pakistan) this
could have been achieved by creating employment opportunities for women and
by improving participation of women in the labour force in export industries
trading with the EU. Third, it has been demonstrated that the EU's leverage in
countries that benefit from GSP+ has been increased due to the close monitoring of them. More specifically, this refers to the power of pushing these countries
towards the effective implementation of the 27 relevant international conventions.[74] Besides, it has created the opportunities for truly constructive dialogue
and has enabled the EU to engage with beneficiary countries on all areas which
are marked by poor and ineffective implementation.

On the other hand, the problem can be approached from a somewhat different direction. As we are aware, the GSP has a very close connection with labour
rights. Yap has pointed out that this is because the GSP contributes to economic
activity generation necessary to sustain labour, and in turn violations of labour
rights, thus producing a vicious circle. The example of Bangladesh is given to
illustrate how the rise of the garment industry has been triggered partly by the
country's primary competitive advantage – the infringements of labour rights and
low labour costs. According to the author, this advantage is further enhanced by
the GSP benefits, identified as Bangladesh's second most significant competitive
advantage. The author ponders the question whether GSP conditionality system
can be an effective instrument of promotion of labour rights. He highlights that
the answer cannot be confined to whether the GSP's labour rights conditionality
mechanism can have a minimal net positive impact on labour rights, but it 'must

---

74 Some authors, however, stress that it cannot always be said that the GSP+ improves the
implementation of labour rights in a certain country. For example, as Peru had ratified the
relevant ILO conventions in 2002, it would be difficult to conclude that the GSP+ has contributed to such implementation. See: Jan Orbie, Lore Van den Putte and Deborah Martens,
'The Impact of Labour Rights Commitments in EU Trade Agreements: The Case of Peru'
in Gerda Van Roozendaal and Jan Orbie (eds), *Labour Standards in a Global Environment*
(2017) 5(4) *Politics and Governance* 6, 8 <http://dx.doi.org/10.17645/pag.v5i4.1091>
accessed 26 November 2020. On the other hand, as pointed out by Leenknegt, even some
ILO officers engage in polemics with the view that granting trade preferences generally
does not entail improvements in the implementation of core labour standards by beneficiary
countries. Indeed, attention is paid to the increasing number of countries which are engaging with the EU on labour standards. Sometimes the EU only needs to wait a little longer
for effects. Pieter Leenknegt, 'EU Trade Policy and International Labour Standards: The
View from the ILO' in Roger Blanpain (ed), Jan Wouters, Glenn Rayp, Laura Beke and Axel
Marx (guest eds), *Protecting Labour Rights in a Multi-Polar Supply Chain and Mobile Global
Economy* (Alphen aan den Rijn: Wolters Kluwer 2015) 79.

also assess whether the conditionality scheme enables the GSP as a whole to foster economic development that does not leave labour rights behind'.[75]

In the view of other authors, ineffective conditionality of GSP programmes deserves considerable criticism,[76] but it is just the tip of the iceberg. Some of them go even further by listing other disadvantages of the GSP, thus putting the GSP programmes out of a reliable tool. GSP labour clauses may entail a danger of having double standard practices as they are developed and applied unilaterally. A country which has introduced a GSP labour clause is the only decision-maker on which country and when would be subject to a GSP investigation and may eventually be excluded from trade benefits.[77] Thus, unequal treatment is used in comparable circumstances. It has been correctly observed that we are dealing here with a 'dichotomy between norms and interests', which means that in determining whether to enforce norms, the EU is motivated by its own interest.[78] In fact, many observers claim that the EU uses the GSP scheme discretionally and instrumentally with the purpose of pursuing foreign policy goals rather than for safeguarding labour rights.[79] We must realise that general safeguards common to all arrangements are indeed a manifestation of protectionism and they are designed to protect 'EU producers of like or directly competing products'. It is thereby evident that the confines of this arrangement should be sought in purely economic calculations.[80] At the margin, even with respect to ILO standards in the EU GSP, it has been noted that their application may prompt accusations of hypocrisy, ineffectuality and inconsistency.[81]

The GSP has also faced a barrage of criticism over the 'lesser entity of affected countries', as it has been named by Ojeda-Avilés. We are talking here about developing countries, very often the smaller ones that fail to respect labour rights, but countries characterised by the enormous economic importance. The latter makes them free of any restrictions and enables them to 'maintain their paradigm' without worrying about consequences to their trade. For this reason, Ojeda-Avilés presents the most efficient way to find the proper solution, which is the creation

75 Yap (n 2) 241–242.
76 Razavi (n 8) 888; see the cited literature. John Hilary, 'European Trade Unions and Free Trade: Between International Solidarity and Perceived Self-Interest' in Andreas Bieler, Bruno Ciccaglione, John Hilary and Ingemar Lindberg (eds), *Free Trade and Transnational Labour* (London, New York: Routledge 2015) 50–51.
77 Bronstein (n 1) 110.
78 Beke and Hachez (n 58) 193.
79 Samantha Velluti, 'The EU's Social Dimension and Its External Trade Relations' in Axel Marx, Jan Wouters, Glenn Rayp and Laura Beke (eds), *Global Governance of Labour Rights. Assessing the Effectiveness of Transnational Public and Private Policy Initiatives* (Cheltenham, Northampton: Edward Elgar Publishing 2015) 50; see the cited literature.
80 See also: Weiss (n 53) 127.
81 Tonia Novitz, 'Trading in Services – Commodities and Beneficiaries' in Adelle Blackett and Anne Trebilcock (eds), *Research Handbook on Transnational Labour Law* (Cheltenham, Northampton: Edward Elgar Publishing 2015) 501; see the cited literature.

of a universal system under which a social clause would be included in trade agreements of a majority of countries.[82]

The EU's GSP labour provisions has already been used in Myanmar's case (withdrawal from the whole scheme). It was deprived of trade privileges because of the widespread use of forced labour by the government.[83] A similar method was deployed in case of trade union rights infringements in Belarus.[84] However, this did not give rise to any significant policy change regarding labour standards.[85] Benefits have been also withdrawn in 2010 against Sri Lanka (withdrawal from GSP+),[86] which failed to implement human rights conventions.[87]

Of course, there have been many more occasions to suspend GSP preferences, for example, decision-makers have debated such a step in regard to China, Russia, Pakistan and India.[88] However, it has never materialised. The rare enforcement of conditionality provisions has become an impulse for further criticism, which is focused on imbalance between positive and negative conditionality (the former used widely, and the latter only to a minor extent).[89] In this type of argument, it is worth remembering that supporters of EU sanctions highlight their positive consequences, which even go further beyond the sanctioned country. Zhou and Cuyvers emphasise that sanctions can be perceived as contributing to 'the international definition, promulgation, recognition, and domestic internalization of human rights norms'.[90] They believe in the sanction's deterrent potential, that is, that other countries refrain from violating human rights. Moreover, the authors

---

82 Ojeda-Avilés (n 16) 112.
83 Bronstein (n 1) 109. More: Tonia Novitz, 'Labour Standards and Trade: Need We Choose Between "Human Rights" and "Sustainable Development"?' in Henner Gött (ed), *Labour Standards in International Economic Law* (Cham: Springer 2018) 126–127.
84 Evgeny Postnikov, 'Valued Exports: Social Standards in EU and U.S. Trade Agreements' (A dissertation submitted to the faculty of the Graduate School of Public and International Affairs in partial fulfillment of the requirements for the degree of Doctor of Philosophy, University of Pittsburgh 2014) 56.
85 David Cheong and Franz Christian Ebert, 'Labour Law and Trade Policy: What Implications for Economic and Human Development?' in Shelley Marshall and Colin Fenwick (eds), *Labour Regulation and Development: Socio-Legal Perspectives* (Cheltenham, Northampton: Edward Elgar Publishing 2016) 107; Myant (n 36) 55; see the cited literature; Weifeng Zhou and Ludo Cuyvers, 'Linking International Trade and Labour Standards: The Effectiveness of Sanctions Under the European Union's GSP' (2011) 45(1) *Journal of World Trade* 63, 64, 77–78.
86 Axel Marx and Jadir Soares, 'Does Integrating Labour Provisions in Free Trade Agreements Make a Difference? An Exploratory Analysis of Freedom of Association and Collective Bargaining Rights in 13 EU Trade Partners' in Jan Wouters, Axel Marx, Dylan Geraets and Bregt Natens (eds), *Global Governance Through Trade: EU Policies and Approaches* (Cheltenham, Northampton: Edward Elgar Publishing 2015) 161; Beke and Hachez (n 58) 192. See also: Yap (n 2) 224–227.
87 Francis Maupain, *The Future of the International Labour Organization in the Global Economy* (Oxford, Portland OR: Hart Publishing 2013) 199.
88 Portela and Orbie (n 53) 64.
89 Beke and Hachez (n 58) 192.
90 Zhou and Cuyvers (n 85) 78.

see sanctions as an institutionalised expression of the EU's commitment to core labour standards.[91] This apotheosis, however, cannot obscure the fact that trade measures can cause a lot of harm and, as a general rule, should be used with particular caution. Sometimes postulates are developed for impact assessment before imposing sanctions. Negative conditionality and sanctions can only be considered as the final solution because 'it hurts populations more than it does the governments that violate human rights'.[92]

Taking into account these drawbacks, it should be noted that the idea behind the Regulation (EU) No 978/2012 was to solve many of these problems. In particular, the latest reforms have reduced the number of eligible beneficiary countries to 75. Consequently, the Commission will be able to focus only on those that are most in need of help and, what is important, deserve it.[93] Next, the rules of the Regulation are devised to contribute to allaying the criticism connected to the lack of legal security, objectivity, stability, predictability and transparency in the GSP scheme. Procedural simplification and enhanced monitoring can help to level out these defects.[94] As rightly stated by Portela and Orbie, the Regulation (EU) No 978/2012 places a stronger focus on guaranteeing compliance in comparison to the previous regulation, which concentrated on the ratification requirement leaving behind the implementation of the conventions.[95]

Last but not least, in carrying out the general evaluation of the GSP, we must refer to the latest research of Tobin and Busch who have developed a unique approach to the negative interaction between GSP and the GATT/WTO. More specifically, the authors have sought to explain why the GATT/WTO's interaction with GSP undermines trade. They have demonstrated that by itself, GSP contributes to export growth in developing countries, but when these countries join the GATT or the WTO, their imports decrease. If compared to GSP recipients that do not get GATT/WTO membership, their total trade produces fewer gains. Tobin and Busch have explained this by the fact that joining and participating in the GATT/WTO regime 'make GSP more predictable by making it non-discriminatory, in the sense that exporters in recipient countries are less vulnerable to the programme's ad hoc conditionality. This leads these exporters to lobby less against domestic protectionism, yielding higher trade barriers at home, and thus fewer imports'.[96] From the point of view of this research, these findings are not without significance because our fundamental questions are: how to

91 ibid.
92 Beke and Hachez (n 58) 192–193; see the cited literature.
93 Yap (n 2) 217; Beke and Hachez (n 58) 198. See also: Jan Wouters, Axel Marx, Dylan Geraets and Bregt Natens, 'Conclusion: Possibilities and Limitations of Governing Through Trade' in Jan Wouters, Axel Marx, Dylan Geraets and Bregt Natens (eds), *Global Governance Through Trade: EU Policies and Approaches* (Cheltenham, Northampton: Edward Elgar Publishing 2015) 352.
94 See also: Beke and Hachez (n 58) 196.
95 Portela and Orbie (n 53) 66; see the cited literature.
96 Tobin and Busch (n 28) 133, 157.

improve the regulation of global processes towards providing not only economic growth but also social justice and the effectiveness of labour rights?, and how to find a balance between protective function of labour law and the attempt for flexibility, that is, between strengthening the workers' rights standards and free trade and investment?

4 Concluding remarks: a comparison of the EU's and the US's GSP schemes

The presented characteristics of the US and the EU schemes reveal some important differences between them. The issue which should be at the forefront of the discussion is connected to their motivation. The operation of the US GSP scheme, relying much on a sanction-based strategy, is often referred to as 'aggressive unilateralism' and is in contrast to the EU approach called 'soft unilateralism'.[97] The latter is mainly motivated by the will to ensure that poor countries have preferential access to the EU market. The linking of trade liberalisation with, inter alia, protection of workers' rights plays an important role in the whole concept. Clearly, even if protectionism is not the central part of the EU's approach, economic calculations are also taken into consideration. This is explicitly reflected in the provisions related to general safeguards common to all arrangements.

The EU's GSP scheme has been applied since 1971 and has been governed by a number of regulations. By way of comparison, the US GSP programme was implemented in 1976, and must be periodically renewed by the Congress. What is important, only the US GSP programme is designed to give organisations the possibility to file petitions with the office of the USTR in the framework of the GSP petition process.[98] Thus, organisations can ask the US government to verify the state of compliance with labour rights in a given country in order to decide about the possibility of the suspension of its GSP privileges. For example, on 30 May 2018, a new country practice review of Thailand was announced, and was based on a petition from the National Pork Producers Council. This trade association raised an argument regarding the failure to meet the GSP eligibility criterion to provide equitable and reasonable market access. Similarly, the AFL-CIO's petition became the basis for an ongoing eligibility review of Kazakhstan. The Federation has alleged that this country's government restricts the right to form trade unions and other internationally recognised worker rights.[99] In the case of the EU, it is possible for stakeholders to give information which can only be added to the List of Issues.

---

97 Contrary to the US, the EU concentrates more on a 'carrot' than on a 'stick'. Church Albertson and Compa (n 12) 476.
98 Of course, one should not forget about new enforcement priorities for GSP, announced in 2017.
99 Congressional Research Service (n 35) 20–21.

Making further comparisons, it is important that the US GSP legislation has adopted the concept of 'internationally recognised worker rights', and the EU GSP scheme has adopted the ILO core labour standards.[100] The first four 'internationally recognised worker rights' practically coincide with those of the ILO Declaration. However, it should be noted that the elimination of discrimination in employment and occupation, which is present in the ILO Declaration, has not been included in the US law.[101] On the other hand, the US has included acceptable conditions of work with respect to wages, hours of work and occupational health and safety. Mosley and Tello suggest that it can be interpreted softly as 'a difference in emphasis', or more acutely as 'an indication of the contestation that surrounds the specifics of labour rights'.[102] It finds confirmation in the fact that the US withdrew from the ILO in November 1977 because of selective concerns for human rights, the erosion of tripartitism, disregard of due process and because the ILO was becoming too 'politicised', and allowing political campaigning against the US and Western nations generally.[103] Naturally, during the 1980s, the US was not willing to make references to ILO conventions in its labour legislation.

It must also be observed here that the EU requires developing countries to comply only with conventions which have been ratified by EU member states. Obviously, in the case of the US the situation is quite different. The US has ratified only 14 of 189 ILO Conventions[104] including only two of the ILO's core labour standards – Convention No. 105 (on forced labour) and Convention No. 182 (on the worst forms of child labour). Conventions concerning wages, hours of work or occupational safety and health (except Convention No. 176 on safety and health in mines) have not been ratified. Van den Putte and Velluti argue that practice indicates that monitoring officials' work is regularly based on ILO assessments.[105]

As Weiss rightly points out, the US and the EU differ also in their approaches with regard to the functioning of the monitoring system. The EU GSP scheme, in contrast to the US, has introduced in its system a clear link between the EU monitoring procedure and the 'case law' of the ILO's and the UN's monitoring bodies. Besides, refusal or withdrawal of preferences must be preceded, in the case of the EU, by transparent and fair procedures.[106] It has also been

100 Ojeda-Avilés (n 16) 111; Lore Van den Putte and Samantha Velluti, 'The Promotion of Social Trade by the European Union in Its External Trade Relations' in Sangeeta Khorana and María García (eds), *Handbook on the EU and International Trade* (Cheltenham, Northampton: Edward Elgar Publishing 2018) 230; Elliott and Freeman (n 46) 75, 153.

101 Van den Putte and Velluti (n 100) 230.

102 Mosley and Tello (n 36) 65.

103 Departments of Commerce, Justice, and State, the Judiciary, and Related Agencies Appropriations for 1983, *Hearings Before a Subcommittee of the Committee on Appropriations, House of Representatives, Ninety-Seventh Congress* (Washington DC: U.S. Government Printing Office 1982) 1176; Jack Peel, *The Real Power Game: A Guide to European Industrial Relations* (Maidenhead: McGraw-Hill Book Company 1979) 46.

104 Violence and Harassment Convention No. 190 adopted on the 108th ILC session (21 June 2019) will enter into force 12 months after two member states have ratified it.

105 Van den Putte and Velluti (n 100) 230.

106 Weiss (n 53) 127.

demonstrated that due to the EU's enhanced monitoring of the implementation of the international conventions relating to GSP+, the most recent version of GSP has contributed to the promotion of sustainable development and good governance.

Taking into consideration, inter alia, the use of aggressive unilateralism, the term 'internationally recognised worker rights', the monitoring system functioning, the approach towards ratification of ILO's core labour conventions, the desirable effectiveness, the Trump administration's steps relating to certain beneficiary countries, it seems clear that the EU system pretends to be far better organised. However, it is doubtful if the US would ever take a cue from the EU.

Bibliography

Adalberto Perulli and Vania Brino, *Manuale di diritto internazionale del lavoro* (Turin: Giappichelli 2015).

Alan Hyde, 'A Game-Theory Account and Defence of Transnational Labour Standards – a Preliminary Look at the Problem' in John DR Craig and Michael Lynk (eds), *Globalization and the Future of Labour Law* (Cambridge, New York, Melbourne, Madrid, Cape Town, Singapore, São Paulo: Cambridge University Press 2006).

Alessandra Zanobetti, *Diritto internazionale del lavoro: Norme universali, regionali e dell'Unione europea* (Milan: Giuffrè 2011).

André Raynauld and Jean-Pierre Vidal, *Labour Standards and International Competitiveness: A Comparative Analysis of Developing and Industrialized Countries* (Cheltenham, Northampton: Edward Elgar Publishing 1998).

André Sapir, 'The Impact of Globalization on Employment in Europe' in Mathias Dewatripont, André Sapir and Khalid Sekkat (eds), *Trade and Jobs in Europe: Much Ado About Nothing?* (Oxford: Oxford University Press 1999).

Angel Torres, 'A Wishful Thought: Enforceability and Avoidance of Labor Provisions in Foreign Trade Agreements' (2014) 20(4) *Law and Business Review of the Americas* 617.

Aneta Tyc, 'The US's and the EU's Generalised System of Preferences: A Comparison in the Context of Workers' Rights' 2020 (2) *Studia z Zakresu Prawa Pracy i Polityki Społecznej* 115.

Anne CL Davies, 'Should the EU Have the Power to Set Minimum Standards for Collective Labour Rights in the Member States?' in Philip Alston (ed), *Labour Rights as Human Rights* (Oxford: Oxford University Press 2005).

Annelien Gansemans, Deborah Martens, Marijke D'Haese and Jan Orbie, 'Do Labour Rights Matter for Export? A Qualitative Comparative Analysis of Pineapple Trade to the EU' in Gerda Van Roozendaal and Jan Orbie (eds), *Labour Standards in a Global Environment* (2017) 5(4) *Politics and Governance* 93 <http://dx.doi.org/10.17645/pag.v5i4.1082> accessed 26 November 2020.

Anthony N Cole, 'Labor Standards and the Generalized System of Preferences: The European Labor Incentives' 2003 (25)1 *Michigan Journal of International Law* 179.

Antonio Ojeda-Avilés, *Transnational Labour Law* (Alphen aan den Rijn: Wolters Kluwer Law & Business 2015).

Arturo Bronstein, *International and Comparative Labour Law: Current Challenges* (Geneva: Palgrave Macmillan, International Labour Office 2009).

Axel Marx and Jadir Soares, 'Does Integrating Labour Provisions in Free Trade Agreements Make a Difference? An Exploratory Analysis of Freedom of Association and Collective Bargaining Rights in 13 EU Trade Partners' in Jan Wouters, Axel Marx, Dylan Geraets and Bregt Natens (eds), *Global Governance Through Trade: EU Policies and Approaches* (Cheltenham, Northampton: Edward Elgar Publishing 2015).

Brooke Ringel, 'President Trump Suspends Preferential Trade Treatment for Thailand' *Trade and Manufacturing Monitor* (28 October 2019) <www.ustrademonitor.com/2019/10/president-trump-suspends-preferential-trade-treatment-for-thailand/> accessed 21 November 2020.

Christine Kaufmann, *Globalisation and Labour Rights: The Conflict Between Core Labour Rights and International Economic Law* (Oxford, Portland OR: Hart Publishing 2007).

Clara Portela and Jan Orbie, 'Sanctions Under the EU Generalised System of Preferences and Foreign Policy: Coherence by Accident?' (2014) 20(1) *Contemporary Politics* 63 <http://10.1080/13569775.2014.881605> accessed 25 November 2020.

Cleopatra Doumbia-Henry and Eric Gravel, 'Free Trade Agreements and Labour Rights: Recent Developments' (2006) 145(3) *International Labour Review* 185.

Clotilde Granger and Jean-Marc Siroën, 'Core Labour Standards in Trade Agreements: From Multilateralism to Bilateralism' (2006) 40(5) *Journal of World Trade* 813.

Congressional Research Service, *Generalized System of Preferences (GSP): Overview and Issues for Congress* (Report RL33663, 2019) <https://fas.org/sgp/crs/misc/RL33663.pdf> accessed 25 November 2020.

David Cheong and Franz Christian Ebert, 'Labour Law and Trade Policy: What Implications for Economic and Human Development?' in Shelley Marshall and Colin Fenwick (eds), *Labour Regulation and Development: Socio-Legal Perspectives* (Cheltenham, Northampton: Edward Elgar Publishing 2016).

Departments of Commerce, Justice, and State, the Judiciary, and Related Agencies Appropriations for 1983, Hearings Before a Subcommittee of the Committee on Appropriations, House of Representatives, Ninety-Seventh Congress (Washington DC: U.S. Government Printing Office 1982).

Edmé Domínguez, Rosalba Icaza, Cirila Quintero, Silvia López and Åsa Stenman, 'Women Workers in the Maquiladoras and the Debate on Global Labor Standards' (2010) 16(4) *Feminist Economics* 185 <http://dx.doi.org/10.1080/13545701.2010.530603> accessed 22 November 2020.

Emily Blanchard and Shushanik Hakobyan, 'The US Generalised System of Preferences in Principle and Practice' (2015) 38(3) *The World Economy* 399 <https://doi.org/10.1111/twec.12216> accessed 22 November 2020.

European Commission, Report from the Commission to the European Parliament and the Council on the Application of Regulation (EU) No 978/2012 Applying a Scheme of Generalised Tariff Preferences and Repealing Council Regulation (EC) No 732/2008 (COM(2018) 665 final, Brussels, 4 October 2018.

European Communities – *Conditions for the Granting of Tariff Preferences to Developing Countries: Report of the Appellate Body* (7 April 2004) WT/DS246/AB/R.

Evgeny Postnikov, 'Valued Exports: Social Standards in EU and U.S. Trade Agreements' (A dissertation submitted to the faculty of the Graduate School of Public and International Affairs in partial fulfillment of the requirements for the degree of Doctor of Philosophy, University of Pittsburgh 2014).

Francis Maupain, *The Future of the International Labour Organization in the Global Economy* (Oxford, Portland OR: Hart Publishing 2013).

George Tsogas, 'Labour Standards in the Generalized Systems of Preferences of the European Union and the United States' (2000) 6(3) *European Journal of Industrial Relations* 349.

The International Corporate Accountability Roundtable, Tools of Trade. *The Use of U.S. Generalized System of Preferences to Promote Labor Rights for All* (2018) <https://static1.squarespace.com/static/583f3fca725e25fcd45aa446/t/5a72 3ff1ec212d3d586635d9/1517436916673/ICAR+GSP+Report+FINAL.pdf> accessed 21 November 2020.

Jack Peel, *The Real Power Game: A Guide to European Industrial Relations* (Maidenhead: McGraw-Hill Book Company 1979).

James Yap, 'One Step Forward: The European Union Generalised System of Preferences and Labour Rights in the Garment Industry in Bangladesh' in Jan Wouters, Axel Marx, Dylan Geraets and Bregt Natens (eds), *Global Governance Through Trade: EU Policies and Approaches* (Cheltenham, Northampton: Edward Elgar Publishing 2015).

Jan Orbie, Lore Van den Putte and Deborah Martens, 'The Impact of Labour Rights Commitments in EU Trade Agreements: The Case of Peru' in Gerda Van Roozendaal and Jan Orbie (eds), *Labour Standards in a Global Environment* (2017) 5(4) *Politics and Governance* 6 <http://dx.doi.org/10.17645/pag.v5i4.1091> accessed 26 November 2020.

Jan Orbie and Olufemi Babarinde, 'The Social Dimension of Globalization and EU Development Policy: Promoting Core Labour Standards and Corporate Social Responsibility' (2008) 30(3) *European Integration* 459 <https://doi.org/10.1080/07036330802142178> accessed 25 November 2020.

Jan Wouters, Axel Marx, Dylan Geraets and Bregt Natens, 'Conclusion: Possibilities and Limitations of Governing Through Trade' in Jan Wouters, Axel Marx, Dylan Geraets and Bregt Natens (eds), *Global Governance Through Trade: EU Policies and Approaches* (Cheltenham, Northampton: Edward Elgar Publishing 2015).

Jane A Winzer, 'Expanding the Scope of Multilateral Regimes: The Uruguay Round of GATT Negotiations' (A dissertation or thesis submitted to the Faculty of the Graduate School of Emory University in partial ulfillment of the requirements for the degree of Doctor of Philosophy, Department of Political Science 2006).

Jeffrey S Vogt, 'The Bangladesh Sustainability Compact: An Effective Tool for Promoting Workers' Rights?' in Gerda Van Roozendaal and Jan Orbie (eds), *Labour Standards in a Global Environment* (2017) 5(4) *Politics and Governance* 80 <http://dx.doi.org/10.17645/pag.v5i4.1093> accessed 25 November 2020.

Jennifer L Tobin and Marc L Busch, 'The Disadvantage of Membership: How Joining the GATT/WTO Undermines GSP' (2019) 18(1) *World Trade Review* 133 <https://doi.org/10.1017/S1474745618000034> accessed 22 November 2020.

Jeremy B Grace, 'Environment and Labor Standards in World Trade: Cognitive Approaches to Changes in Regime Scope' (A dissertation submitted to the Faculty of the School of International Service of the American University in partial fulfillment of the requirements for the degree of Master of Arts in International Affairs 1995).

John Hilary, 'European Trade Unions and Free Trade: Between International Solidarity and Perceived Self-Interest' in Andreas Bieler, Bruno Ciccaglione, John Hilary and Ingemar Lindberg (eds), *Free Trade and Transnational Labour* (London, New York: Routledge 2015).

Joris Larik, 'Good Global Governance Through Trade: Constitutional Moorings' in Jan Wouters, Axel Marx, Dylan Geraets and Bregt Natens (eds), *Global Governance Through Trade: EU Policies and Approaches* (Cheltenham, Northampton: Edward Elgar Publishing 2015).

Kevin Kolben, 'A Development Approach to Trade and Labor Regimes' (2010) 45(2) *Wake Forest Law Review* 355.

Kimberly A Elliott and Richard B Freeman, *Can Labour Standards Improve Under Globalization?* (Washington DC: Peterson Institute for International Economics 2003).

Kofi Addo, *Core Labour Standards and International Trade: Lessons from the Regional Context* (Heidelberg, New York, Dordrecht, London: Springer 2015).

Lance Compa and Jeffrey S Vogt, 'Labor Rights in the Generalized System of Preferences: A 20-Year Review' (2001) 22(2–3) *Comparative Labor Law & Policy Journal* 199.

Laura Beke and Nicolas Hachez, 'The EU GSP: A Preference for Human Rights and Good Governance? The Case of Myanmar' in Jan Wouters, Axel Marx, Dylan Geraets and Bregt Natens (eds), *Global Governance Through Trade: EU Policies and Approaches* (Cheltenham, Northampton: Edward Elgar Publishing 2015).

Layna Mosley and Lindsay Tello, 'Labor Rights, Material Interests, and Moral Entrepreneurship' (2015) 37(1) *Human Rights Quarterly* 53.

Lore Van den Putte and Samantha Velluti, 'The Promotion of Social Trade by the European Union in Its External Trade Relations' in Sangeeta Khorana and María García (eds), *Handbook on the EU and International Trade* (Cheltenham, Northampton: Edward Elgar Publishing 2018).

Ludo Cuyvers, 'The Sustainable Development Clauses in Free Trade Agreements of the EU with Asian Countries: Perspectives for ASEAN?' (2014) 22(4) *Journal of Contemporary European Studies* 427 <https://doi.org/10.1080/14782804.2014.923752> accessed 26 November 2020.

Manfred Weiss, 'The EU Generalised Scheme of Preferences and the Special Incentive Arrangement for Sustainable Development and Good Governance' in Adalberto Perulli and Tiziano Treu (eds), *Sustainable Development, Global Trade and Social Rights* (Alphen aan den Rijn: Kluwer Law International 2018).

Marley S Weiss, 'International Labor and Employment Law: From Periphery to Core' (2010) 25 *ABA Journal of Labor & Employment Law* 487.

Martin Gassebner and Arevik Gnutzmann-Mkrtchyan, 'Politicized Trade: What Drives Withdrawal of Trade Preferences?' (2018) 167(C) *Economics Letters* 10 <https://doi.org/10.1016/j.econlet.2017.12.005> accessed 25 November 2020.

Martin Myant, *The Impact of Trade and Investment Agreements on Decent Work and Sustainable Development* (Brussels: European Trade Union Institute 2017).

Michael Gadbaw and Michael T Medwig, 'Multinational Enterprises and International Labor Standards: Which Way for Development and Jobs?' in Lance A Compa and Steven F Diamond (eds), *Human Rights, Labor Rights, and International Trade* (Philadelphia: University of Pennsylvania Press 1996).

Office of the United States Trade Representative, Executive Office of the President, *U.S. Generalized System of Preferences Guidebook* (Washington DC 2019) <https://ustr.gov/sites/default/files/IssueAreas/gsp/GSP_Guidebook-December_2019.pdf?utm_source=google&utm_medium=google&utm_term=(not%20 provided)&utm_content=undefined&utm_campaign=(not%20set)&gclid=undefin ed&dclid=undefined&GAID=false> accessed 21 November 2020.

Paul Alois, 'Better Work and Global Governance' (A dissertation submitted to the Graduate faculty in Political Science in partial fulfillment of the requirements for the degree of Doctor of Philosophy, The City University of New York 2016).

Paula Church Albertson and Lance Compa, 'Labour Rights and Trade Agreements in the Americas' in Adelle Blackett and Anne Trebilcock (eds), *Research Handbook on Transnational Labour Law* (Cheltenham, Northampton: Edward Elgar Publishing 2015).

Peter S Liapis, *Preferential Trade Agreements. How Much Do They Benefit Developing Economies?* (Paris: OECD Publishing 2007) <https://doi. org/10.1787/9789264033696-en> accessed 21 November 2020.

Peter-Tobias Stoll, 'International Economic and Social Dimensions: Divided or Connected?' in Henner Gött (ed), *Labour Standards in International Economic Law* (Cham: Springer 2018).

Philip Alston, 'Labor Rights Provisions in U.S. Trade Law: "Aggressive Unilateralism"?' in Lance A Compa and Stephen F Diamond (eds), *Human Rights, Labor Rights, and International Trade* (Philadelphia: University of Pennsylvania Press 1996).

Pieter Leenknegt, 'EU Trade Policy and International Labour Standards: The View from the ILO' in Roger Blanpain (ed), Jan Wouters, Glenn Rayp, Laura Beke and Axel Marx (guest eds), *Protecting Labour Rights in a Multi-Polar Supply Chain and Mobile Global Economy* (Alphen aan den Rijn: Wolters Kluwer 2015).

Robert JS Ross, 'Bringing Labor Rights to Bangladesh' *The American Prospect* (12 July 2015) <https://prospect.org/labor/bringing-labor-rights-back-bangladesh/> accessed 25 November 2020.

Sabrina Zajak, *Transnational Activism, Global Labor Governance, and China* (Basingstoke: Palgrave Macmillan 2017).

Samantha Velluti, 'The EU's Social Dimension and Its External Trade Relations' in Axel Marx, Jan Wouters, Glenn Rayp and Laura Beke (eds), *Global Governance of Labour Rights: Assessing the Effectiveness of Transnational Public and Private Policy Initiatives* (Cheltenham, Northampton: Edward Elgar Publishing 2015).

Scott Cooper, 'Global Supply Chain Governance: ILO, ISO & Worker Safety' (October 2018) 63(10) *Professional Safety* 70.

Seyed Mohamad Hassan Razavi, 'Labour Standards and WTO – Dilemma of Legitimacy and Efficacy' (2010) 11(5) *The Journal of World Investment & Trade* 879.

Stephanie Luce, 'The Case for International Labour Standards: A "Northern" Perspective' (2005) *Institute of Development Studies Working Paper* 250 <www.ids. ac.uk/files/Wp250.pdf> accessed 22 November 2020.

Stephen Herzenberg, 'In from the Margins: Morality, Economics, and International Labor Rights' in Lance A Compa and Steven F Diamond (eds), *Human Rights, Labor Rights, and International Trade* (Philadelphia: University of Pennsylvania Press 1996).

Steve Charnovitz, 'International Trade and Worker Rights' (1987) 7(1) *Steve SAIS Review* 185.

Tamara Kay, *NAFTA and the Politics of Labor Transnationalism* (New York: Cambridge University Press 2011).

Terry Collingsworth, 'International Worker Rights Enforcement: Proposals Following a Test Case' in Lance A Compa and Stephen F Diamond (eds), *Human Rights, Labor Rights, and International Trade* (Philadelphia: University of Pennsylvania Press 1996).

Thomas R Donahue, 'Workers' Rights in the Global Village: Observations of an American Trade Unionist' in Werner Sengenberger and Duncan Campbell (eds), *International Labour Standards and Economic Interdependence: Essays in Commemoration of the 75th Anniversary of the International Labour Organization and the 50th Anniversary of the Declaration of Philadelphia* (Geneva: International Institute for Labour Studies 1994).

Tonia Novitz, 'Trading in Services: Commodities and Beneficiaries' in Adelle Blackett and Anne Trebilcock (eds), *Research Handbook on Transnational Labour Law* (Cheltenham, Northampton: Edward Elgar Publishing 2015).

Tonia Novitz, 'Labour Standards and Trade: Need We Choose Between "Human Rights" and "Sustainable Development"?' in Henner Gött (ed), *Labour Standards in International Economic Law* (Cham: Springer 2018).

United Nations, *Generalized System of Preferences: Handbook on the Scheme of the European Union* (New York, Geneva: United Nations 2015).

Weifeng Zhou and Ludo Cuyvers, 'Linking International Trade and Labour Standards: The Effectiveness of Sanctions Under the European Union's GSP' (2011) 45(1) *Journal of World Trade* 63.

William A Douglas, John P Ferguson and Erin Klett, 'An Effective Confluence of Forces in Support of Workers' Rights: ILO Standards, US Trade Laws, Unions, and NGOs' (May 2004) 26(2) *Human Rights Quarterly* 273.

5 The US's and the EU's international trade agreements

1 Introduction

The global financial crisis, which erupted in 2008, was one of the causes of the rise in the number of international trade agreements.[1] More than a decade later, as the world experiences the COVID-19 pandemic, we are allowed to ask questions about the potential of these instruments in offsetting the effects of the crisis. International Labour Organization research shows that generally trade liberalisation can trigger economic growth and increase employment opportunities in both developing countries and advanced economies, that it impacts on global supply chains and the role of businesses to address decent work deficits.[2] Questions about international trade agreements are crucial in the context of the changing face of globalisation and in the light of some reflections arising during the pandemic. Are we entering an epoch of 'the solstice of civilisation', which will entail a change of paradigms? Are we going to witness the phenomenon of pushing China out of markets, and shortening supply chains? Are we heading from one global village towards several villages with supply chains as the focal point of the game? Will the world be divided into zones of influence where a technological race leads the way? Even if we cannot answer these questions today, one thing is certain – all this will influence the global division of labour. If trade agreements should constitute a solution for workers, labour provisions included in them have to effectively protect workers' rights. There is already now some evidence of the positive impact of labour provisions in trade agreements on labour market access (e.g. for working age women) and on the narrowing of the gender wage gap. Importantly, it has been proved that labour provisions in trade agreements do not divert or decrease trade flows.[3]

1 Sebastian Benz and Erdal Yalcin, 'Productivity Versus Employment: Quantifying the Economic Effects of an EU – Japan Free Trade Agreement' (2015) 38(6) *The World Economy* 935, 936 <https://doi.org/10.1111/twec.12205> accessed 26 November 2020.
2 ILO, *Handbook on Assessment of Labour Provisions in Trade and Investment Agreements* (Geneva: ILO 2017) 1, 4.
3 ibid 3.

According to the ILO, labour provisions in trade agreements[4] have proliferated over the last two decades – from only four in 1995, the number of trade agreements that include labour provisions increased to 21 in 2005, 58 in June 2013,[5] 77 in 2016 and 85 in 2019.[6] Thus, the share of trade agreements including labour provisions has increased from 7.3% of the total number of trade agreements in 1995 to 28.8% in 2016 and 29% in 2019. In total, 72% of labour provisions in trade agreements make reference to ILO instruments.[7] The question is how to increase their positive impact and make them guarantee effective enforcement of labour rights. Is the mere reference to the ILO sufficient?

Before scrutinising the US's and the EU's international trade agreements in more detail, let me first note that the approaches of both of them to labour provisions in trade agreements show some significant differences. Indeed, the US model mostly refers to the ILO 1998 Declaration and involves FTAs that use a conditional approach. This amounts to the fact that FTAs contain labour provisions that make the conclusion of a trade agreement conditional upon respect for particular labour standards (pre-ratification conditionality) and/or provisions in the concluded trade agreements that authorise sanctions if labour standards are infringed (post-ratification conditionality).[8]

The EU relies more on the ILO agenda, including a commitment towards ratifying its core conventions. The EU model involves a promotional approach. It means that labour provisions included in FTAs 'do not link compliance to economic consequences but provide a framework for dialogue, cooperation, and/or monitoring'.[9]

EU countries have all ratified the eight core labour conventions in full, while the US has ratified only two and its labour law and practice deviate considerably from the core labour conventions in several respects. The US ratifications do not include Convention No. 87 concerning Freedom of Association and Protection of the Right to Organise and Convention No. 98 on the Right to Organise and Collective Bargaining.

4 Trade-related labour provisions are defined by the ILO as: 'references to any standard that addresses labour relations or working terms or conditions; mechanisms for monitoring or promoting compliance with labour standards, such as consultative groups; and/or a framework for cooperation, such as the sharing of best practices, seminars and forums', ibid 11.
5 ILO, *Social Dimensions of Free Trade Agreements: Studies on Growth with Equity* (Geneva: ILO 2013) 5.
6 ILO, *Labour Provisions in G7 Trade Agreements: A comparative perspective* (Geneva: ILO 2019) 15.
7 ILO (n 2) 5, 11.
8 ILO (n 5) 1; Liam Campling, James Harrison, Ben Richardson and Adrian Smith, 'Can Labour Provisions Work Beyond the Border? Evaluating the Effects of EU Free Trade Agreements' (2016) 155(3) *International Labour Review* 357, 360–361.
9 ILO (n 5) 1.

2 The US international trade agreements

2.1 The NAFTA

The negotiations over the NAFTA lasted from 1990 to 1992 and took place during the administrations of US President Republican George Bush, Canadian Prime Minister Brian Mulroney, and Mexican President Carlos Salinas. They signed the agreement in August 1992, the US Congress approved it in November 1993 and finally the NAFTA came into effect in 1994. Meanwhile, after winning the elections in November 1992, Bill Clinton and his administration began negotiations on the side agreement concerning labour, and in August 1993, the heads of three states signed the North American Agreement on Labor Cooperation (NAALC).[10] The labour agreement includes labour principles, six obligations, an organisational structure and a complaint mechanism for reviewing compliance. It embraces a broad, by contrast to a 'core', elaboration of norms.[11] The NAALC's 11 'Labor Principles' are as follows:

1   freedom of association and protection of the right to organise;
2   the right to bargain collectively;
3   the right to strike;
4   prohibition of forced labour;
5   labour protection for children and young persons;
6   minimum employment standards, such as minimum wages and overtime pay;
7   non-discrimination in employment;
8   equal pay for women and men;
9   occupational safety and health;
10 compensation in cases of occupational injuries and illnesses;
11 migrant worker protection.

The three signatory countries commit themselves to 'promoting' these principles, indicating at the same time that they 'do not establish common minimum standards for their domestic law', which is one of the main characteristics of the NAALC.

Alongside of 11 'Labor Principles', the US, Canada and Mexico adopt six 'obligations', the fulfilment of which should give effect to the labour principles. These are as follows:

1   'high labor standards, consistent with high quality and productivity workplaces' within a framework of national sovereignty, that is, affirming full respect for each Party's constitution, and recognising the right of each Party

---

10 The NAALC was the first trade agreement to include a binding labour provision.
11 Lance Compa and Tequila Brooks, *NAFTA and the NAALC: Twenty Years of North American Trade-Labour Linkage* (Alphen aan den Rijn: Kluwer Law International 2015) 20–21, 25.

to establish its own domestic labour standards, and to adopt or modify accordingly its labour laws and regulations (Article 2);

2   effective enforcement of national labour law (according to Article 3, each Party shall promote compliance with and effectively enforce its labour law through appropriate government action. Each Party shall also ensure that its competent authorities give due consideration in accordance with its law to any request by an employer, employee or their representatives, or other interested person, for an investigation of an alleged violation of the Party's labour law);

3   appropriate access to administrative, quasijudicial, judicial or labour tribunals providing redress for violations of national law (Article 4);

4   due process in labour law proceedings (Article 5);[12]

5   assurance that each Party's laws, regulations, procedures and administrative rulings of general application respecting any matter covered by the Agreement are promptly published or otherwise made available in such a manner as to enable interested persons and Parties to become acquainted with them (Article 6);

6   promotion of public awareness of labour law (Article 7).

As regards the complaint mechanism, there is no new supranational labour law enforcement system with remedies established under the NAALC. As pointed out by Compa, the cross-border complaint system means nothing else than that

12   Procedural guarantees are as follows:

1   Each Party shall ensure that its administrative, quasiiudicial, judicial and labor tribunal proceedings for the enforcement of its labour law are fair, equitable and transparent. . . .

2   Each Party shall provide that final decisions on the merits of the case in such proceedings are:

   a) in writing and preferably state the reasons on which the decisions are based;
   b) made available without undue delay to the parties to the proceedings and, consistent with its law, to the public; and
   c) based on information or evidence in respect of which the parties were offered the opportunity to be heard.

3   Each Party shall provide, as appropriate, that parties to such proceedings have the right, in accordance with its law, to seek review and, where warranted, correction of final decisions issued in such proceedings.

4   Each Party shall ensure that tribunals that conduct or review such proceedings are impartial and independent and do not have any substantial interest in the outcome of the matter.

5   Each Party shall provide that the parties to administrative, quasijudicial, judicial or labor tribunal proceedings may seek remedies to ensure the enforcement of their labor rights. . . .

6   Each Party may, as appropriate, adopt or maintain labor defense offices to represent or advise workers or their organisations.

7   Nothing in Article 5 shall be construed to require a Party to establish, or to prevent a Party from establishing, a judicial system for the enforcement of its labour law distinct from its system for the enforcement of laws in general.

8   For greater certainty, decisions by each Party's administrative, quasijudicial, judicial or labour tribunals, or pending decisions, as well as related proceedings shall not be subject to revision or reopened under the provisions of the Agreement.

human rights groups, trade unions and other civil society groups have to cooperate with the aim of finding new ways of communication, collaboration and solidarity. This mechanism is triggered by advocates in the country where violations
took place, who join with their counterparts in the country where the complaint
was lodged. The complaint goes to the labour department, which performs an
initial review. There are then three steps to be taken in the framework of the
complaint mechanism. They include:

1   consultations between National Administrative Officers (NAOs) or govern-
    ment ministers, and 'cooperation' steps taken with the aim of addressing
    problems;
2   a committee of independent experts' evaluation and recommendations;
3   dispute resolution – a remedial plan, and trade sanctions, which depend on
    decisions of an arbitral panel.[13]

Interestingly, only three of the aforementioned 'Labor Principles' (namely
child labour, minimum wage standards, and workplace health and safety) are
susceptible to dispute resolution. If a government fails to adopt an action plan
recommended by an arbitral panel after the panel finds a persistent pattern of
failure to effectively enforce its laws related to one of these three principles, a
fine of up to 0.007% of the volume of trade between two disputing countries
can be imposed. It means that the NAALC is the first international labour agreement which provides for the possibility of imposing trade sanctions as a means of
enforcing labour rights.[14] However, as raised by Compa, none of the complaints
lodged by civil society advocates ever moved beyond the 'first cut' review phase
and the consultation step, no evaluation committee of experts was ever established, and no arbitral panel ever took up a case.[15] Hence, this enforcement
mechanism is neither regarded as having the potential for ensuring the states'
compliance with domestic standards, nor as preventing a 'race to the bottom' of
labour standards.[16] However, it should not be assessed solely as a stand-alone
tool, but rather in conjunction with other tactics, for example picketing of company headquarters or union organising.[17]

---

13 Lance Compa, 'Trump, Trade, and Trabajo: Renegotiating NAFTA's Labor Accord in
   a Fraught Political Climate' (2019) 26(1) *Indiana Journal of Global Legal Studies* 263,
   269–270.
14 Compa and Brooks (n 11) 26.
15 Compa (n 13) 270.
16 John Anthony VanDuzer, Penelope Simons and Graham Mayeda, *Integrating Sustainable
   Development into International Investment Agreements: A Guide for Developing Country
   Negotiators* (London: Commonwealth Secretariat 2013) 369.
17 Jonathan Graubart, 'Giving Teeth to NAFTA's Labour Side Agreement' in John J Kirton
   and Virginia W Maclaren (eds), *Linking Trade, Environment, and Social Cohesion: NAFTA
   Experiences, Global Challenges* (London, New York: Routledge 2018) 204.

In fact, some of the joint actions achieved high visibility. One of the most vivid examples is a complaint alleging sex discrimination in export-processing 'maquiladora' factories, which was filed in 1997 with the National Administrative Office of the United States (NAO) by Human Rights Watch and the International Labor Rights Forum, together with the Mexican National Association of Democratic Lawyers (Asociación Nacional de Abogados Democráticos, ANAD). The complaint alleged that pregnancy tests of all female job candidates were required, and pregnant women were denied employment. The submission also highlighted that such practices were tolerated by the state. The US labour department accepted the case and public hearings were organised. There was much ado in the media about the case. This contributed to the Mexican federal government's ban on pregnancy testing in the case of women applying for employment in federal ministries. Besides, many of the US companies stopped such testing in their factories.[18] Subsequent studies, however, indicated that these practices were not completely eliminated.[19]

According to the information provided by the US Department of Labor, 40 complaints against governments were lodged under the NAALC.[20] A broad spectrum of submissions, for example, Mexico NAO Submission 9501 (Sprint), Mexico Submission 2011–1 (H-2B Visa Workers), US NAO Submissions 940001 and 940002 (Honeywell & General Electric), US NAO Submission 9602 (Maxi-Switch), US NAO Submission 9804 (Rural Mail Couriers), US NAO Submission 9703 (Itapsa), US NAO Submission 9803 (McDonald's), US NAO Submission 9901 (TAESA), Canadian NAO Submission CAN 98–1 (Itapsa),[21] has demonstrated that many different results are possible when using the complaint mechanism, and not always does it entail reinstatement of workers, compensation payment or union recognition. What is certain, however, is that the NAALC does not preclude the possibility of transnational social actors organising campaigns, publicising cases in the media, pursuing cooperation with NGOs, requesting public hearings or government consultations.

18 Lance Compa, 'From Chile to Vietnam: International Labour Law and Workers' Rights in International Trade' in Gráinne de Búrca, Claire Kilpatrick and Joanne Scott (eds), *Critical Legal Perspectives on Global Governance: Liber Amicorum David M Trubek* (Oxford, Portland OR: Hart Publishing 2014) 151–152.
19 Mark Thomas, 'Regulating Labour Standards in the Global Economy: Emerging Approaches to Global Governance' in Gary Teeple and Stephen McBride (eds), *Relations of Global Power: Neoliberal Order and Disorder* (Toronto: University of Toronto Press 2011) 101; Carolyn Tuttle, *Mexican Women in American Factories: Free Trade and Exploitation on the Border* (Austin: University of Texas Press 2012) 182 et seq.
20 <www.dol.gov/agencies/ilab/submissions-under-north-american-agreement-labor-cooperation-naalc-print> accessed 26 November 2020.
21 All cases can be found at: <www.dol.gov/agencies/ilab/submissions-under-north-american-agreement-labor-cooperation-naalc-print> accessed 26 November 2020.

2.2 The other US agreements and their compliance with the ILO standards

The US–Jordan agreement (2000) for the first time incorporated ILO standards, referring to the 1998 Declaration on Fundamental Principles and Rights at Work, and obligated the parties to 'strive to ensure' that ILO core standards are reflected in national law. From that time, the US negotiated several trade agreements which maintained the 'strive to ensure' clause (CAFTA-DR, agreements with Chile, Singapore, Australia, Morocco, Bahrain and Oman). These agreements were negotiated pursuant to the trade objectives enumerated in the Bipartisan Trade Promotion Authority Act of 2002. This Act embraced the promotion of 'worker rights and the rights of children consistent with the core labor standards of the ILO' and 'universal ratification and full compliance with ILO Convention No. 182'.[22]

A year after the US Democrat Party won a majority in the House and Senate in November 2006, the Bipartisan Agreement on Trade Policy (10 May Agreement) between Congress and the White House was reached. According to its new trade template, each party was required to 'adopt and maintain in its statutes, regulations, and practices' the 'rights as stated in the ILO Declaration on Fundamental Principles and Rights at Work and its Follow-Up (1998)'.[23] It constituted an important progress in comparison to the prior 'strive to ensure' formulation. Effective enforcement of laws reflecting the ILO core labour standards was required. The US renegotiated labour chapters of trade agreements with Peru, Panama, Colombia and South Korea. These standards had to be achieved in future trade agreements as well.

In spite of this, the compliance with international trade agreements in relation to ILO standards is not satisfactory (the few optimistic examples include Panama, which eliminated restrictions on collective bargaining, and Cambodia where a significant increase in the possibility of forming trade unions has been noted).[24] While the US has made the commitments, they exist only in writing. Employers still have permission to replace workers who exercise their right to strike with new personnel. They can also aggressively campaign against workers to prevent them from exerting their right to organise.[25]

---

22 ILO, *Assessment of Labour Provisions in Trade and Investment Arrangements* (Geneva: ILO 2016) 43.

23 Jeffrey S Vogt, 'The Evolution of Labor Rights and Trade: A Transatlantic Comparison and Lessons for the Transatlantic Trade and Investment Partnership' (2015) 18(4) *Journal of International Economic Law* 827, 833 <https://doi.org/10.1093/jiel/jgv046> accessed 26 November 2020.

24 See: Paula Church Albertson and Lance Compa, 'Labour Rights and Trade Agreements in the Americas' in Adelle Blackett and Anne Trebilcock (eds), *Research Handbook on Transnational Labour Law* (Cheltenham, Northampton: Edward Elgar Publishing 2015) 478–479, 485–486; Martin Myant, *The Impact of Trade and Investment Agreements on Decent Work and Sustainable Development* (Brussels: European Trade Union Institute 2017) passim.

25 Lance Compa, 'Labor Rights and Labor Standards in Transatlantic Trade and Investment Negotiations: A US Perspective' (2015) 2 *Economia & Lavoro* 87, 94.

The implication of the US position seems to be that restricting trade unions' rights in some parts of a free trade area may result in unfair competition for other parts. Consequently, it may further aggravate the weakening of trade unions' bargaining power. It is hard to disagree with De Ville et al.[26] that if there is no request for ratification of ILO core conventions, the benchmarking and monitoring of labour conditions can be restrained in the case of non-ratification by partner countries all core conventions.

Referring to the experience of the labour provisions under the Central America Free Trade Agreement (CAFTA) and the Trans-Pacific Partnership (TPP), the former does not require labour law of states' parties to be consistent with the rules laid down in the basic ILO conventions. Trade unions, human and labour rights organisations have criticised its labour chapter for doing little to improve labour laws and law enforcement or to restrain future abuses.[27] In relation to the TPP, the president of the AFL-CIO has pointed out that: 'After much talk about labor standards, the TPP falls woefully short. It retains the totally discretionary nature of enforcement and does nothing to streamline the process so labor cases will be addressed without delay, leaving workers with no assurance of improved conditions'.[28] The TPP's chapter 19 on labour follows the US approach to labour provisions in trade agreements[29] and it reiterates the aforementioned 10 May model. The AFL-CIO has declared its opposition to the TPP, emphasising the lack of enforceable labour provisions.[30]

According to the recent US's FTAs with the Republic of Korea, Colombia and Peru: 'each party shall adopt and maintain in its statutes and regulations, and practices thereunder' the rights stated in the 1998 Declaration. Nonetheless, caution is required as regards the footnote included in the FTAs which states that 'the obligations set out in [this Article], as they relate to the ILO, refer only to the ILO Declaration'. As rightly stated by Plasa: 'While this declaration lists the CLS, it does not specify the conventions defining them. Apparently, the purpose of this footnote is to clarify that the FTAs do not commit the signatories to respect the terms of these conventions'.[31]

---

26 Ferdi De Ville, Jan Orbie and Lore Van den Putte, *TTIP and Labour Standards* (Study for the EMPL Committee, European Parliament 2016) 47 <www.europarl.europa.eu/RegData/etudes/STUD/2016/578992/IPOL_STU(2016)578992_EN.pdf> accessed 26 November 2020.
27 Vogt (n 23) 831–832.
28 Richard Trumka, 'TPP: A New Low' *The Hill* (2 February 2016) <http://thehill.com/opinion/op-ed/267968-tpp-a-new-low> accessed 26 November 2020.
29 De Ville, Orbie and Van den Putte (n 26) 39.
30 Vogt (n 23) 835–836.
31 Wolfgang Plasa, *Reconciling International Trade and Labor Protection: Why We Need to Bridge the Gap Between ILO Standards and WTO Rules* (Lanham, Boulder, New York, London: Lexington Books 2015) 115–116.

2.3 The USMCA

Concerns about NAFTA labour provisions were often raised in the context of worker's rights in Mexico. Not only 'maquiladora' factories are problematic in this country. Unfortunately, ghost unions or protection contracts (contractual agreements between corrupt unions and employers) are also a characteristic feature of its labour relations that has increased rapidly since economic liberalisation in the 1980s and has been even more intense since NAFTA. These contracts equip employers with an absolute authority over the determination of wages and other working conditions.[32] In 2020, minimum wage workers in Mexico earn around $6.50 per day. Even if a great increase is clearly visible, Mexico's daily minimum wage is still around half of the hourly minimum wage in Arizona and California.[33] It was crucial under new negotiations that decision-makers put pressure on labour agreements that raise wages in Mexico and strengthen protection of labour rights not only in Mexico but also in Canada and the US (where, especially in the latter country, there is also much to be done).

On 30 September 2018, the US, Canada and Mexico announced they had reached a trilateral free trade agreement in the renegotiation of the NAFTA, concluding more than 13 months of negotiations.[34] USTR Robert Lighthizer has called the USMCA 'the gold standard by which all future trade agreements will be judged, and citizens of all three countries will benefit for years to come'. The USMCA has been ratified by all three countries[35] and has taken effect as of 1 July 2020.[36]

In comparison to the NAALC, the USMCA uses more far-reaching language. The Parties shall now 'adopt and maintain' in their 'statutes and regulations, and practices thereunder, the . . . rights, as stated in the ILO Declaration on Rights at Work'. The same formulations ('adopt and maintain statutes and regulations, and practices thereunder') is used in reference to 'acceptable conditions of work with respect to minimum wages, hours of work, and occupational safety and

32   Norman Caulfield, *NAFTA and Labor in North America* (Urbana: University of Illinois Press 2010) 53; International Business Publications, *Mexico Labor Laws and Regulations Handbook: Strategic Information and Basic Laws* (Washington DC: International Business Publications 2019) 51.

33   Nathaniel Parish Flannery, 'Will A Minimum Wage Hike Boost Mexico's Struggling Economy?' *Forbes* (3 January 2020) <www.forbes.com/sites/nathanielparishflannery/2020/01/03/will-a-minimum-wage-hike-boost-mexicos-struggling-economy/#67d6e36b18ed> accessed 26 November 2020.

34   <https://ustr.gov/trade-agreements/free-trade-agreements/united-states-mexico-canada-agreement> accessed 26 November 2020. The US–Mexico–Canada Agreement (USMCA) was subsequently amended in the 'Protocol of Amendment to the Agreement between the United States of America, the United Mexican States, and Canada' of 10 December 2019.

35   <https://ustr.gov/about-us/policy-offices/press-office/press-releases/2020/march/ambassador-lighthizer-statement-canadas-approval-usmca> accessed 26 November 2020.

36   Reuters Staff, 'New North American Trade Pact to Take Effect July 1: USTR' *Reuters* (25 April 2020) <www.reuters.com/article/us-usa-trade-usmca/new-north-american-trade-pact-to-take-effect-july-1-ustr-idUSKCN2263H0> accessed 26 November 2020.

health'. Footnote 1 adds the 'greater certainty' clause, namely, it states that for greater certainty a Party's labour laws regarding 'acceptable conditions of work with respect to minimum wages' include requirements under that Party's labour laws to provide wage-related benefit payments to, or on behalf of, workers, such as those for profit sharing, bonuses, retirement and healthcare.

It is worth noting that any previous trade agreement has ever provided for such a precise provision, according to which 'for greater certainty, the right to strike is linked to the right to freedom of association, which cannot be realized without protecting the right to strike' (footnote 6). The Parties clearly affirm the right to strike and suggest that it has always been their view that any reference to freedom of association in trade agreements implicitly included the right to strike.[37]

Four further optimistic perspectives emerge from completely new provisions related to forced or compulsory labour, violence against workers, migrant workers and discrimination in the workplace.

The USMCA labour chapter sets out that

> the Parties recognize the goal of eliminating all forms of forced or compulsory labor, including forced or compulsory child labor. Accordingly, each Party shall prohibit the importation of goods into its territory from other sources produced in whole or in part by forced or compulsory labor, including forced or compulsory child labor (Article 23.6).

It is also surely correct to support the content of Article 23.7, which obligates the Parties not to fail to address violence or threats of violence against workers, directly related to the exercise of labour rights, in a manner affecting trade or investment between the Parties. It has been clarified that for purposes of dispute settlement, a panel shall presume that a failure is in a manner affecting trade or investment between the Parties, unless the responding Party demonstrates otherwise (a rebuttable presumption). The article uses formulations that have never been used before in such agreements. It provides that the Parties recognise that workers and labour organisations must be able to exercise labour rights 'in a climate that is free from violence, threats, and intimidation'. Consequently, governments are required to effectively address incidents of violence, threats and intimidation against workers.

As indicated earlier, one of the NAALC's 11 'Labor Principles' assumes migrant worker protection. Similarly, the USMCA introduces one provision related to migrant workers. It stipulates that 'the Parties recognize the vulnerability of migrant workers with respect to labor protections'. Accordingly, each

37 See also: Jeffrey Vogt, Janice Bellace, Lance Compa, Keith D Ewing, John Hendy QC, Klaus Lörcher and Tonia Novitz, *The Right to Strike in International Law* (Chicago: Hart Publishing, an Imprint of Bloomsbury Publishing 2020) 132.

Party is obliged to ensure that migrant workers are protected under its labour laws, whether they are nationals or non-nationals of the Party (Article 23.8).

Interestingly, the USMCA labour chapter also establishes a non-discrimination provision (Article 23.9), which aims at eliminating discrimination in employment and occupation, and promoting equality of women in the workplace. It requires the Parties to implement policies that they consider appropriate to protect workers against employment discrimination on the basis of sex (including with regard to sexual harassment), pregnancy, sexual orientation, gender identity and caregiving responsibilities; provide job-protected leave for birth or adoption of a child and care of family members; and protect against wage discrimination. It is worth stressing that the catalogue of legally protected characteristics listed in this provision is broader than the one envisaged by Title VII of the Civil Rights Act of 1964, 42 US Code §§ 2000e-2(a) to (d) (2012). The latter does not include sexual orientation, gender identity or caregiving responsibilities.[38] On the other hand, however, there is an issue that could be better regulated. The provision under discussion embraces footnote 15, according to which the US's existing federal agency policies regarding the hiring of federal workers are sufficient to fulfil the obligations set forth in Article 23.9. The Article thus requires no additional action on the part of the US, including any amendments to Title VII of the Civil Rights Act of 1964, in order for the US to be in compliance with the obligations set forth in Article 23.9. As rightly pointed out by Charnovitz, the formulation, according to which 'no additional action on the part of' the US is required seems rather enigmatic. Besides, the wording that the Parties implement policies that they 'consider appropriate' suggests 'more of a subjective rather than an objective legal standard'. Finally, the provision requires the Parties to 'implement policies', and not laws, so it may be applicable to federal policies related to cities and states.[39]

The USMCA is generally a perfect example of how footnotes are important in trade agreements. The US–Guatemala CAFTA labour arbitration ruling of 2017, in which an arbitral panel under the CAFTA-DR found that Guatemala's alleged failure to enforce domestic labour legislation was not done 'in a manner affecting trade',[40] has definitely influenced the shape of footnotes 8 and 9 of the USMCA labour chapter. Taking into account that Article

---

38 See: Compa (n 13) 301.
39 Steve Charnovitz, 'The Labor Rights Rationale to Approve the USMCA' *International Economic Law and Policy Blog* (13 December 2019) <https://ielp.worldtradelaw.net/2019/12/the-labor-rights-rationale-to-approve-the-usmca.html> accessed 26 November 2020.
40 See: International Centre for Trade and Sustainable Development, 'Trade Dispute Panel Issues Ruling in US–Guatemala Labour Law Case' (6 July 2017) 21(24) *Bridges* <https://ictsd.iisd.org/bridges-news/bridges/news/trade-dispute-panel-issues-ruling-in-us-guatemala-labour-law-case> accessed 26 November 2020. More: Eric Gottwald, Jeffrey Vogt and Lance Compa, 'Wrong Turn for Workers' Rights: The US–Guatemala CAFTA Labor Arbitration Ruling – And What to Do About It' *International Labor Rights Forum* (12 April 2018) <https://laborrights.org/publications/wrong-turn-workers%E2%80%99-rights-us-guatemala-cafta-labor-arbitration-ruling-%E2%80%93-and-what-do> accessed 27 November 2020.

23.4 considers it inappropriate if the Parties encourage trade or investment by weakening or reducing the protections afforded in each Party's labour laws, that is, it requires the Parties not to waive or otherwise derogate from their statutes or regulations implementing the labour rights Article in a manner affecting trade or investment between the Parties, footnote 8 seems of utter importance. It introduces the 'greater certainty' clause, clarifying that a waiver or derogation is 'in a manner affecting trade or investment between the Parties' if it involves:

a)   a person or industry that produces a good or supplies a service traded between the Parties or has an investment in the territory of the Party that has failed to comply with this obligation; or
b)   a person or industry that produces a good or supplies a service that competes in the territory of a Party with a good or a service of another Party.

This means that there is no more need to 'prove that a company involved in trade changed its price structure because of the government's failure to effectively enforce labor law, which is what the Guatemala arbitral panel demanded'.[41] Moreover, footnote 9 establishes a rebuttable presumption that a failure is in a manner affecting trade or investment between the Parties.

In addition, Article 23.5 obliges the Parties to effectively enforce its labour laws through a sustained or recurring course of action or inaction in a manner affecting trade or investment. A panel shall presume that a failure is in a manner affecting trade or investment between the Parties, unless the responding Party demonstrates otherwise.

When assessing the USMCA, it should be also be appreciated that 'in a dispute arising under Chapter 23 (Labor), panelists other than the chair shall have expertise or experience in labor law or practice' (Article 31.8 of Chapter 31 on dispute settlement). Consider that the panel comprises five members (ius dispositivum; Article 31.9 of Chapter 31 on dispute settlement), it follows from the new provision that four of them shall have expertise or experience in labour law or practice. This should be viewed as a major advance with respect to the US–Guatemala case, in which the majority of panellists were trade law practitioners with no expertise or experience in labour law or practice.[42]

There are several other important provisions in the USMCA that strongly influence the situation of workers. These include the following: Annex 23-A entitled 'Worker Representation in Collective Bargaining in Mexico' (Chapter 23 'Labor'); Annex 31-A 'Facility-specific rapid response labor mechanism'

41 Compa (n 13) 302.
42 Compa (n 13) 302.

(Chapter 31 'Dispute Settlement'[43]); and a new 'Labor Value Content' provision (Chapter 4 'Rules of Origin').

According to the new Annex 23-A, 'Mexico shall adopt and maintain the measures. . ., which are necessary for the effective recognition of the right to collective bargaining'. Mexico has been obliged, inter alia, to provide

> in its labor laws the right of workers to engage in concerted activities for collective bargaining or protection and to organize, form, and join the union of their choice, and prohibit, in its labor laws, employer domination or interference in union activities, discrimination, or coercion against workers for union activity or support, and refusal to bargain collectively with the duly recognized union.

Under the new Annex, Mexico has been supposed to establish and maintain impartial and independent bodies authorised to register union elections and resolve disputes relating to collective bargaining agreements and the recognition of unions. In this regard, it is worth noting that in order to achieve compliance with the Annex 23-A, Mexico has introduced a serious labour law reform, that is, on 1 May 2019, 'Decreto por el que se reforman, adicionan y derogan diversas disposiciones de la Ley Federal del Trabajo, de la Ley Orgánica del Poder Judicial de la Federación, de la Ley Federal de la Defensoría Pública, de la Ley del Instituto del Fondo Nacional de la Vivienda para los Trabajadores y de la Ley del Seguro Social, en materia de Justicia Laboral, Libertad Sindical y Negociación Colectiva' was published.[44] Moreover, on 23 November 2018, Mexico ratified the Right to Organise and Collective Bargaining Convention, 1949 (No. 98).[45]

One of the crucial characteristics of the USMCA is a facility-specific rapid response labour mechanism, which purpose is to ensure remediation of a 'Denial of Rights' of free association and collective bargaining for workers at a Covered Facility in Mexico or the US, and to ensure that remedies are lifted immediately once a Denial of Rights is remediated. It has been admitted that Annex 31-A creates 'the strongest labor rights monitoring and enforcement mechanisms in any U.S. free trade agreement concluded to date'.[46] The mechanism allows the complainant Party to request the formation of a 'Rapid Response Labor Panel' (the

---

43 It should be noted that no Party shall have recourse to dispute settlement under Chapter 31 for a matter arising under Chapter 23 'Labor' without first seeking to resolve the matter in accordance with Article 23.17 ('Labor Consultations').
44 *Diario Oficial* (1 May 2019) <www.diputados.gob.mx/LeyesBiblio/ref/lft/LFT_ref30_01may19.pdf> accessed 27 November 2020.
45 <www.ilo.org/dyn/normlex/en/f?p=1000:11300:0::NO:11300:P11300_INSTRU-MENT_ID:312243> accessed 27 November 2020.
46 Shara Aranoff, Cindy Owens, John K Veroneau and Kate McNulty, 'Companies Should Understand USMCA's Labor Obligations as They Are Significant and Likely to Be Enforced' *Global Policy Watch* (28 January 2020) <www.globalpolicywatch.com/2020/01/companies-should-understand-usmcas-labor-obligations-as-they-are-significant-and-likely-to-be-enforced/> accessed 27 November 2020.

'panel'). Its competences include conducting on-site verifications at the facility in question (if the respondent Party agrees to the verification). Based on the findings of the panel, the complainant Party may impose remedies that are the most appropriate to remedy the Denial of Rights. Remedies may include suspension of preferential tariff treatment for goods manufactured at the Covered Facility or the imposition of penalties on goods manufactured at or services provided by the Covered Facility. In cases where a Covered Facility or a Covered Facility owned or controlled by the same person producing the same or related goods or providing the same or related services has received a prior Denial of Rights determination, remedies may include suspension of preferential tariff treatment for such goods or the imposition of penalties on such goods or services. If the Covered Facility has received at least two prior Denial of Rights determinations, remedies may include suspension of preferential tariff treatment for such goods; the imposition of penalties on such goods or services; or the denial of entry of such goods. It must be acknowledged that when comparing the mechanism concerned with previous trade agreements, a novel pattern emerges, which consists of on-site verifications at a given facility. In comparison, labour law clauses included in trade agreements to date provided an opportunity to address the failure of a government to ensure effective enforcement of labour laws.[47]

What is also of note is that an important anti-abuse provision has been incorporated in Article 31-A.11, according to which if one Party considers that the other has not acted in good faith in its use of the facility-specific rapid response labour mechanism, that Party may have recourse to the dispute settlement mechanism under Chapter 31. If a panel shares these concerns, within 45 days from receipt of the final panel report, the Parties shall endeavour to agree to the resolution of the dispute. If the Parties are unable to resolve the dispute, the complainant Party may elect either to prevent the responding Party from using the mechanism for a period of two years or another remedy permitted under Chapter 31. Such a provision actually eliminates concerns of lodging unjustified complaints or abusing the mechanism with the aim of restricting trade.

What is extremely characteristic is that Title VII 'Labor Monitoring and Enforcement' of the USMCA Implementation Act of 2020 requires the US President to establish 'the Interagency Labor Committee for Monitoring and Enforcement' within 90 days of the enactment of the USMCA Implementation Act, to coordinate US efforts with respect to each USMCA country:

- to monitor the implementation and maintenance of the labour obligations;
- to monitor the implementation and maintenance of Mexico's labour reform; and
- to request enforcement actions with respect to a USMCA country that is not in compliance with such labour obligations.

---

47 See: Christoph Scherrer, 'Novel Labour-Related Clauses in a Trade Agreement: From NAFTA to USMCA' (2020) 11(3) *Global Labour Journal* 291, 297–298.

The USMCA Implementation Act of 2020 (section 712) enumerates the duties of the Interagency Labour Committee for Monitoring and Enforcement, which are divided into groups: coordination, consultation, recommendation and review duties.[48] The Interagency Labour Committee for Monitoring and Enforcement is also required to complete assessments of Mexico's compliance with the USMCA labour obligations on a biannual basis for the first five years after the USMCA Implementation Act is enacted. The assessment shall include an information whether Mexico is providing adequate funding to implement and enforce Mexico's labour reform (section 714). Moreover, the Interagency Labour Committee for Monitoring and Enforcement is required to recommend enforcements actions to the Trade Representative when it determines that a USMCA country has failed to meet its labour obligations, including with respect to obligations under Annex 23-A of the USMCA. More specifically, the Committee may recommend that the Trade Representative initiate enforcement actions relating to: cooperative labour dialogue and labour consultations; dispute settlement consultations; or the rapid response labour mechanism (section 715).

What refers to procedures for submissions by the public to the Interagency Labour Committee for Monitoring and Enforcement of information with respect to potential failures to implement the labour obligations of a USMCA country, they have been laid down in section 716. If the Interagency Labour Committee for Monitoring and Enforcement receives a petition requesting an enforcement action under Annex 31-A, it shall determine whether there is sufficient, credible evidence of a Denial of Rights enabling the good-faith invocation of enforcement mechanisms under Annex 31-A. If its determination is negative, it shall certify such determination to the Committee on Ways and Means and the Senate Finance Committee, and the petitioner. On the other hand, if the Committee in question reaches an affirmative determination, the Trade Representative shall submit a request for review, pursuant to Annex 31-A, with respect to the Covered Facility and shall inform the petitioner and the appropriate congressional committees of the submission of such request. No later than 60 days after the date of an affirmative determination, the Trade Representative is required to determine whether to request the establishment of a rapid response labour panel under Annex 31-A. If the Trade Representative's determination is negative, the Trade Representative is required to certify such determination to the Committee on Ways and Means and the Senate Finance Committee in conjunction with the reasons for such determination and the details of any agreed-upon remediation plan. Besides, section 716 establishes a petition process for allegations of non-compliance with the USMCA labour obligations not related to Annex 31-A.

When seeking the best solutions for workers one should pay attention to the hotline envisaged in the USMCA Implementation Act. To be precise, the Interagency Labour Committee for Monitoring and Enforcement is required

---

48 For details, please see: <www.congress.gov/bill/116th-congress/house-bill/5430/text> accessed 27 November 2020.

to establish a web-based hotline to receive confidential information regarding labour issues in USMCA countries from interested parties, including Mexican workers (section 717).

The next contribution of the USMCA Implementation Act toward resolution of Mexican workers' problems is the appointment of labour attachés. Strictly speaking, the Secretary of Labour will hire up to five additional full-time officers or employees of the Department of Labour who will be detailed or assigned to work on behalf of the US government in Mexico. They will not only assist the Interagency Labour Committee for Monitoring and Enforcement in monitoring and enforcing the labour obligations of Mexico but also submit to this Committee on a quarterly basis reports on the efforts undertaken by Mexico to comply with its labour obligations (sections 721–722).

We should also concentrate on section 741 that requires the president to establish a 'Forced Labor Enforcement Task Force' to monitor US enforcement of the prohibition on importation of goods made by or with forced labour under section 307 of the Tariff Act of 1930 (19 U.S.C. 1307). The Task Force shall be chaired by the Secretary of Homeland Security and shall be comprised of the Trade Representative, the Department of Labour, and other agencies with relevant expertise. The Forced Labor Enforcement Task Force is required to establish timelines for responding to petitions alleging that goods are being imported by or with forced or child labour (section 742). Details of such procedures are specified by sections 742–744.

Unfortunately, the USMCA – similarly to NAFTA – does not give a right (with some exceptions) to make a private case against government. Charnovitz has rightly concluded that 'such a private right of action would be a much more effective way to enhance worker rights than expecting governments to lodge cases against each other'.[49] This could be achieved through the extension of ISDS with the aim of allowing workers to bring complaints before independent arbitrators when an alleged violation of their rights, committed by foreign corporations, occurs. Such a proposal has a potential to give increased legitimacy to a dispute settlement mechanism, in the framework of which only corporations have a private right of action.[50]

Last but not least, the USMCA tries to correct the great wage differential between Mexico on the one hand, and the US and Canada on the other hand. Article 7 (Chapter 4) requires the vehicle producer to certify that its production meets a 'Labor Value Content' requirement, which means 30 to 40% of vehicle value being produced by workers earning wages of at least US\$16.00 per hour. In addition, it is required that certain automobile elements be produced in the

---

49 Charnovitz (n 39).
50 See more: Kimberly Ann Elliott, 'Developing a More Inclusive US Trade Policy at Home and Abroad' (2019) *Center for Global Development Policy Paper* 146, 20 <www.cgdev.org/publication/developing-more-inclusive-us-trade-policy-home-and-abroad> accessed 27 November 2020.

region, as must 70% of all steel and aluminium content. As it seems, these provisions are established with the aim of increasing production in North America, at the same time reducing it in other supply chains, especially in Asia.[51] As regards US$16.00 per hour, one could only postulate that it should be a minimum, and not an average wage, as is presently the case.

3 The EU international trade agreements

3.1 *The commitments to labour standards in the four generations of the EU international trade agreements*

The first generation of EU trade agreements, referring to labour especially in the context of migrant workers, and concluded between 1995 and 2002, embraces the following: the Euro-Med (Euro-Mediterranean Association Agreements) concluded by the EU with Tunisia, Morocco, Israel and the EU-Med (Euro-Mediterranean Cooperation Agreements) with Algeria, Egypt, Jordan and Lebanon.[52] The Barcelona Declaration of November 1995 (a non-binding instrument) constituted the ground for the conclusion of these agreements. The document put emphasis on the protection of the rights of legally resident migrant workers. It established 14 principles as the basis for the Partnership in Social, Cultural and Human Affairs, two of which (the 10th and 11th) related to migration. All concerned countries decided to strengthen cooperation with the aim of reducing migratory pressures, for example, by undertaking vocational training programmes and plans of assistance for job creation (the 10th principle). The obligation of all countries to ensure the protection of the rights of migrants legally residing in their territory (which are recognised under national legislation) was also established. Illegal immigration was the issue raised in the 11th principle. However, these obligations were to be envisaged in bilateral or multilateral (ratified) agreements in order to have a mandatory character.[53]

51 Álvaro Santos, 'Reimagining Trade Agreements for Workers: Lessons from the USMCA' (2019) 113 *American Journal of International Law Unbound* 407, 411 <www.cambridge.org/core/services/aop-cambridge-core/content/view/AF9056844AEAF8085CA-7F594AFB32B3C/S2398772319000746a.pdf/reimagining_trade_agreements_for_workers_lessons_from_the_usmca.pdf> accessed 27 November 2020.

52 Helen Freeman, 'Special Trade Arrangements to Improve Market Access' in Merlinda Ingco and John D Nash (eds), *Agriculture and the WTO: Creating a Trading System for Development* (Washington DC: World Bank and Oxford University Press 2004) 293; ILO (n 22) 39. More: Caroline Freund and Carlos A Primo Braga, 'The Economics of Arab Transitions' in Cesare Merlini and Olivier Roy (eds), *Arab Society in Revolt: The West's Mediterranean Challenge* (Washington DC: Brookings Institution Press 2012) 137 et seq.; Lorand Bartels, 'A Legal Analysis of Human Rights Clauses in the European Union's Euro-Mediterranean Association Agreements' 2004 9(3) *Mediterranean Politics* 368 <https://doi.org/10.1080/1362939042000259933> accessed 27 November 2020.

53 Konstantinos D Magliveras, 'Protecting the Rights of Migrant Workers in the Euro-Mediterranean Partnership' in Iván Martín and Iain Byrne (eds), *Special Issue on Economic and*

The agreements with Morocco, Algeria and Tunisia are very similar to each other. They all establish the prohibition of discrimination on the grounds of nationality as regards working conditions, remuneration and dismissal, and they also include social security issues. Moreover, they give priority to reducing migratory pressure by improving living conditions, creating new job opportunities and developing training in those countries from which immigrants originated.[54]

The agreement with Israel can be characterised as having only a rather restrictive social dialogue, which is related to, inter alia, unemployment, rehabilitation of disabled persons, equal treatment for women and men, vocational training, work safety and hygiene. The agreements with Egypt, Jordan and Lebanon include neither social security provisions nor protections for workers of either side, who are legally employed in the respective territory. They only mention the establishment of a social dialogue among the partners and social cooperation actions.[55]

Respect for basic social rights through the promotion of cooperative activities related to international labour standards, also appear in the 1999 Trade, Development and Cooperation Agreement (TDCA) with South Africa,[56] which represents a second generation of trade agreements. However, explicit commitments to labour standards have been included in the 2000 Cotonou Partnership Agreement with the African, Caribbean and Pacific states.[57] The important status attained by the Cotonou Agreement is due to the fact that both the EU and the African, Caribbean and Pacific countries have equally committed themselves to respect core labour standards and to enhance cooperation in this area.[58] Clear commitments to labour standards have been also included in the FTA with Chile (2003).[59]

Concluded in 2008, the economic partnership agreement between the EU and the Forum of Caribbean Group of African, Caribbean and Pacific States (the EU-Cariforum EPA) is treated as a third-generation agreement, and as a special category of agreements because of its different rationale, which goes beyond traditional free trade agreements. This EPA is the first in which the parties reaffirm their commitment to core labour standards, as defined by the relevant ILO

Social Rights in the Euro-Mediterranean Partnership (2004) 9(3) Mediterranean Politics 459, 462, 464 <www.academia.edu/2068195/_2004_Economic_and_Social_Rights_in_the_Euro_Mediterranean_Partnership> accessed 27 November 2020.

54 ibid 464–467.

55 ibid 468–469.

56 See more on TDCA: Stefaan Smis and Stephen Kingah, 'EU South African Trade, Developmentand Cooperation Agreement: Bane or Boon for Socio-Economic Rights Under the South African Constitution?' (November 2014) 20(6) *European Law Journal* 793 <https://doi.org/10.1111/eulj.12106> accessed 27 November 2020.

57 Campling, Harrison, Richardson and Smith (n 8) 362; see the cited literature.

58 Samantha Velluti, 'The EU's Social Dimension and Its External Trade Relations' in Axel Marx, Jan Wouters, Glenn Rayp and Laura Beke (eds), *Global Governance of Labour Rights. Assessing the Effectiveness of Transnational Public and Private Policy Initiatives* (Cheltenham, Northampton: Edward Elgar Publishing 2015) 57.

59 Campling, Harrison, Richardson and Smith (n 8) 362.

Conventions. Thus, the parties commit themselves to the respect of fundamental principles and rights at work, as recognised by the 1998 ILO Declaration. Besides, the EU-Cariforum EPA includes labour provisions relating to foreign investors in the investment chapter. It is also the only EU agreement that submits labour provisions to sanction-based arbitral dispute settlement and establishes the first ad hoc dispute settlement mechanism for labour provisions in an EU trade agreement.[60]

The EU–South Korea FTA, which was signed in 2010, and has been applied since 2011, has given rise to the EU's current (fourth) generation of trade agreements. It is not in dispute that the main characteristic of the fourth generation of trade agreements is that they contain a 'trade and sustainable development' chapter which aims at integrating labour provisions into them. For example, Article 13.4.3 of the EU–South Korea FTA highlights 'respecting, promoting and realising, in their laws and practices, the principles concerning the fundamental rights', 'the commitment to effectively implementing the ILO Conventions that Korea and the Member States of the EU have ratified respectively', and making 'continued and sustained efforts towards ratifying the fundamental ILO Conventions as well as the other Conventions that are classified as "up-to-date" by the ILO'. Not only the agreement with the Republic of Korea but also agreements with Central America, Colombia and Peru, Georgia, Moldova and Ukraine, all refer to the 1998 ILO Declaration, the UN Declaration on Full Employment and Decent Work, the goal of achieving high levels of labour protection, commitments with regard to the fundamental principles and rights at work and the eight fundamental ILO Conventions[61] (in terms of substantive standards). When it comes to institutional structures, the 'trade and sustainable development' chapters establish the Committee on Trade and Sustainable Development.[62] For example, such a Committee has been created under the agreement with Korea in order to monitor implementation of the trade and sustainable development chapter.[63] Besides, according to the Article 13.12.4 of the EU–South Korea FTA, the parties are required to 'establish a Domestic Advisory Group(s) on sustainable development (environment and labour) with the task of advising on the implementation of this Chapter', and with the aim of making national and EU civil society actors participate in its structure. If there is a dispute that the parties are not able to resolve themselves, they can involve a Panel of Independent Experts,

---

60 ILO (n 22) 40.
61 ibid 41.
62 Campling, Harrison, Richardson and Smith (n 8) 363.
63 Analysing the EU-Colombia trade agreement, Marx, Lein and Brando highlight that there is no monitoring mechanism to track compliance with the human rights clause, nor a Subcommittee dedicated to human rights. The authors point out that because of the lack of a specialised human rights Subcommittee, human rights and democracy issues would fall under the auspices of the Trade Committee, which excludes any participation of civil society. See: Axel Marx, Brecht Lein and Nicolás Brando, 'The Protection of Labour Rights in Trade Agreements: The Case of the EU-Colombia Agreement' (2016) 50(4) *Journal of World Trade* 587, 591.

the conclusions of which are, however, non-binding. Furthermore, there is no provision for sanctions. As rightly stated by Campling et al.:

> There is some initial evidence suggesting that the combination of weak domestic advisory groups, 'a trade and sustainable development' chapter that lacks any mechanism to arbitrate disputes or impose penalties, and the absence of political will on the part of the EU means that the EU–South Korea FTA does not thus far provide a particularly effective mechanism for resolving labour disputes.[64]

Given this context, it should be highlighted that the standard dispute settlement procedure for dealing with complaints does not appear in any of the FTAs. For this reason, one party cannot bring an action that would result in the suspension of trade preferences against the other party.[65]

As pointed out by Van Roozendaal, with respect to the ratification, there is no intermediate impact of the FTAs. In fact, the Republic of Korea has not ratified the following fundamental Conventions: Forced Labour Convention, 1930 (No. 29); Freedom of Association and Protection of the Right to Organise Convention, 1948 (No. 87); Right to Organise and Collective Bargaining Convention, 1949 (No. 98); Abolition of Forced Labour Convention, 1957 (No. 105).[66] Van Roozendaal stresses that – what refers to other kinds of impact – the FTAs have not made a difference in the field of enabling rights. There are considerable problems connected to the freedom of association, the right to collective action, and the right to strike. She highlights that the lack of impact is due to the absence of political willingness on the part of the Korean side, and an equal absence of 'readiness on the trade partners' sides to either include strong wording and a strong instrument to back up any commitment, or to actually use the available instruments in a way which would lead to improvement'.[67]

However, in the near future, we will witness the outcome of the EU–Korea dispute settlement over workers' rights,[68] in which the panel was established and started its work on 30 December 2019.[69] It was supposed to present its report

---

64 Campling, Harrison, Richardson and Smith (n 8) 370–371.
65 ibid 363–364.
66 <www.ilo.org/dyn/normlex/en/f?p=1000:11210:0::NO:11210:P11210_COUNTRY_ID:103123> accessed 27 November 2020.
67 Gerda Van Roozendaal, 'Where Symbolism Prospers: An Analysis of the Impact on Enabling Rights of Labour Standards Provisions in Trade Agreements with South Korea' (2017) 5(4) *Politics and Governance* 19, 24–25, 27.
68 <https://trade.ec.europa.eu/doclib/press/index.cfm?id=2095> accessed 27 November 2020.
69 This step was not so obvious to make as a lack of political will on the part of the EU to enforce labour standards provisions was symptomatic for a long time. As it was pointed out by a Commission official: 'It is important to have a positive forward looking agenda. Confrontation would lead to a backlash on behalf of Korea. We want to add investment protection into the agreement. If we took action under this chapter, we might lose benefits

to the Parties by the end of March 2020; however, in light of COVID-19 travel restrictions, Parties and panel have agreed to postpone the hearing on the EU–Korea dispute on workers' rights in Korea.[70] Clearly, much is to be reported, as South Korea – what has been mentioned previously – has so far failed to ratify four of eight ILO core Conventions. It should also be highlighted that on 20 January 2020 the EU made its first submission in the dispute, requesting for findings and recommendations.[71] It will soon become clear whether the EU's approach has the potential of influencing the process of ratification of the ILO core Conventions.

In 2014, the EU and Canada concluded negotiations on the Comprehensive Economic and Trade Agreement (CETA), which is another example of the fourth generation of trade agreements, and which, if we speak about adopted labour norms, is very similar to the EU–Korea FTA. Already at the beginning of Chapter 23 entitled 'Trade and Labour', we can read:

> Affirming the value of greater policy coherence in decent work, encompassing core labour standards, and high levels of labour protection, coupled with their effective enforcement, the Parties recognise the beneficial role that those areas can have on economic efficiency, innovation and productivity, including export performance. In this context, they also recognise the importance of social dialogue on labour matters among workers and employers, and their respective organisations, and governments, and commit to the promotion of such dialogue.

What is more, the parties have agreed to ensure that their national laws conform to the ILO core labour standards and commit themselves to the respect of fundamental principles and rights at work, as recognised by the 1998 ILO Declaration, the 2008 ILO Declaration on Social Justice for a Fair Globalisation, the 2006 Ministerial Declaration of the UN Economic and Social Council on Full Employment and Decent Work, and the OECD Guidelines for Multilateral Enterprises.

However, all the lofty phrases, the reaffirmation of the parties' commitment to the ILO 1998 Declaration and to the core labour standards are perceived as seriously undermined if, the 'Trade and Labour' Chapter lacks effectiveness and 'is not able to automatically ensure a protection of labour rights among the two sides of the Atlantic Ocean'.[72]

---

elsewhere. So we do need to think about the bigger context'. See: James Harrison, Mirela Barbu, Liam Campling, Ben Richardson and Adrian Smith, 'Governing Labour Standards Through Free Trade Agreements: Limits of the European Union's Trade and Sustainable Development Chapters' (2019) 57(2) *Journal of Common Market Studies* 260, 269 <https://doi.org/10.1111/jcms.12715> accessed 27 November 2020.

70 <www.porgeslaw.com/rta-disputes> accessed 27 November 2020.
71 <https://trade.ec.europa.eu/doclib/docs/2020/january/tradoc_158585.pdf> accessed 27 November 2020.
72 Silvio Bologna, 'The Comprehensive Economic and Trade Agreement (CETA): What Kind of Space Is Given to Fair Trade and Labour Rights?' (2017) 9(1) Temilavoro.it Sinossi Internet di Diritto del Lavoro e della Sicurezza Sociale 1, 4, 10 <https://iris.unipa.it/retrieve/handle/10447/241968/452354/CETA_Temilavoro.pdf> accessed 27 November 2020.

As in case of the EU–Korea FTA, the Committee on Trade and Sustainable Development – established under Article 26.2.1(g) (Specialised committees) – shall, inter alia, oversee the implementation of the Chapter entitled 'Trade and Labour' and review the progress achieved under it, including its operation and effectiveness. Besides, the CETA establishes a 'Civil Society Forum' to conduct a dialogue on the sustainable development aspects of the agreement. A party may request consultations with the other party regarding any matter arising under the 'Trade and Labour' Chapter by delivering a written request to the contact point of the other party. For any matter that is not satisfactorily addressed through such consultations, a party may request that a 'Panel of Experts' be convened to examine that matter. Unfortunately, mechanisms to ensure effective enforcement are absent for disputes concerning labour rights infringements. There is no possibility to access the national jurisdiction.[73] The CETA excludes access to its regular dispute settlement mechanism, which allows for the imposition of sanctions. In addition, no trade or other sanctions are projected. Consequently, compliance with any panel findings is, to a great extent, left to the discretion of the party concerned.[74]

It is worth stressing that the reaffirmation of the parties' commitment to the core labour standards is not clearly linked to other chapters of the CETA where it should be relevant, for example, the one concerning regulatory cooperation. This means that labour matters are not treated as generally relevant but only when consistent with specific sections, for example, on the liberalisation of trade.[75]

3.2 The EU and Japan's Economic Partnership Agreement as an example of the fourth generation of trade agreements

3.2.1 The background

After years of 'economic friction' between Europe and Japan, which was experienced from the 1960s to the late 1980s, and after a 'qualitative transformation' of their relationship in the 1990s, which was triggered by the Hague Declaration

---

73 See: Vincenzo Ferrante, 'Social Concerns in Free Trade Agreements' (2016) 5(2 May–June) E-Journal of International and Comparative Labour Studies 1, 8; Michele Faioli, 'Atlantic Transitions for Law and Labor: CETA First and TTIP Second?' in Adalberto Perulli and Tiziano Treu (eds), *Sustainable Development, Global Trade and Social Rights* (Alphen aan den Rijn: Wolters Kluwer 2018) 88; Lorand Bartels, 'Human Rights, Labour Standards, and Environmental Standards in CETA' in Stefan Griller, Walter Obwexer and Erich Vranes (eds), *Mega-Regional Trade Agreements: CETA, TTIP, and TiSA. New Orientations for EU External Economic Relations* (Oxford: Oxford University Press 2017) 208.
74 See: Franz Christian Ebert, 'The Comprehensive Economic and Trade Agreement (CETA): Are Existing Arrangements Sufficient to Prevent Adverse Effects on Labour Standards?' (2017) 33(2) *International Journal of Comparative Labour Law and Industrial Relations* 295, 307.
75 E.g. Bologna (n 72) 4–5; see the cited literature.

of 1991,[76] the countries have taken a political step forward. A case in point is the EU and Japan's Economic Partnership Agreement (EPA), which entered into force on 1 February 2019.[77] It was concluded between two of the world's biggest economies with hope that the position of EU exporters and investors on Japan's large market would improve and, at the same time, strong guarantees for the protection of EU standards and values would be preserved.[78] The EU and Japan's EPA removes the majority of duties incurred by EU companies, which sum up to €1 billion annually. As it is declared, it opens the Japanese market to key EU agricultural exports and increases opportunities in a range of sectors.[79] According to the European Commission website, in the first ten months following the implementation of the EU and Japan's EPA, EU exports to Japan grew by 6.6% in comparison to the same period a year earlier, and Japanese exports to Europe went up by 6.3% in the same period.[80]

Similarly to other free trade agreements, the Parties to the EPA have devoted one chapter, inter alia, to labour provisions. This is Chapter 16 entitled 'Trade and sustainable development'.[81]

3.2.2 Labour laws and labour provisions

Already at first glance, the Chapter entitled 'Trade and sustainable development' seems to correspond with other recent EU trade agreements. However, given the very different legal traditions between EU and Japan, Article 16.1, paragraph 2 states that 'The Parties . . . recognise that the purpose of this Chapter is to

---

76 Yuko Hosoi, 'Japan-EU Relations After World War II and Strategic Partnership' (2019) 17(3) Asia Europe Journal 295, 298–302 <https://doi.org/10.1007/s10308-019-00555-1> accessed 27 November 2020. See more: Aiko Morii, 'Dialogue Without Cooperation? Diplomatic Implications of EU–Japan Summits' (2015) 13(4) *Asia Europe Journal* 413, 418 et seq. <https://doi.org/10.1007/s10308-015-0429-7> accessed 27 November 2020.

77 Comparing to the EU negotiations with the US and Canada, the EU–Japan EPA negotiations encountered few critics from civil society organisations. See: Hitoshi Suzuki, 'The New Politics of Trade: EU–Japan' (2017) 39(7) *Journal of European Integration* 875, passim <https://doi.org/10.1080/07036337.2017.1371709> accessed 27 November 2020.

78 <https://ec.europa.eu/commission/presscorner/detail/en/MEMO_18_6784> accessed 27 November 2020.

79 <https://trade.ec.europa.eu/doclib/docs/2006/december/tradoc_118238.pdf> accessed 27 November 2020.

80 <https://ec.europa.eu/commission/presscorner/detail/en/ip_20_161> accessed 27 November 2020. It should be however noted that, even after EPA, market access in Japan is not easy for European companies because of informal market barriers. These are as follows: difficulties with adaptation to the Japanese business culture and the closed nature of Japanese society; legal system and practice, which tend to discriminate against foreign companies; top tax rates of more than 50%; high prices for land and property; considerable market entry and operational costs; and significant sales and distribution costs. As a result, the below-average integration of Japan into the global economic division of labour is clearly discernable. See more: Hanns Günther Hilpert, 'The Japan-EU Economic Partnership Agreement – Economic Potentials and Policy Perspectives' (2018) 16(4) *Asia Europe Journal* 439, 445 <https://doi.org/10.1007/s10308-017-0496-z> accessed 27 November 2020.

81 <https://trade.ec.europa.eu/doclib/press/index.cfm?id=1684> accessed 27 November 2020.

strengthen the trade relations and cooperation between the Parties in ways that promote sustainable development, and is not to harmonise the environment or labour standards of the Parties'. In fact, it must be observed that the important characteristics of the Japanese system differ from those in Europe or the US, and are related to a lifetime employment system,[82] the large gender gap in earnings,[83] and enterprise unionism, where each unionised enterprise has its own union with which it undertakes collective bargaining independently. In this respect, it should be noted, however, that the unionisation rate is only about 18%.[84]

---

82 Haruo Takeuchi, 'The Present Situation in the Japanese Employment System, with Special Reference to the Problems Regarding Temporary Workers' in Hans-Heinrich Bass, Toshihiko Hozumi and Uwe Staroske (eds), *Labor Markets and Labor Market Policies Between Globalization and World Economic Crisis: Japan and Germany* (München: Rainer Hampp Verlag 2010) 166; Mariana Pargendler, 'The Grip of Nationalism on Corporate Law' (2020) 95(2) *Indiana Law Journal* 533, 557. Lifetime employment and seniority-based wages constitute the characteristics of a stable long-term employment, that is, regular employment (a regular worker is called 'seishain' in Japanese). See: Nobuko Nagase and Mary C Brinton, 'The Gender Division of Labor and Second Births: Labor Market Institutions and Fertility in Japan' (2017) 36 *Demographic Research* 339, 346, 342 <www.demographic-research.org/volumes/vol36/11/> accessed 27 November 2020. On the other hand, however, Japan's labour market includes non-standard employment, consisting of part-time workers, arubaito workers, temporary contract workers, dispatch workers, and entrusted workers. As explained by Diamond, arubaito is similar to part-time employment but very often relates to college or high school students. Dispatch workers are employed by a temporary employment agency. Finally, entrusted workers are those who are usually retained by the company after mandatory retirement on relatively long fixed-term contracts. Importantly, there are great differences in wages between regular and non-standard workers. Jess Diamond, 'Employment Status Persistence in the Japanese Labour Market' (2018) 69(1) *The Japanese Economic Review* 69, 72 <https://doi.org/10.1111/jere.12148> accessed 27 November 2020.

83 See for example: Sagiri Kitao and Minamo Mikoshiba, 'Females, the Elderly, and also Males: Demographic Aging and Macroeconomy in Japan' (2020) 5 *Journal of the Japanese and International Economies* 1, 9 <https://doi.org/10.1016/j.jjie.2020.101064> accessed 27 November 2020. Moreover, in the light of the 2011 data provided by the Japanese Ministry of Health, Labour and Welfare, 45.9% of Japanese women are in part time work, compared with only 13.8% of Japanese men. See: European Commission, *Trade Sustainability Impact Assessment of the Free Trade Agreement Between the European Union and Japan* (Final Report, Brussels 2016) 196 <http://trade.ec.europa.eu/doclib/docs/2016/may/tradoc_154522.pdf> accessed 27 November 2020. In addition, it should be noted that Japan was ranked 121 out of 153 countries in the Global Gender Gap Index 2020. See: World Economic Forum, *Global Gender Gap Report 2020* (Cologny: World Economic Forum 2019) 9. For previous research, see: John Benson, Masae Yuasa and Philippe Debroux, 'The Prospect for Gender Diversity in Japanese Employment' (2007) 18(5) *International Journal of Human Resource Management* 890, 892 <https://doi.org/10.1080/09585190701249495> accessed 27 November 2020.

84 Marcus Rebick, 'The Japanese Economy' in James D Babb (ed), *The Sage Handbook of Modern Japanese Studies* (Los Angeles, London, New Delhi, Singapore, Washington DC: Sage Publishing 2015) 510; Lonny E Carlile, 'The Labor Movement' in Alisa Gaunder (ed), *Routledge Handbook of Japanese Politics* (London, New York: Routledge 2011) 162. See also: Heidi Gottfried, 'Precarious Work in Japan: Old Forms, New Risks?' (2014) 44(3) *Journal of Contemporary Asia* 464, 467 <http://dx.doi.org/10.1080/00472336.2013.867523> accessed 27 November 2020. Even though the establishment of Rengō (Japanese Trade Union Confederation) in 1989 helped labour unions achieve substantial unification of

What is also interesting is that, admittedly, in accordance with the Civil Code of Japan, the employer has the power of dismissing the worker without reason, but the jurisprudence of abuse of dismissals has introduced significant and rigorous limitations on the employer's dismissal rights in practice.[85]

Chapter 16 establishes the prohibition of relaxing or lowering the level of protection provided by domestic labour laws to encourage trade or investment,[86] and it also introduces the provision on non-discrimination ('The Parties shall not use their respective environmental or labour laws and regulations in a manner which would constitute a means of arbitrary or unjustifiable discrimination against the other Party, or a disguised restriction on international trade', Article 16.2, paragraph 3).

The EU and Japan's EPA refers to the spectrum of international instruments (Article 16.1, paragraph 1), in particular to the ILO Declaration on Fundamental Principles and Rights at Work and its Follow-up. The Parties reaffirm their commitments with regard to this document (Article 16.3, paragraph 2). However, the EPA does not require the ratification of the ILO Conventions in order to conclude an agreement ('Each Party shall make continued and sustained efforts on its own initiative to pursue ratification of the fundamental ILO Conventions and other ILO Conventions which each Party considers appropriate to ratify', Article 16.3, paragraph 3). In common with many other agreements such as the Transatlantic Trade and Investment Partnership (TTIP), the EU and Japan's EPA includes lofty phrases, but the question is, whether it is able to ensure

---

the labour movement, union density has been declining, in particular since the 1990s, when the government's implementation of labour market deregulation took place. Hiroaki Richard Watanabe, 'Labour Market Dualism and Diversification in Japan' (2018) 56(3) *British Journal of Industrial Relations* 579, 593 <https://doi.org/10.1111/bjir.12258> accessed 27 November 2020; Hiroaki Richard Watanabe, 'The Struggle for Revitalisation by Japanese Labour Unions: Worker Organising After Labour-Market Deregulation' (2015) 45(3) *Journal of Contemporary Asia* 510, 510 <http://dx.doi.org/10.1080/00472336.2015.10 07388> accessed 27 November 2020. For an overview of changes, see: Susumu Watanabe, 'The Japan Model and the Future of Employment and Wage Systems' (2000) 139(3) *International Labour Review* 307.

85 Li Yu-Chun, 'Law Review and Comparison of Dismissal Regulations' in Tatsuo Hatta and Shinya Ouchi (eds), *Severance Payment and Labor Mobility: A Comparative Study of Taiwan and Japan* (Singapore: Springer 2018) 126; Shinya Ouchi, 'Why Should the Monetary Compensation System Be Introduced in Japanese Dismissal Regulation?' in Tatsuo Hatta and Shinya Ouchi (eds), *Severance Payment and Labor Mobility: A Comparative Study of Taiwan and Japan* (Singapore: Springer 2018) 4–6.

86 'The Parties shall not encourage trade or investment by relaxing or lowering the level of protection provided by their respective environmental or labour laws and regulations. To that effect, the Parties shall not waive or otherwise derogate from those laws and regulations or fail to effectively enforce them through a sustained or recurring course of action or inaction in a manner affecting trade or investment between the Parties' (Article 16.2, paragraph 2) <http://trade.ec.europa.eu/doclib/docs/2018/august/tradoc_157228.pdf#page=440> accessed 28 November 2020.

enforcement of labour standards.[87] Unfortunately, soft, promotional formulations (e.g. 'Recognising the right of each Party to . . . establish its own levels of
domestic . . . labour protection. . ., each Party shall strive to ensure that its laws,
regulations and related policies provide high levels of . . . labour protection and
shall strive to continue to improve those laws and regulations and their underlying levels of protection' as in Article 16.2 paragraph 1) may not achieve this
effect. It should be clearly stated that Japan has only ratified six out of eight ILO
core Conventions. It has not ratified Conventions No. 105 (Abolition of Forced
Labour Convention)[88] and No. 111 (Convention concerning Discrimination
in Respect of Employment and Occupation).[89] The EU and Japan's EPA places
greater emphasis on the implementation of ILO Conventions that have been
already ratified ('Each Party reaffirms its commitments to effectively implement
in its laws, regulations and practices ILO Conventions ratified by Japan and the
Member States of the European Union respectively', Article 16.3 paragraph 5).

3.2.3 Japan's difficulties with ratifications

One may wonder what is the reason for the lack of ratification of the two core
Conventions. While such state of affairs in regard to the Convention concerning
Discrimination in Respect of Employment and Occupation seems to be related
to cultural backgrounds, the situation connected with the Abolition of Forced
Labour Convention is quite different. Since 1995, the CEACR has been examining the issues of wartime industrial forced labour and sexual slavery (so-called
'comfort women') during the Second World War. The CEACR, noting the observations of the All Japan Shipbuilding and Engineering Union, refers in particular
to a decision of the Korean Supreme Court of Justice of 24 May 2012 which
reversed the decisions of lower courts rejecting the demands for compensation
by forced labour victims against two leading Japanese industries. Consequently,
the Retrial Courts (the Seoul and Pusan High Courts of Justice) ordered the
industries to pay compensation to former victims of forced labour. Unfortunately
for the victims, the defendants filed an appeal to the Supreme Court of Justice.
This means that plaintiffs who have since passed away will not know the outcome of their complaint. It has been highlighted that a number of lawsuits have
been initiated recently concerning wartime industrial forced labour following the
retrial judgement of the Supreme Court of Justice. According to further observations of the All Japan Shipbuilding and Engineering Union, officials of these
companies declared that they considered that the issue of compensation had been
settled by the conclusion of the 1965 Agreement on the Settlement of Problems

---

87 Aneta Tyc, 'Workers' Rights and Transatlantic Trade Relations: The TTIP and Beyond'
(2017) 28(1) *The Economic and Labour Relations Review* 113, 121–122.
88 <www.ilo.org/dyn/normlex/en/f?p=NORMLEXPUB:11310:0::NO:11310:P11310_
INSTRUMENT_ID:312250:NO> accessed 28 November 2020.
89 <www.ilo.org/dyn/normlex/en/f?p=NORMLEXPUB:11310:0::NO:11310:P11310_
INSTRUMENT_ID:312256:NO> accessed 28 November 2020.

Concerning Property and Claims and on Economic Cooperation between Japan and the Republic of Korea, for which reason they filed the appeal. The CEACR notes with concern that no concrete outcome has been achieved. At the same time, the CEACR expresses the firm hope that, given the seriousness and long-standing nature of the case, the government will make every effort to achieve reconciliation with the victims, and that measures will be taken, without further delay, to respond to the expectations and claims made by the aged surviving victims of wartime industrial forced labour and military sexual slavery. Another factor to consider if analysing the lack of ratification of the Abolition of Forced Labour Convention is a CEACR Direct Request adopted 2018, published 108th ILC session (2019), and related to the trafficking in persons. The CEACR requested the government to indicate the measures taken to raise awareness and strengthen the capacities of the authorities responsible for enforcing the law to ensure that sufficiently dissuasive and effective penalties are applied to perpetrators of trafficking for both labour and sexual exploitation. The CEACR remained concerned, inter alia, about the low number of prison sentences imposed on perpetrators.[90]

3.2.4 The Committee on Trade and Sustainable Development

Article 22.3 of the EU and Japan's EPA establishes the Committee on Trade and Sustainable Development, which shall be responsible for the effective implementation and operation of Chapter 16. According to Article 16.13 paragraph 2, the Committee shall have the following functions:

a)   reviewing and monitoring the implementation and operation of Chapter 16 and, when necessary, making appropriate recommendations to the Joint Committee for its consideration;
b)   considering any other matter related to Chapter 16 as the Parties may agree;
c)   interacting with civil society (independent economic, social and environmental stakeholders, including employers' and workers' organisations and environmental groups) on the implementation of Chapter 16;
d)   carrying out other functions as may be delegated by the Joint Committee comprising representatives of both Parties (it may allocate responsibilities to specialised committees, working groups or other bodies); and
e)   seeking solutions to resolve differences between the Parties as to the interpretation or application of Chapter 16.

The first meeting of the Committee on Trade and Sustainable Development took place on 29–30 January 2020 in Tokyo.[91] Corporate social responsibility, responsible business conduct, engagement with civil society, and – quite

---

90   <www.ilo.org/dyn/normlex/en/f?p=1000:13101:0::NO:13101:P13101_COMMENT_ ID:3081910> accessed 28 November 2020.
91   <https://trade.ec.europa.eu/doclib/docs/2020/january/tradoc_158594.pdf> accessed 28 November 2020.

mysterious – 'other issues' have been listed in agenda as the priorities for cooperation. During the meeting there was also a dedicated session on labour and trade,
which focused on update on ratification and implementation of ILO Conventions and potential cooperative activities.

What comes to mind, however, is a critique of the poor transparency of work of
the Committee on Trade and Sustainable Development. What we have access to
is only a one-page agenda prepared for its first meeting. The same consideration
applies to the Joint Dialogue with civil society convened on 31 January 2020.

3.2.5 Civil society's involvement

The EU and Japan's EPA ensures the involvement of civil society in the implementation of Chapter 16. This can take two forms: first, domestic advisory group
(Article 16.15); and second, Joint Dialogue with civil society (Article 16.16). As
regards domestic advisory group, both Parties to the Agreement shall convene
meetings of their own new or existing domestic advisory group or groups on
economic, social and environmental issues related to Chapter 16 and consult with
the group or groups in accordance with their laws, regulations and practices. The
advisory group should consist of a balanced representation of independent economic, social and environmental stakeholders, including employers' and workers'
organisations and environmental groups. An important competence conferred
upon the advisory group of each Party is that it may meet on its own initiative
and express its opinions on the implementation of Chapter 16 independently
of the Party and submit those opinions to that Party. In this regard, it is worth
noting that the EU and Japan's EPA provides a more complex explanation of
domestic advisory group than other agreements do, for example, the EU and
South Korea FTA of 2009. The document specifies its composition, consultative
role and other important functions and powers.

With respect to what the EU and Japan's EPA terms 'Joint Dialogue with
civil society' (Article 16.16), the Parties shall convene the Joint Dialogue with
civil society organisations situated in their territories, including members of their
domestic advisory groups, to conduct a dialogue on Chapter 16. The Parties shall
promote in the Joint Dialogue a balanced representation of relevant stakeholders,
including independent organisations which are representative of economic, environmental and social interests as well as other relevant organisations as appropriate. The EPA requires the Parties to provide the Joint Dialogue with information
on the implementation of Chapter 16. The views and opinions of the Joint Dialogue may be submitted to the Committee and may be made publicly available.
As indicated earlier, the Parties convened the Joint Dialogue with civil society on
31 January 2020 in Tokyo[92] (no later than one year after the date of entry into
force of the Agreement, Article 16.16, paragraph 3). The Joint Dialogue shall be
convened regularly, unless the Parties agree otherwise.

92 ibid.

3.2.6 Dispute resolution

It is worth noting that the EU and Japan's EPA includes Chapter 21 entitled 'Dispute settlement', however, the provisions of Chapter 16 shall not be subject to dispute settlement under Chapter 21. Instead, Chapter 16 offers the special dispute settlement mechanism, which provides two special tools for dispute resolution, namely governmental consultations (Article 16.17) and recourse to the panel of experts (Article 16.18). The latter shall interpret the relevant Articles of Chapter 16 in accordance with customary rules of interpretation of public international law, including those codified in the Vienna Convention on the Law of Treaties, done at Vienna on 23 May 1969. The panel of experts shall issue an interim and a final report setting out the findings of facts, the interpretation or the applicability of the relevant Articles and the basic rationale behind any findings and suggestions. The final report shall be made publicly available. The Parties shall discuss actions or measures to resolve the matter in question, taking into account the panel's final report and its suggestions. Each Party shall inform the other Party and its own domestic advisory group or groups of any follow-up actions or measures, which – by the way – shall be monitored by the Committee. The domestic advisory group or groups and the Joint Dialogue may submit their observations in this regard to the Committee.

The dispute resolution mechanism does not establish sanctions for breaching the obligations included in Chapter 16, but relies on cooperation on the part of the country that has breached the EPA's provisions.[93] Such a solution may raise the question of enforceability of labour provisions. By way of comparison, according to the Comprehensive and Progressive Trans-Pacific Partnership (CPTPP) to which Japan is a party, a panel can be established and sanctions (even compensation and suspension of benefits) can be imposed towards the CPTPP member in case of non-compliance on labour provisions. The CPTPP does not envisage a special dispute settlement mechanism but only stipulates that in any dispute arising under Chapter 19 (Labour), panellists other than the chair shall have expertise or experience in labour law or practice.[94]

---

93 This reflects the EU's approach to hard enforcement mechanisms in trade agreements in general. See for example, Billy Melo Araujo, 'Labour Provisions in EU and US Mega-Regional Trade Agreements: Rhetoric and Reality' (2018) 67(1) *International & Comparative Law Quarterly* 233, 241–242.

94 <www.mfat.govt.nz/en/trade/free-trade-agreements/free-trade-agreements-in-force/cptpp/comprehensive-and-progressive-agreement-for-trans-pacific-partnership-text-and-resources/#chapters> accessed 28 November 2020. See also: Alice Poidevin and Hosuk Lee-Makiyama, 'The EU–Japan EPA: Freer, Fairer and More Open Trading System: Conference Note' (2018) *European Centre for International Political Economy Policy Brief* 10, 4 <www.econstor.eu/bitstream/10419/202512/1/104346235X.pdf> accessed 28 November 2020.

4 The EU and the US: the Transatlantic Trade and Investment Partnership (TTIP)

Not to be overlooked is the fact that in November 2011, the initiative to establish the Transatlantic Trade and Investment Partnership (TTIP) between the EU and the US was taken, but the negotiations were frozen after the 2016 US presidential election. From the historical perspective, neither of the documents, namely 'Directives for the negotiation on a comprehensive trade and investment agreement, called the transatlantic trade and investment partnership, between the European Union and the United States of America' and the EU's initial proposal for legal text on 'Trade and sustainable development' was able to ensures effective workers' rights protection. As regards the directives, even if they included lofty phrases, they could not ensure enforcement of labour standards. Indeed, they appeared to provide only soft, promotional formulations, for example, 'the Agreement will include provisions to promote adherence to and effective implementation of internationally agreed standards and agreements in the labour and environmental domain as a necessary condition for sustainable development', and 'the Agreement will include mechanisms to support the promotion of decent work through effective domestic implementation of ILO core labour standards, as defined in the 1998 ILO Declaration of Fundamental Principles and Rights at Work'. At that time, directives for the negotiation on the TTIP raised serious concerns not only about the possibility of the implementation and proper enforcement but also about the ratification by the US of the eight ILO core conventions.

On the other hand, assessing the EU's proposed chapter on 'Trade and sustainable development' from the perspective of the European Parliament resolution of 8 July 2015,[95] it should be mentioned that it failed to observe an important recommendation 'to ensure that the sustainable development chapter is binding and enforceable and aims at the full and effective ratification, implementation and enforcement' of the eight fundamental ILO conventions and their content, and the ILO's Decent Work Agenda. Rather than complying with the recommendation, the Commission's proposal did not guarantee the enforceability of the labour provisions, and only stated that: 'each Party shall continue to make sustained efforts towards ratifying the fundamental ILO Conventions', 'each Party shall ensure that its laws and practices respect, promote, and realise within an integrated strategy, in its whole territory and for all, the internationally recognised core labour standards, which are the subject of the fundamental ILO Conventions', or 'each Party shall effectively implement in its laws and practices and in its whole territory the ILO Conventions it has ratified'. Yet according to

---

95 European Parliament resolution of 8 July 2015 containing the European Parliament's recommendations to the European Commission on the negotiations for the Transatlantic Trade and Investment Partnership.

the European Parliament resolution, the parties should 'ensure that the implementation of and compliance with labour provisions is subjected to an effective monitoring process, involving social partners and civil society representatives and to the general dispute settlement which applies to the whole agreement'. No such provisions existed in the submitted proposal.

Of course, the TTIP project is currently outdated and now much in the EU-US trade relations will depend on the US post-November 2020 situation. In the EU a new document was issued on 15 April 2019, that is, a 'Council decision authorising the opening of negotiations with the United States of America for an agreement on the elimination of tariffs for industrial goods',[96] which states that the negotiating directives for the TTIP are obsolete and no longer relevant. One can search in vain for any provisions on labour standards in the Annex to the 'Recommendation for a Council Decision authorising the opening of negotiations of an agreement with the United States of America on the elimination of tariffs for industrial goods' entitled 'Directives for the negotiation of an agreement with the United States of America on the elimination of tariffs for industrial goods'.[97]

5 Concluding remarks

In conclusion, the new face of globalisation – with coronavirus as a catalyst of change – seems inescapable. The COVID-19 pandemic can be regarded as a black swan, which has triggered a profound recession on a worldwide scale. International trade agreements seem to be a useful tool to help pave the way out of this crisis. In the new version of globalisation, the USMCA can be perceived as a new model agreement and a symbol of a shift in perspective from long global supply chains to a focus on regional ones, local production, jobs and a rise in wages. 'The gold standard' has taken a step forward as it comes to negotiating trade agreements. The USMCA consists of many crucial elements, including: considerably stronger language as regards labour rights; clear footnotes introducing the 'greater certainty' clauses; new, hopeful provisions related to forced or compulsory labour, violence against workers, migrant workers and discrimination in the workplace; Annex 23-A entitled 'Worker Representation in Collective Bargaining in Mexico'; Annex 31-A 'Facility-specific rapid response labor mechanism'; the activity of 'the Interagency Labor Committee for Monitoring and Enforcement' and other provisions included in the USMCA Implementation Act of 2020; or new 'Labor Value Content' requirements. In the era of COVID-19, when unemployment is skyrocketing, the USMCA's quick implementation can be a chance to alleviate economic depression and create a framework not only for a new US medical supply chain, but also – and more generally – economic growth.

---

96 No. 6052/19 <https://ec.europa.eu/trade/policy/in-focus/ttip/index_pl.htm> accessed 28 November 2020.
97 <https://eur-lex.europa.eu/legal-content/EN/TXT/?uri=COM:2019:016:FIN> accessed 28 November 2020.

What about the other agreements? Considering them very useful in the process of mitigating the effects of the crisis, one should wonder how to change them and make them guarantee effective enforcement of labour rights. The point here is to concentrate on the ways, in which labour provisions may be strengthened to better promote ILO fundamental labour rights.

Focusing on free trade agreements concluded by the US, the EU agreements and the TTIP, and on the compliance of international trade agreements with the ILO standards, this chapter has highlighted some limitations of labour provisions. For example, as pointed out by Brown, the EU-Republic of Korea and the EU-Peru/Colombia FTAs and also the other agreements, have tackled 'tough issues associated with trade while capitalizing on economic ones', and have embraced the model of dual commitment – both to the ILO Declaration and to the core ILO labour standards. Therefore, these FTAs were considered stepping stones for the future of globalisation.[98] However, as discussed here, it is not sufficient to accept the model of dual commitment. It seems proved under several different circumstances that the compliance with international trade agreements in relation to ILO standards is not satisfactory. The parties' discretion in applying labour provisions should be limited.

This chapter makes it clear that we should not simply assume that lofty phrases (e.g. the Parties 'reaffirm their obligations deriving from' the ILO membership or 'The Parties further reaffirm their respective commitments with regard to the ILO Declaration on Fundamental Principles and Rights at Work and its Follow-up') translate easily into policies with teeth. I entertain considerable doubts whether soft formulations of a promotional nature (e.g. 'strive to ensure'; 'strive to continue to improve'; 'make continued and sustained efforts on its own initiative to pursue ratification') have the potential to ensure effective enforcement of labour standards. There is little doubt that the EU should have pushed more on stronger provisions in the trade and sustainable development chapters. It is clear that language in these chapters should have been stronger, and a more decisive tone should have been used.[99]

As the issues set out in this chapter are – to a large extent – the task of governments and the EU's policy, it seems that lack of political will is an important obstacle to compliance. However, over the past few months things have started

---

98 Ronald C Brown, 'Promoting Labour Rights in the Global Economy: Could the United States' New Model Trade and Investment Frameworks Advance International Labour Standards in Bangladesh?' (2016) 155(3) *International Labour Review* (Special Issue: Enforcing Global Labour Rights) 383, 396 <https://doi.org/10.1111/j.1564-913X.2015.00038.x> accessed 28 November 2020.

99 For example, according to research conducted by Marx, Lein and Brando, a considerable majority of the stakeholders interviewed in Brussels and Bogotá answered that the EU labour rights language in the EU-Colombia trade agreement is too broad to be meaningful. They added that 'labour provisions were not formulated in a Specific Measurable Achievable Relevant and Time-bound (SMART) way, which hampers their monitoring, progress tracking and benchmarking'. See: Marx, Lein and Brando (n 63) 606.

taking a different turn. As it has been mentioned earlier, we will soon observe the outcome of the EU–Korea dispute settlement over workers' rights. Of course, what the EU should also do is put pressure on Japan to make every possible effort to resolve its difficulties and to ratify all the ILO core Conventions. Nevertheless, one should remember that both the EPA and the EU–South Korea Free Trade Agreement have rejected a sanctions-based approach to labour standards. Such a situation provokes a threat of creating serious problems with enforcement of the 'Trade and sustainable development' chapter.

Focusing specifically on the need to ensure compliance with international trade agreements in relation to ILO standards, we could articulate a series of goals in order to animate reforms and signal a set of proposals. Given the need to correct compliance shortcomings, I do not think that different approaches to labour standards in the US and the EU can be upheld. On the one hand, the EU should include in its FTAs labour provisions that make the conclusion of a trade agreement conditional upon respect for particular labour standards and/or provisions that authorise sanctions if labour standards are infringed (pre-ratification and/or post-ratification conditionality). As rightly pointed out by Hepple, persuasion and conciliation will not function unless there is ultimately a sanction which can be invoked.[100] On the other hand, following the EU framework, the US's model should obligate the US to comply with the Declaration and the ILO's core labour standards.[101] Moreover, the ratification of core labour conventions should be mandatory.[102]

At the margin, establishing Labour Development Plans as suggested by the ILO seems too weak. According to this proposal, labour-related development objectives could be included in trade agreements. The idea employs combining, where appropriate, 'labour development plans' with economic incentives, rather than sanctions. Thus, the regulatory focus of labour provisions would be placed on positive rather than negative conditionality.[103] Nevertheless, as rightly pointed out by Granger and Siroën, in certain circumstances, both types of sanctions – positive, such as preferential concessions or incremental aid to

100 Bob Hepple, *Labour Laws and Global Trade* (Oxford: Hart Publishing 2005) 274.
101 Brown (n 98) 396.
102 However, ratification itself is not a synonym of a proper implementation of those conventions. A recent impact assessment study by Orbie, Van den Putte and Martens shows the poor impact of labour rights commitments in the EU – Peru – Colombia agreement, on the example of the agricultural sector in Peru. Jan Orbie, Lore Van den Putte and Deborah Martens, 'The Impact of Labour Rights Commitments in EU Trade Agreements: The Case of Peru' (2017) 5(4) *Politics and Governance* 6 <http://dx.doi.org/10.17645/pag.v5i4.1091> accessed 28 November 2020. Peru has ratified the ILO's eight fundamental conventions. Unfortunately, the authors identify considerable shortcomings with their implementation and indicate that practices of child labour, forced labour, discrimination and breaches of trade union rights still exist in Peru. Orbie, Van den Putte and Martens (n 102) 7, 9–10.
103 ILO (n 5) 97.

countries improving their labour standards, and negative, such as duties or import prohibition – can be used simultaneously.[104]

It is correct to support combining cooperation (e.g. in the form of technical assistance or funding) with binding enforcement and monitoring (e.g. by the partner countries, civil society, organisations such as the ILO, a new body which could be created and which could follow the model of the NAALC Secretariat).[105] What the parties to the FTAs should do is to embrace a clear unitary dispute settlement and enforcement mechanism, which would allow them to bring a claim.[106] On the other hand, the involvement of civil society is perceived as already existing infrastructure to promote agency, dialogue and participation within trade agreements. The US–Guatemala CAFTA labour arbitration ruling of 2017 is a perfect example of this. In fact, during the dispute, many NGOs submitted amicus briefs. Making better use of the already existing mechanism could significantly reinforce the trade-labour linkage, which is visible in the case of international trade agreements.[107]

The chapter also supports Ebert's claim, resulting from the analysis of the CETA (but true also in reference to many other agreements), about the role of stakeholders in CETA's institutional setting. While it is admittedly true that the participation of trade unions is provided for under the chapters on Sustainable Development and Labour, their involvement under other chapters is up to the parties' discretion. However, it appears that the involvement of trade unions and related stakeholders should be integrated into CETA's institutional setting as a whole and should be mandatory for the parties. This is because the relevant risks for labour standards result from a variety of the agreement's chapters, for example, chapters on Cross-Border Trade in Services, on Regulatory Cooperation, on Financial Services, on International Maritime Transport Services.[108] As indicated previously, the same can apply to other agreements.

---

104 Clotilde Granger and Jean-Marc Siroën, 'Core Labour Standards in Trade Agreements: From Multilateralism to Bilateralism' (2006) 40(5) *Journal of World Trade* 813, 835.

105 See: Lars Engen, 'Labour Provisions in Asia-Pacific Free Trade Agreements' (2017) *Background Paper No. 1* (Economic and Social Commission for Asia and the Pacific, United Nations) 61–63 <www.unescap.org/sites/default/files/Background%20Material%20-%20Labour%20provisions%20in%20Asia-Pacific%20PTAs.pdf> accessed 28 November 2020; Vogt (n 23) passim.

106 Brown (n 98) 403. Similarly, analysing the EU-Colombia trade agreement, Marx, Lein and Brando identify the absence of a binding enforcement mechanism, and the lack of adequate engagement with Civil Society Organisations as factors hampering the agreement's 'overall contribution when it comes to following up on, and contributing to, a better de facto compliance with labour provisions'. See: Marx, Lein and Brando (n 63) 606.

107 Clair Gammage, '(Re)Imagining the Trade-Labour Linkage: The Capabilities Approach' in Brian Langille (ed), *The Capability Approach to Labour Law* (Oxford: Oxford Scholarship Online 2019) <DOI:10.1093/oso/9780198836087.003.0015> accessed 28 November 2020.

108 Ebert (n 74) 302, 328–329.

Last but not least, to my mind, it is correct to support an interesting view presented by Marx, Brando and Lein who propose to strengthen the labour rights provisions in trade agreements by linking them to existing voluntary sustainability standards. The latter are an instrument to govern transnational supply chains. Most such initiatives have

> an organization that defines social and ecological standards, and include a set of procedures to assess conformity with those standards. When products or production processes comply with the standards, a certificate is awarded which may or may not be used for external communication (a label).

It is argued that such a solution would allow the EU to better govern the global protection of labour rights through its trade agreements. It is predicted that this kind of linkage could close a regulatory gap since contracting partners do not have jurisdiction over each other's compliance with the agreed commitments, and it could help enforce labour standards through monitoring, sanctioning and withdrawing certificates. The level of accountability and credibility of these sustainability chapters could noticeably increase as an independent third party would be allowed to monitor and evaluate compliance with trade provisions. Besides, the responsibility for implementing the labour rights provisions in trade agreements – instead of relying only on states – would be expanded to firms as well. On the other hand, the integration of voluntary sustainability standards in trade agreements offers public regulators the opportunity to demand a strengthening of the quality of voluntary sustainability standards in terms of their design and procedures.[109] It is therefore worth examining in more detail a private standard-setting, an analysis of which is the objective of Chapter 6.

Bibliography

Aiko Morii, 'Dialogue Without Cooperation? Diplomatic Implications of EU–Japan Summits' (2015) 13(4) *Asia Europe Journal* 413 <https://doi.org/10.1007/s10308-015-0429-7> accessed 27 November 2020.

Alice Poidevin and Hosuk Lee-Makiyama, 'The EU–Japan EPA: Freer, Fairer and More Open Trading System: Conference Note' (2018) *European Centre for International Political Economy Policy Brief* 10 <www.econstor.eu/bitstream/10419/2 02512/1/104346235X.pdf> accessed 28 November 2020.

Álvaro Santos, 'Reimagining Trade Agreements for Workers: Lessons from the USMCA' (2019) 113 *American Journal of International Law Unbound* 407 <www.cambridge.org/core/services/aop-cambridge-core/content/view/AF9056844AEAF8085CA7F594AFB32B3C/S2398772319000746a.pdf/

---

109 Axel Marx, Nicolás Brando and Brecht Lein, 'Strengthening Labour Rights Provisions in Bilateral Trade Agreements: Making the Case for Voluntary Sustainability Standards' (2017) 8(Supplement 3) *Global Policy* 78, 78–79, 85 <https://doi.org/10.1111/1758-5899.12397> accessed 28 November 2020.

reimagining_trade_agreements_for_workers_lessons_from_the_usmca.pdf> accessed 27 November 2020.

Aneta Tyc, 'Workers' Rights and Transatlantic Trade Relations: The TTIP and Beyond' (2017) 28(1) *The Economic and Labour Relations Review* 113.

Axel Marx, Brecht Lein and Nicolás Brando, 'The Protection of Labour Rights in Trade Agreements: The Case of the EU-Colombia Agreement' (2016) 50(4) *Journal of World Trade* 587.

Axel Marx, Nicolás Brando and Brecht Lein, 'Strengthening Labour Rights Provisions in Bilateral Trade Agreements: Making the Case for Voluntary Sustainability Standards' (2017) 8(Supplement 3) *Global Policy* 78 <https://doi.org/10.1111/1758-5899.12397> accessed 28 November 2020.

Billy Melo Araujo, 'Labour Provisions in EU and US Mega-Regional Trade Agreements: Rhetoric and Reality' (2018) 67(1) *International & Comparative Law Quarterly* 233.

Bob Hepple, *Labour Laws and Global Trade* (Oxford: Hart Publishing 2005).

Caroline Freund and Carlos A Primo Braga, 'The Economics of Arab Transitions' in Cesare Merlini and Olivier Roy (eds), *Arab Society in Revolt: The West's Mediterranean Challenge* (Washington DC: Brookings Institution Press 2012).

Carolyn Tuttle, *Mexican Women in American Factories: Free Trade and Exploitation on the Border* (Austin: University of Texas Press 2012).

Christoph Scherrer, 'Novel Labour-Related Clauses in a Trade Agreement: From NAFTA to USMCA' (2020) 11(3) *Global Labour Journal* 291.

Clair Gammage, '(Re)Imagining the Trade-Labour Linkage: The Capabilities Approach' in Brian Langille (ed), *The Capability Approach to Labour Law* (Oxford: Oxford Scholarship Online 2019) <DOI:10.1093/oso/9780198836087.003.0015> accessed 28 November 2020.

Clotilde Granger and Jean-Marc Siroën, 'Core Labour Standards in Trade Agreements: From Multilateralism to Bilateralism' (2006) 40(5) *Journal of World Trade* 813.

Diario Oficial (1 May 2019) <www.diputados.gob.mx/LeyesBiblio/ref/lft/LFT_ref30_01may19.pdf> accessed 27 November 2020.

Eric Gottwald, Jeffrey Vogt and Lance Compa, 'Wrong Turn for Workers' Rights: The US–Guatemala CAFTA Labor Arbitration Ruling – and What to Do About It' *International Labor Rights Forum* (12 April 2018) <https://laborrights. org/publications/wrong-turn-workers%E2%80%99-rights-us-guatemala-cafta-labor-arbitration-ruling-%E2%80%93-and-what-do> accessed 27 November 2020.

European Commission, *Trade Sustainability Impact Assessment of the Free Trade Agreement Between the European Union and Japan* (Final Report, Brussels 2016) <http://trade.ec.europa.eu/doclib/docs/2016/may/tradoc_154522.pdf> accessed 27 November 2020.

Ferdi De Ville, Jan Orbie and Lore Van den Putte, *TTIP and Labour Standards* (Study for the EMPL Committee, European Parliament 2016) <www.europarl.europa.eu/RegData/etudes/STUD/2016/578992/IPOL_STU(2016)578992_EN.pdf> accessed 26 November 2020.

Franz Christian Ebert, 'The Comprehensive Economic and Trade Agreement (CETA): Are Existing Arrangements Sufficient to Prevent Adverse Effects on Labour Standards?' (2017) 33(2) *International Journal of Comparative Labour Law and Industrial Relations* 295.

Gerda Van Roozendaal, 'Where Symbolism Prospers: An Analysis of the Impact on Enabling Rights of Labour Standards Provisions in Trade Agreements with South Korea' (2017) 5(4) *Politics and Governance* 19.

Hanns Günther Hilpert, 'The Japan-EU Economic Partnership Agreement: Economic Potentials and Policy Perspectives' (2018) 16(4) *Asia Europe Journal* 439 <https://doi.org/10.1007/s10308-017-0496-z> accessed 27 November 2020.

Haruo Takeuchi, 'The Present Situation in the Japanese Employment System, with Special Reference to the Problems Regarding Temporary Workers' in Hans-Heinrich Bass, Toshihiko Hozumi and Uwe Staroske (eds), *Labor Markets and Labor Market Policies Between Globalization and World Economic Crisis: Japan and Germany* (München: Rainer Hampp Verlag 2010).

Heidi Gottfried, 'Precarious Work in Japan: Old Forms, New Risks?' (2014) 44(3) *Journal of Contemporary Asia* 464 <http://dx.doi.org/10.1080/00472336.2013.867523> accessed 27 November 2020.

Helen Freeman, 'Special Trade Arrangements to Improve Market Access' in Merlinda Ingco and John D Nash (eds), *Agriculture and the WTO: Creating a Trading System for Development* (Washington DC: World Bank and Oxford University Press 2004).

Hiroaki Richard Watanabe, 'The Struggle for Revitalisation by Japanese Labour Unions: Worker Organising After Labour-Market Deregulation' (2015) 45(3) *Journal of Contemporary Asia* 510 <http://dx.doi.org/10.1080/00472336.2015.1007388> accessed 27 November 2020.

Hiroaki Richard Watanabe, 'Labour Market Dualism and Diversification in Japan' (2018) 56(3) *British Journal of Industrial Relations* 579 <https://doi.org/10.1111/bjir.12258> accessed 27 November 2020.

Hitoshi Suzuki, 'The New Politics of Trade: EU–Japan' (2017) 39(7) *Journal of European Integration* 875 <https://doi.org/10.1080/07036337.2017.1371709> accessed 27 November 2020.

ILO, *Social Dimensions of Free Trade Agreements: Studies on Growth with Equity* (Geneva: ILO 2013).

ILO, *Assessment of Labour Provisions in Trade and Investment Arrangements* (Geneva: ILO 2016).

ILO, *Handbook on Assessment of Labour Provisions in Trade and Investment Agreements* (Geneva: ILO 2017).

ILO, *Labour Provisions in G7 Trade Agreements: A Comparative Perspective* (Geneva: ILO 2019).

International Business Publications, *Mexico Labor Laws and Regulations Handbook: Strategic Information and Basic Laws* (Washington DC: International Business Publications 2019).

International Centre for Trade and Sustainable Development, 'Trade Dispute Panel Issues Ruling in US–Guatemala Labour Law Case' (6 July 2017) 21(24) *Bridges* <https://ictsd.iisd.org/bridges-news/bridges/news/trade-dispute-panel-issues-ruling-in-us-guatemala-labour-law-case> accessed 26 November 2020.

James Harrison, Mirela Barbu, Liam Campling, Ben Richardson and Adrian Smith, 'Governing Labour Standards Through Free Trade Agreements: Limits of the European Union's Trade and Sustainable Development Chapters' (2019) 57(2) *Journal of Common Market Studies* 260 <https://doi.org/10.1111/jcms.12715> accessed 27 November 2020.

Jan Orbie, Lore Van den Putte and Deborah Martens, 'The Impact of Labour Rights Commitments in EU Trade Agreements: The Case of Peru' (2017) 5(4) *Politics and Governance* 6 <http://dx.doi.org/10.17645/pag.v5i4.1091> accessed 28 November 2020.

Jeffrey S Vogt, 'The Evolution of Labor Rights and Trade – A Transatlantic Comparison and Lessons for the Transatlantic Trade and Investment Partnership' (2015) 18(4) *Journal of International Economic Law* 827 <https://doi.org/10.1093/jiel/jgv046> accessed 26 November 2020.

Jeffrey S Vogt, Janice Bellace, Lance Compa, Keith D Ewing, John Hendy QC, Klaus Lörcher and Tonia Novitz, *The Right to Strike in International Law* (Chicago: Hart Publishing, an Imprint of Bloomsbury Publishing 2020).

Jess Diamond, 'Employment Status Persistence in the Japanese Labour Market' (2018) 69(1) *The Japanese Economic Review* 69 <https://doi.org/10.1111/jere.12148> accessed 27 November 2020.

John Anthony VanDuzer, Penelope Simons and Graham Mayeda, *Integrating Sustainable Development into International Investment Agreements: A Guide for Developing Country Negotiators* (London: Commonwealth Secretariat 2013).

John Benson, Masae Yuasa and Philippe Debroux, 'The Prospect for Gender Diversity in Japanese Employment' (2007) 18(5) *International Journal of Human Resource Management* 890 <https://doi.org/10.1080/09585190701249495> accessed 27 November 2020.

Jonathan Graubart, 'Giving Teeth to NAFTA's Labour Side Agreement' in John J Kirton and Virginia W Maclaren (eds), *Linking Trade, Environment, and Social Cohesion: NAFTA Experiences, Global Challenges* (London, New York: Routledge 2018).

Kimberly Ann Elliott, 'Developing a More Inclusive US Trade Policy at Home and Abroad' (2019) *Center for Global Development Policy Paper* 146 <www.cgdev.org/publication/developing-more-inclusive-us-trade-policy-home-and-abroad> accessed 27 November 2020.

Konstantinos D Magliveras, 'Protecting the Rights of Migrant Workers in the Euro-Mediterranean Partnership' in Iván Martín and Iain Byrne (eds), *Special Issue on Economic and Social Rights in the Euro-Mediterranean Partnership* (2004) 9(3) *Mediterranean Politics* 459 <www.academia.edu/2068195/_2004_Economic_and_Social_Rights_in_the_Euro_Mediterranean_Partnership> accessed 27 November 2020.

Lance Compa, 'From Chile to Vietnam: International Labour Law and Workers' Rights in International Trade' in Gráinne de Búrca, Claire Kilpatrick and Joanne Scott (eds), *Critical Legal Perspectives on Global Governance: Liber Amicorum David M Trubek* (Oxford, Portland OR: Hart Publishing 2014).

Lance Compa, 'Labor Rights and Labor Standards in Transatlantic Trade and Investment Negotiations: A US Perspective' (2015) 2 *Economia & Lavoro* 87.

Lance Compa, 'Trump, Trade, and Trabajo: Renegotiating NAFTA's Labor Accord in a Fraught Political Climate' (2019) 26(1) *Indiana Journal of Global Legal Studies* 263.

Lance Compa and Tequila Brooks, *NAFTA and the NAALC: Twenty Years of North American Trade-Labour Linkage* (Alphen aan den Rijn: Kluwer Law International 2015).

Lars Engen, 'Labour Provisions in Asia-Pacific Free Trade Agreements' (2017) *Background Paper no. 1* (Economic and Social Commission for Asia and the Pacific, United Nations) <www.unescap.org/sites/default/files/Background%20Material%20-%20Labour%20provisions%20in%20Asia-Pacific%20PTAs.pdf> accessed 28 November 2020.

Li Yu-Chun, 'Law Review and Comparison of Dismissal Regulations' in Tatsuo Hatta and Shinya Ouchi (eds), *Severance Payment and Labor Mobility: A Comparative Study of Taiwan and Japan* (Singapore: Springer 2018).

Liam Campling, James Harrison, Ben Richardson and Adrian Smith, 'Can Labour Provisions Work Beyond the Border? Evaluating the Effects of EU Free Trade Agreements' (2016) 155(3) *International Labour Review* 357.

Lonny E Carlile, 'The Labor Movement' in Alisa Gaunder (ed), *Routledge Handbook of Japanese Politics* (London, New York: Routledge 2011).

Lorand Bartels, 'A Legal Analysis of Human Rights Clauses in the European Union's Euro-Mediterranean Association Agreements' 2004 9(3) *Mediterranean Politics* 368 <https://doi.org/10.1080/1362939042000259933> accessed 27 November 2020.

Lorand Bartels, 'Human Rights, Labour Standards, and Environmental Standards in CETA' in Stefan Griller, Walter Obwexer and Erich Vranes (eds), *Mega-Regional Trade Agreements: CETA, TTIP, and TiSA. New Orientations for EU External Economic Relations* (Oxford: Oxford University Press 2017).

Marcus Rebick, 'The Japanese Economy' in James D Babb (ed), *The Sage Handbook of Modern Japanese Studies* (Los Angeles, London, New Delhi, Singapore, Washington DC: Sage Publishing 2015).

Mariana Pargendler, 'The Grip of Nationalism on Corporate Law' (2020) 95(2) *Indiana Law Journal* 533.

Mark Thomas, 'Regulating Labour Standards in the Global Economy: Emerging Approaches to Global Governance' in Gary Teeple and Stephen McBride (eds), *Relations of Global Power: Neoliberal Order and Disorder* (Toronto: University of Toronto Press 2011).

Martin Myant, *The Impact of Trade and Investment Agreements on Decent Work and Sustainable Development* (Brussels: European Trade Union Institute 2017).

Michele Faioli, 'Atlantic Transitions for Law and Labor: CETA First and TTIP Second?' in Adalberto Perulli and Tiziano Treu (eds), *Sustainable Development, Global Trade and Social Rights* (Alphen aan den Rijn: Wolters Kluwer 2018).

Nathaniel Parish Flannery, 'Will A Minimum Wage Hike Boost Mexico's Struggling Economy?' *Forbes* (3 January 2020) <www.forbes.com/sites/nathanielparishflannery/2020/01/03/will-a-minimum-wage-hike-boost-mexicos-struggling-economy/#67d6e36b18ed> accessed 26 November 2020.

Nobuko Nagase and Mary C Brinton, 'The Gender Division of Labor and Second Births: Labor Market Institutions and Fertility in Japan' (2017) 36 *Demographic Research* 339 <www.demographic-research.org/volumes/vol36/11/> accessed 27 November 2020.

Norman Caulfield, *NAFTA and Labor in North America* (Urbana: University of Illinois Press 2010).

Paula Church Albertson and Lance Compa, 'Labour Rights and Trade Agreements in the Americas' in Adelle Blackett and Anne Trebilcock (eds), *Research Handbook on Transnational Labour Law* (Cheltenham, Northampton: Edward Elgar Publishing 2015).

Reuters Staff, 'New North American Trade Pact to Take Effect July 1: USTR' *Reuters* (25 April 2020) <www.reuters.com/article/us-usa-trade-usmca/

new-north-american-trade-pact-to-take-effect-july-1-ustr-idUSKCN2263H0> accessed 26 November 2020.

Richard Trumka, 'TPP: A New Low' *The Hill* (2 February 2016) <http://the-hill.com/opinion/op-ed/267968-tpp-a-new-low> accessed 26 November 2020.

Ronald C Brown, 'Promoting Labour Rights in the Global Economy: Could the United States' New Model Trade and Investment Frameworks Advance International Labour Standards in Bangladesh?' (2016) 155(3) *International Labour Review* (Special Issue: Enforcing Global Labour Rights) 383 <https://doi.org/10.1111/j.1564-913X.2015.00038.x> accessed 28 November 2020.

Sagiri Kitao and Minamo Mikoshiba, 'Females, the Elderly, and also Males: Demographic Aging and Macroeconomy in Japan' (2020) 5 *Journal of the Japanese and International Economies* 1 <https://doi.org/10.1016/j.jjie.2020.101064> accessed 27 November 2020.

Samantha Velluti, 'The EU's Social Dimension and Its External Trade Relations' in Axel Marx, Jan Wouters, Glenn Rayp and Laura Beke (eds), *Global Governance of Labour Rights: Assessing the Effectiveness of Transnational Public and Private Policy Initiatives* (Cheltenham, Northampton: Edward Elgar Publishing 2015).

Sebastian Benz and Erdal Yalcin, 'Productivity Versus Employment: Quantifying the Economic Effects of an EU – Japan Free Trade Agreement' (2015) 38(6) *The World Economy* 935 <https://doi.org/10.1111/twec.12205> accessed 26 November 2020.

Shara Aranoff, Cindy Owens, John K Veroneau and Kate McNulty, 'Companies Should Understand USMCA's Labor Obligations as They Are Significant and Likely to Be Enforced' *Global Policy Watch* (28 January 2020) <www.globalpolicywatch.com/2020/01/companies-should-understand-usmcas-labor-obligations-as-they-are-significant-and-likely-to-be-enforced/> accessed 27 November 2020.

Shinya Ouchi, 'Why Should the Monetary Compensation System Be Introduced in Japanese Dismissal Regulation?' in Tatsuo Hatta and Shinya Ouchi (eds), *Severance Payment and Labor Mobility: A Comparative Study of Taiwan and Japan* (Singapore: Springer 2018).

Silvio Bologna, 'The Comprehensive Economic and Trade Agreement (CETA): What Kind of Space is Given to Fair Trade and Labour Rights?' (2017) 9(1) *Temilavoro.it Sinossi Internet di Diritto del Lavoro e della Sicurezza Sociale* 1 <https://iris.unipa.it/retrieve/handle/10447/241968/452354/CETA_Temilavoro.pdf> accessed 27 November 2020.

Stefaan Smis and Stephen Kingah, 'EU South African Trade, Development and Cooperation Agreement: Bane or Boon for Socio-Economic Rights Under the South African Constitution?' (November 2014) 20(6) *European Law Journal* 793 <https://doi.org/10.1111/eulj.12106> accessed 27 November 2020.

Steve Charnovitz, 'The Labor Rights Rationale to Approve the USMCA' International *Economic Law and Policy Blog* (13 December 2019) <https://ielp.worldtradelaw.net/2019/12/the-labor-rights-rationale-to-approve-the-usmca.html> accessed 26 November 2020.

Susumu Watanabe, 'The Japan Model and the Future of Employment and Wage Systems' (2000) 139(3) *International Labour Review* 307.

Vincenzo Ferrante, 'Social Concerns in Free Trade Agreements' (2016) 5(2 May–June) *E-Journal of International and Comparative Labour Studies* 1.

Wolfgang Plasa, *Reconciling International Trade and Labor Protection: Why We Need to Bridge the Gap Between ILO Standards and WTO Rules* (Lanham, Boulder, New York, London: Lexington Books 2015).

World Economic Forum, *Global Gender Gap Report 2020* (Cologny: World Economic Forum 2019).

Yuko Hosoi, 'Japan-EU Relations After World War II and Strategic Partnership' (2019) 17(3) *Asia Europe Journal* 295 <https://doi.org/10.1007/s10308-019-00555-1> accessed 27 November 2020.

6 Private standard-setting

The impact of CSR instruments on labour rights

1 Introduction

In the era of global value chains and turbulent debates on trade policies, we have to consider how to ensure decent work for all. Within the powerful machinery of world trade, social concerns can be expressed in many ways. Labour standards can, inter alia, be included in the entire spectrum of private norms. The aim of this chapter is to assess to what extent self-regulation within the corporate social responsibility (CSR) framework contributes to improving workers' rights worldwide. The chapter aims at providing an overview of some crucial instruments in the field of CSR: corporate codes of conduct, transnational company agreements, NGOs' social accountability standards, ISO standards, the Dow Jones Sustainability Index and the Global Reporting Initiative.

Before scrutinising this in more detail, let me first define the term CSR. It is understood as

> an umbrella term for a variety of theories and practices all of which recognize the following: (a) that companies have a responsibility for their impact on society and the natural environment, sometimes beyond legal compliance and the liability of individuals; (b) that companies have a responsibility for the behavior of others with whom they do business (e.g., within supply chains); and (c) that business needs to manage its relationship with wider society, whether for reasons of commercial viability or to add value to society.[1]

---

1 Michael Blowfield and Jedrzej G. Frynas, 'Editorial. Setting New Agendas: Critical Perspectives on Corporate Social Responsibility in the Developing World' (2005) 81 *International Affairs* 503. Quoted from: Peter Lund-Thomsen and Adam Lindgreen, 'Corporate Social Responsibility in Global Value Chains: Where Are We Now and Where Are We Going?' (2014) 123 *Journal of Business Ethics* 11, 12 <https://doi.org/10.1007/s10551-013-1796-x> accessed 28 November 2020. For more definitions see: Alexander Dahlsrud, 'How Corporate Social Responsibility is Defined: An Analysis of 37 Definitions' (2008) 15(1) *Corporate Social Responsibility and Environmental Management* <https://doi.org/10.1002/csr.132> accessed 28 November 2020. Some parts of this chapter were published previously in Poland: Aneta Tyc, 'Corporate Social Responsibility Instruments and Their Impact on Labour Rights' (2020) 29(1) *Acta Iuris Stetinensis*.

2 Corporate codes of conduct

2.1 Historical background

Corporate codes of conduct can be defined as 'unilateral recommendations through which the main decision-making bodies of companies set up rules of behaviour for managers and employees (sometimes also for suppliers and subcontractors) that reflect the principles and values of corporate social responsibility'.[2] In the 1970s, the number of reports concerning unethical or illegal activities of multinational corporations increased and led to discussions within international organisations.[3] The UN Centre on Transnational Corporations (UNCTC), set up in 1974, developed the UN Draft Code of Conduct on TNCs.[4] In 1976, the OECD was first to adopt its Guidelines for Multinational Enterprises. The ILO adopted its Tripartite Declaration of Principles concerning Multinational Enterprises (MNEs) and Social Policy in 1977.[5] Subsequently, many codes of conduct have been established to provide a stable framework in which MNEs conduct their business.[6] In 1977, the Sullivan Principles were launched. The Principles played a role of a code of conduct for companies with operations in apartheid South Africa. Their goal was to achieve equal opportunity for employees in a particular company. Instead of withdrawing their activities from a country, companies were to remain and act as drivers of change by committing themselves to a number of principles concerning non-discrimination.[7] However, the Sullivan Principles illustrate 'how severely Western-written codes can miss the practicalities of local issues'. Despite its objective, they 'blur[red] definitions of race in measuring the racial composition of the workforce or racial patterns in hiring'.[8]

The second wave of codes appeared in the early 1990s and concentrated its attention on labour conditions.[9] In 1992, Levi Strauss adopted so-called 'Global

---

2   Stefania Marassi, 'Globalization and Transnational Collective Labour Relations. International and European Framework Agreements at Company Level' in Roger Blanpain (general ed), *Bulletin for Comparative Labour Relations* (Alphen aan den Rijn: Kluwer Law International 2015) 21.

3   Christine Kaufmann, *Globalisation and Labour Rights. The Conflict Between Core Labour Rights and International Economic Law* (Oxford, Portland OR: Hart Publishing 2007) 156.

4   Rhys Jenkins, Ruth Pearson and Gill Seyfang, 'Introduction' in Rhys Jenkins, Ruth Pearson and Gill Seyfang (eds), *Corporate Responsibility and Labour Rights: Codes of Conduct in the Global Economy* (London, Sterling VA: Earthscan Publishing Ltd 2002) 2.

5   Peter Tergeist, 'Multinational Enterprises and Codes of Conduct: The OECD Guidelines for MNEs in Perspective' in Roger Blanpain (ed), *Comparative Labour Law and Industrial Relations in Industrialized Market Economies* (11th edn, Alphen aan den Rijn: Kluwer Law International 2014) 213–214.

6   Kaufmann (n 3) 156.

7   Lisbeth Segerlund, *Making Corporate Social Responsibility a Global Concern. Norm Construction in a Globalizing World* (Farnham: Ashgate 2010) 55.

8   Andrew Herman, 'Reassessing the Role of Supplier Codes of Conduct: Closing the Gap Between Aspirations and Reality' (2012) 52(2) *Virginia Journal of International Law* 445, 463.

9   Jenkins, Pearson and Seyfang (n 4) 3.

Sourcing and Operating Guidelines',[10] which were described as belonging to the second generation of codes.[11] This was the first supplier code of conduct for the apparel industry introduced by an MNC.[12] However, the document omitted reference to freedom of association and the right to collective bargaining.[13] Since the early 1990s, a considerable number of MNCs have adopted codes, most of which fully or partly address employment standards.[14]

In 1999, the Global Sullivan Principles were launched in the presence of Kofi Annan, the UN Secretary General. On that occasion, he made a reference to the Global Sullivan Principles as important for the UN Global Compact (UN 2000). The Global Compact, named in the literature as a 'Model Code',[15] includes references to freedom of association and the right to collective bargaining, and 'symbolizes the evolution of the "international human rights regime" to incorporate what is described as the "third generation"'.[16] In the area of labour, the Global Compact establishes the same principles as the ILO Declaration on Fundamental Principles and Rights at Work. However, the intended effect is to ensure that MNCs – rather than governments – comply with them.[17] Interestingly, it does not address issues of monitoring.[18] Moreover, the UN Global Compact Principles

---

10 Kaufmann (n 3) 156. Also known as 'Business Partner Terms of Engagement', Jenkins, Pearson and Seyfang (n 4) 2.
11 Cynthia Stohl, Michael Stohl and Lucy Popova, 'A New Generation of Corporate Codes of Ethics' (2009) 90(4) *Journal of Business Ethics* 607, 614 <https://doi.org/10.1007/s10551-009-0064-6> accessed 28 November 2020.
12 Herman (n 8) 449.
13 Niklas Egels-Zandén and Jeroen Merk, 'Private Regulation and Trade Union Rights: Why Codes of Conduct Have Limited Impact on Trade Union Rights' (2014) 123(3) *Journal of Business Ethics* 461, 463 <https://doi.org/10.1007/s10551-013-1840-x> accessed 28 November 2020.
14 Harry Arthurs, 'Private Ordering and Workers' Rights in the Global Economy: Corporate Codes of Conduct as a Regime of Labour Market Regulation' in Joanne Conaghan, Richard M Fischl and Karl Klare (eds), *Labour Law in an Era of Globalization: Transformative Practices and Possibilities* (Oxford: Oxford University Press 2004) 474; see the cited literature. Jenkins, Pearson and Seyfang (n 4) 1.
15 Arturo Bronstein, *International and Comparative Labour Law: Current Challenges* (Geneva: Palgrave Macmillan, International Labour Office 2009) 112.
16 'Third generation embodies the social and material conditions as well as the reflexivity associated with globalization, and ethical behavior grounded in the larger interconnected environment within which an organization functions', Stohl, Stohl and Popova (n 11) 612. 'Third generation CSR focuses on the rights of a collective that only can be realized through global participation, cooperation, and agreement. Sections mentioning overall social good, such as peace, healthy environment, and the common heritage of mankind, were coded as third generation', Stohl, Stohl and Popova (n 11) 614.
17 Nikita Lyutov, 'Traditional International Labour Law and the New "Global" Kind: Is There a Way To Make Them Work Together?' (2017) 67(1) *Zbornik Pravnog Fakulteta u Zagrebu* 29, 33; Joseph Carby-Hall, 'Labour Aspects of Corporate Social Responsibility Emanating from the United Nations Global Compact: The Global Case and that of the EU and the United Kingdom' (2016) 5(2) *E-Journal of International and Comparative Labour Studies* 1, 15.
18 Bronstein (n 15) 114.

that developed not long after the launch of the UN Global Compact correspond to a significant degree with the Global Sullivan Principles.[19]

As rightly highlighted by Carby-Hall, in order to maintain the Global Compact partnership, companies have to meet some significant commitments. First, they should integrate the Global Compact and its ten principles with the company's strategy, policy, organisational culture and daily operations. Second, they should disseminate the Global Compact concept to customers, clients, consumers, employees and the general public. In the third place, they are required to incorporate the Global Compact and its ten principles at the highest level of the company. Fourth, the method of implementing the Global Compact's principles should be characterised in the annual or sustainability reports. Last, companies are supposed to contribute to wider development goals, inter alia the Millennium Development Goals.[20]

2.2 The main shortcomings of corporate codes of conduct

The purpose of this part is to assess, through the prism of three generations of codes, if self-regulation is sufficient to ensure the effective enforcement of labour rights. It aims at providing an overview of shortcomings of corporate codes of conduct and analysing ways in which codes could be transformed to more effectively address workers' rights. The assurance of scientific integrity requires, however, that there be an explanation of the fact that corporate social responsibility and codes of conduct tend to be viewed differently. It should be clearly stated that some authors prove that they exert some positive impact on the workers' situation (this will be explained later). Besides, according to Toffel, Short and Ouellet, private codes of conduct that implement global labour standards accomplish an important objective consisting of the reinforcement of the norms promoted by the ILO and the provision of a source of enforcement pressure that the ILO lacks.[21] Harrington writes about the 'quite positive results' of codes of conduct, especially in developing countries.[22] Referring to corporate social responsibility policies, the author highlights that they can ensure that progressive labour standards are used even if they are not legally compulsory. She adds that in this

---

19 Segerlund (n 7) 56.
20 Carby-Hall (n 17) 17–18. See more: Joseph Carby-Hall, 'Multinationals, SMEs and Non-Profit Organisations Participating in the UN Global Compact' (2020) 10(2) *Lex Social: Revista de Derechos Sociales* 130 <https://doi.org/10.46661/lexsocial.5067> accessed 28 November 2020.
21 Michael W Toffel, Jodi L Short and Melissa Ouellet, 'Codes in Context: How States, Markets, and Civil Society Shape Adherence to Global Labor Standards' (2015) 9(3) *Regulation & Governance* 205, 208 <https://doi.org/10.1111/rego.12076> accessed 28 November 2020.
22 Alexandra R Harrington, 'Corporate Social Responsibility, Globalization, the Multinational Corporation, and Labor: An Unlikely Alliance' (2011–2012) 75(1) *Albany Law Review* 483, 493; see the cited literature.

manner corporate social responsibility can eventually lead to the future revision of the domestic labour law.[23]

While it is admittedly true that some authors believe in the potential of codes of conduct, there are much more concerns about these instruments. Codes of conduct classified as falling under the first generation differ between companies and across industries. There is little uniformity in their content. Many of such tools use vague language, and for some rights are limited to asking for compliance with the supplier countries' domestic laws. Codes of conduct often lack clear language on the freedom of association and wages and make a 'renvoi' to domestic law.[24] Their underlying values are perceived as obscure.[25] Codes of conduct mainly address marketing aims and respond to unfavourable publicity produced by the media.[26] They are seen as a measure of propaganda and a means of improvement of an MNC's reputation,[27] corporate legitimacy, trust, image or brand.[28] Research indicates that there is a lack of involvement of social partners in the decision-making process leading to the adoption of codes of conduct.[29] Once adopted, they impose lower standards than the public regulatory frameworks. Besides, they are more selective in their choice of labour rights.[30]

When it comes to the second generation, as supplier codes of conduct enjoyed rising popularity in the 1990s, advocates began to focus less on code adoption and more on compliance verification.[31] The aforementioned Sullivan Principles represent the first effort towards the implementation of codes of conduct with, for example, monitoring schemes and independent monitoring in a multi-stakeholder forum.[32] Currently, there are always numerous problems with the implementation, monitoring and enforcement of a corporate code of conduct.[33]

---

23 ibid 508–509.
24 Herman (n 8) 450–451; see the cited literature.
25 Arthurs (n 14) 477.
26 Marassi (n 2) 22.
27 Wolfgang Däubler, 'Corporate Social Responsibility: A Way to Make Deregulation More Acceptable?' in Roger Blanpain and Frank Hendrickx (eds), *Bulletin for Comparative Labour Relations: Labour Law Between Change and Tradition. Liber Amicorum Antoine Jacobs* (Alphen aan den Rijn: Kluwer Law International 2011) 49; Lyutov (n 17) 45; Jerzy Wratny, 'Kodeksy dobrych praktyk jako wyraz społecznej odpowiedzialności korporacji' in Zbigniew Hajn and Dagmara Skupień (eds), *Przyszłość prawa pracy: Liber Amicorum. W pięćdziesięciolecie pracy naukowej Profesora Michała Seweryńskiego* (Łódź: Wydawnictwo Uniwersytetu Łódzkiego 2015) 143; Jerzy Wratny, 'Korporacyjne kodeksy dobrych praktyk z perspektywy prawa pracy' (2016) 3 Praca i Zabezpieczenie Społeczne 2, 4.
28 Egels-Zandén and Merk (n 13) 464.
29 Marassi (n 2) 22.
30 Bob Hepple, *Labour Laws and Global Trade* (Oxford: Hart Publishing 2005) 76.
31 Herman (n 8) 455.
32 Segerlund (n 7) 56.
33 Hepple (n 30) 76; André Sobczak, 'Are Codes of Conduct in Global Supply Chains Really Voluntary? From Soft Law Regulation of Labour Relations to Consumer Law' (2006) 16(2) *Business Ethics Quarterly* 167, 168 <https://doi.org/10.5840/beq200616219> accessed 28 November 2020.

Monitoring may take different forms within which internal staffing, hiring an accounting firm and independent monitoring should be mentioned. Certain MNCs use their own internal compliance staff in order to monitor suppliers.[34] Lyutov rightly compare the situation to a 'fox in the henhouse' scenario – the MNC in the role of the fox controls itself in the worker henhouse.[35] As it comes to accounting firms, it turned out that they were not successful mainly due to the fact that in general, accountants are not trained in monitoring labour conditions, and they are seldom specialists in labour issues. Third-party certification based on independent monitoring performs a little better. Herman points out that certification takes two forms: brand and factory certification. The mode of action of the first one lies in the fact that a brand's products are certified as being produced under acceptable conditions. The latter model assumes that individual supplier factories are certified. The supplier factories bear the responsibility for retaining a monitor, while the brand-name MNC commits to using certified factories. Herman enumerates obstacles that limit the effectiveness of monitoring. They include monitors' conflict of interest, the limited resources available to monitor suppliers, the lack of uniformity in MNCs' codes of conduct, and the suppliers' ability to game monitoring efforts. MNCs benefit from poor labour conditions, so a 'fox in the henhouse' scenario, that is, monitoring to detect their own irregularities constitutes an obvious conflict of interest. Furthermore, sometimes the interest of NGO involved in voluntary labour rights monitoring initiatives is incompatible with the interest of the supplier's workers. After detection of infringements of labour rights, NGO talks about the 'success' and publicises the case. This may result in cancelling the supplier's contracts and workers losing jobs. Next, monitoring codes of conduct consumes significant resources. Then, as it has been highlighted, codes are vague and differ between companies. They not only vary on the relevant labour standards but also conflict on some issues. This seriously hampers the monitoring.[36] However, there are worse problems in trying to game the monitoring system. There are some popular methods for hiding code violations from monitors. Under the first option, suppliers keep two sets of books, an impeccable set for the monitors and an actual set for business. In this way, they manage to conceal actual hours and wages. Moreover, suppliers instruct workers on what to say. They even recourse to handing out scripts. Additionally, they use the services of consulting firms, which engage in cheating on the monitoring firms hired by MNCs. They also use a special software designed with the aim of creating fictitious employee work information. It is also common practice that suppliers share information with each other on how to pass monitoring inspections.[37]

34 Herman (n 8) 456.
35 Lyutov (n 17) 45.
36 Herman (n 8) 456–458, 460. However, the majority of codes of conduct at least address core labour issues like child labour, forced labour, discrimination, harassment and health and safety in the workplace. Herman (n 8) 450.
37 ibid 461. See: Lund-Thomsen and Lindgreen (n 1) 13; Pun Ngai, 'Global Production, Company Codes of Conduct, and Labor Conditions in China: A Case Study of Two Factories'

During the period between the 2000s and the early 2010s, many impact assessment studies revealed that codes of conduct improved tangible work conditions (outcome standards), for example, the reduction of overtime work, the payment of minimum wages, and occupational health and safety. According to the result of research conducted by Yu, the implementation of Reebok labour-related codes at the second largest footwear supplier factory in China during 1997–2005 caused that sweatshop labour abuses, for example, using child labour, imposing corporal punishments to discipline workers, providing unsafe and unhealthy working conditions, forcing workers to take long overtime, after sharp criticism were purged away. Besides, labour practices grievously infringing Chinese labour law, for example, not paying legal minimum wage or forcing workers to take overtime working hours longer than legal maximum work week, were also curbed. A 'race to ethical and legal minimum' effect, as the author calls it, not only saved Reebok from attacks but also contributed to the company's long-term profitability. It did not, however, satisfy workers' expectations concerning labour practices improvement. Indeed, the situation had imposed contradictory impacts on other working conditions. The overwhelming majority of the factory production workers were supposed to work faster and harder for less pay, not sufficient to meet basic needs of workers and their families. What were the reasons for this? The author finds the cause in the fact that Reebok had committed to neither sharing cost for code implementation with the supplier factory nor amending its sourcing policy to make improved labour standards more financially manageable to the factory management, although Reebok benefited from a significant increase in profitability.[38] The supplier factory was evaluated as Reebok's 'best partner' and, as a 'reward', received a relatively higher volume of forward orders. Workers were obliged to work in a more stressful environment in order to fulfil higher production tasks.[39] Ngai argues similarly that codes of conduct were intentionally implemented as a top-down regulatory process, replacing the role of the Chinese state in regulating labour standards in the workplace. This results in maintaining authoritarian factory regimes in which, prima facie MNCs play a paternalistic role in 'protecting' workers from labour exploitation, meanwhile allowing the sweating to continue, in the form of, for example, excessive overtime work or illegally low wages per hour.[40]

On the other hand, what is probably beyond dispute, codes of conduct have limited impact on less tangible issues (process rights), such as freedom of

(2005) 54 *The China Journal* 101, 107 <https://doi.org/10.2307/20066068> accessed 28 November 2020.

38 Xiaomin Yu, 'Impacts of Corporate Code of Conduct on Labor Standards: A Case Study of Reebok's Athletic Footwear Supplier Factory in China' (2008) 81(3) *Journal of Business Ethics* 513, 523–525 <https://doi.org/10.1007/s10551-007-9521-2> accessed 28 November 2020.
39 ibid 519–520.
40 Ngai (n 37) 113.

association and the right to collective bargaining.[41] According to Egels-Zandén and Merk, codes exert little effect on trade union rights because of:

- buyers paying lip service to trade union rights;
- codes not being able to open up space for union organising when leveraged in grassroots struggles (there is a lack of complaints or grievance mechanisms);
- codes introducing parallel means of organising (instead of labour unions), which are not able to guarantee an independent workers' voice, including real worker representation and collective bargaining;
- workers lacking voice in the development of codes of conduct, knowledge of codes, and workers and unions being deprived of possibilities to participate in monitoring processes;
- monitoring being unable to reveal and remedy infringements of trade union rights; and
- suppliers having limited encouragement for compliance. Comparing two alternatives with regard to costs (the higher cost of compliance and the lower cost of non-compliance), greater financial incentives from buyers would be necessary in order to persuade factory managers to comply with trade union rights.[42]

2.3 Ways in which codes could be transformed to more effectively address workers' rights

Codes of conduct seem 'like a weak, uncertain method for improving world labor conditions'.[43] Tough competition for just-in-time production and low-cost products in the world market is unfavourable to codes implementation,[44] and the implementation itself does not grant workers the right to demand that this code be applied.[45] Moreover, once implemented, codes of conduct have limited effectiveness – 58.5% of the variance in the perceived effectiveness of codes (effectiveness of codes measured by the opinion of the respondent),[46] and slightly above

---

41 Lund-Thomsen and Lindgreen (n 1) 13; Egels-Zandén and Merk (n 13) 464; Ngai (n 37) 112.
42 Egels-Zandén and Merk (n 13) passim; see the cited literature.
43 Robert J Flanagan, *Globalization and Labor Conditions: Working Conditions and Worker Rights in a Global Economy* (Oxford: Oxford University Press 2006) 141.
44 Ngai (n 37) 107.
45 Isabelle Martin, 'Corporate Governance Structures and Practices: From Ordeal to Opportunities and Challenges for Transnational Labour Law' in Adelle Blackett and Anne Trebilcock (eds), *Research Handbook on Transnational Labour Law* (Cheltenham, Northampton: Edward Elgar Publishing 2015) 62–63.
46 Jang B Singh, 'Determinants of the Effectiveness of Corporate Codes of Ethics: An Empirical Study' (2011) 101(3) *Journal of Business Ethics* 385, 386, 389, 393 <https://doi.org/10.1007/s10551-010-0727-3> accessed 28 November 2020.

50% compliance with the standards in corporate codes of conduct (as regards corporate audits).[47]

Given these facts, it is worth recalling some viewpoints articulated in the literature, on how codes of conduct could be transformed to more effectively address workers' rights.

Herman argues that a more practical approach to improving workers' labour conditions should be found and introduced in the new generation of codes of conduct. To this end, a better understanding of the role for different organisations (especially local NGOs that should be given a top priority role in monitoring) and of business strategies and the economic motivations of suppliers and MNCs should be adopted. Besides, such an attitude requires a thorough rethinking the types of labour standards that can effectively be improved through codes of conduct.[48] According to the author, adopting a narrower point of view and concentrating on a single 'linchpin' labour condition, that is, a sufficient hourly wage, would better align supplier codes with the objective of improving the labour conditions of supplier workers.[49]

According to Yu, fair distribution among crucial players in global supply chains of the cost of improving labour standards and transformation of codes into supplement initiatives (not the alternatives) to international law and state legislation constitute important conditions for the creation of a new quality approach.[50] This is an interesting view, in particular because the research indicates that currently private and public regulation interact in diverse ways – one time as complements, another time as substitutes. It depends not only on the national contexts but also on the specific matters being addressed.[51] In countries where labour regulations are weakly and irregularly enforced, private compliance initiatives frequently serve as substitutes for government enforcement or national laws and regulations, while in countries with more decisive government enforcement of labour regulations, private compliance efforts often complement stricter government regulation.[52] However, what refers to freedom of association, there is no substitute for effective government enforcement of national labour laws.[53]

47 Harry C Katz, Thomas A Kochan and Alexander JS Colvin, *Labor Relations in a Globalizing World* (Ithaca, London: Cornell University Press 2015) 277.
48 Herman (n 8) 471, 481.
49 ibid 448.
50 Yu (n 38) 526–527.
51 Richard M Locke, Ben A Rissing and Timea Pal, 'Complements or Substitutes? Private Codes, State Regulation and the Enforcement of Labour Standards in Global Supply Chains' (2013) 51(3) *British Journal of Industrial Relations* 519, passim <https://doi.org/10.1111/bjir.12003> accessed 28 November 2020.
52 ibid 543. See also: Tom Campbell, 'A Human Rights Approach to Developing Voluntary Codes of Conduct for Multinational Corporations' (2006) 16(2) *Business Ethics Quarterly* 255, 257 <https://doi.org/10.5840/beq200616225> accessed 28 November 2020.
53 Locke, Rissing and Pal (n 51) 544; Richard Locke, Thomas Kochan, Monica Romis and Fei Qin, 'Beyond Corporate Codes of Conduct: Work Organization and Labour Standards

Another important constant trend is a 'soft law to hard law' trajectory, as codes of conduct are moving to a legally-binding and legally-enforceable sphere.[54] For instance, in 1986, the Sullivan Principles became the basis of US sanctions legislation. This process still takes place today.[55] Optional codes of conduct are more frequently becoming legally-binding through legislation, through contracts and possibly through litigation.[56]

García-Muñoz Alhambra et al. propose a transnational labour inspectorate system, that is, a bow in the direction of publicly based monitoring, complementary to national labour inspectorates. Its premises are featured in the voluntary participation of the MNC (however, after the submission of the application, the rules of monitoring would be entirely binding) and a public root which upholds the independence of the monitoring system. According to this concept, the ILO should provide or control, supervise and/or coordinate the monitoring system, and would be responsible for providing a list of transnational labour inspectors who have been trained and accredited by the Organization. The ILO should establish a special protocol introducing the basic rules and requirements for monitoring, with the aim of ensuring its independence and quality.[57]

In fact, some (e.g. the Worker Rights Consortium, WRC) argue that in order to be effective, monitoring must be completely independent of brands and factories.[58] Others add that not only codes of conduct must be independently monitored but also the trade unions representing the workers at the factories must be involved.[59] Recognising the differences between codes of conduct and international framework agreements (IFAs) in the monitoring process, Schömann et al. point out that a vast majority of codes are implemented, monitored and enforced only by management parties, sometimes with the help of external auditors, whereas IFAs often provide for a certain role for employees' organisations and[60] trade unions in this context. The authors indicate that this affects the effectiveness of labour rights. They give the case of IKEA as one of the exceptional

---

at Nike's Suppliers' (2007) 146(1–2) *International Labour Review* 21, 24 <https://doi.org/10.1111/j.1564-913X.2007.00003.x> accessed 28 November 2020.

54 Lara Blecher, 'Codes of Conduct: The Trojan Horse of International Human Rights Law?' (2017) 38(3) *Comparative Labor Law & Policy Journal* 437.

55 ibid 438.

56 ibid 474.

57 Antonio M García-Muñoz Alhambra, Beryl Ter Haar and Attila Kun, 'Independent Monitoring of Private Transnational Regulation of Labour Standards: A Proposal for a "Transnational Labour Inspectorate" System' in Edoardo Ales and Iacopo Senatori (eds), *The Transnational Dimension of Labour Relations: A New Order in the Making? Atti dell'XI Convegno internazionale in ricordo di Marco Biagi* (Turin: G. Giappichelli Editore 2013) 275–277.

58 Locke, Kochan, Romis and Qin (n 53) 23.

59 Jack Eaton, *Comparative Employment Relations: An Introduction* (Cambridge: Polity Press 2000) 168.

60 Isabelle Schömann, André Sobczak, Eckhard Voss and Peter Wilke, *Codes of Conduct and International Framework Agreements: New Forms of Governance at Company Level* (Dublin: European Foundation for the Improvement of Living and Working Conditions 2008) 74.

examples where, on the one hand, management on its own undertakes extensive action to monitor implementation of the code of conduct, and on the other hand, supports the active involvement of trade unions in this process, including the establishment of a joint monitoring and implementation group with Building Workers International (BWI, formerly IFBWW – International Federation of Building and Wood Workers). An analogous shared monitoring process exists at Bosch and Securitas. According to Schömann et al., the potential added value of a cooperation between management and trade unions is underlined by the fact that at IKEA and Securitas, the IFAs were negotiated with the aim of improving the pre-existing code of conduct or the CSR practice.[61]

In order to avoid a 'fox in the henhouse' scenario, some international organisations and many companies specialised in auditing adopt their own codes of conduct in order to make MNC subscribe. Such codes of conduct are known as 'external' in opposition to 'internal' ones adopted by companies themselves. However, while it is admittedly true that the majority of international employers subscribe to external codes, they keep their internal codes anyway.[62]

Däubler shows great scepticism about the whole CSR concept, even considering its abolition.[63] The author recognises the role of NGOs and public opinion as new agents in industrial relations but only in a small field and with limited possibilities. He highlights that the profit does increase when bad conditions are offered to workers in developing countries, but it decreases even more due to the bad publicity in industrialised countries. Nobody would like to buy T-shirts produced by persons working like slaves and suffering from inhumane conditions, or produced by children. At this point social sanctions are activated.[64]

Däubler proposes a 'stakeholder model' under which an enterprise should balance different interests, give adequate instruments to each stakeholder with the aim of avoiding predominance of one of them (especially the shareholders), endow employees with a right to collective action which can question even management decisions, and consumers with a right to act collectively, mainly to boycott certain products.[65]

2.4 Evaluation

The purpose of this chapter subsection was to explore the main shortcomings of corporate codes of conduct and ways in which codes could be transformed to more effectively address workers' rights, as existing generations of these instruments seem not to be sufficient to ensure the effective enforcement of labour rights. Starting with the positive, codes of conduct are at least able to eliminate

---

61 ibid 75.
62 Lyutov (n 17) 45–46.
63 Däubler (n 27) 50 et seq.
64 ibid 54–55.
65 ibid 56–57.

the worst abuses, such as child labour or corporal punishments. Nevertheless, the analysis of the extant literature reveals that certain labour standards are not suitable for improvement through codes of conduct. It has been stated that there is no substitute for effective government enforcement of national labour laws when it comes to, for example, freedom of association and the right to collective bargaining. However, what if the national labour law does not guarantee any rights? Caution is also required if one, believing in the potential of codes of conduct, wants to treat them as effective supplement initiatives. It would be difficult to supplement effectively something that actually does not exist. In China, for instance, no separate unions are protected by law. The Trade Union Law (dating back to 1992 and amended in 2001) states that the All-China Federation of Trade Union (ACFTU) shall be established as the unified national organisation (Article 10). Although Article 35 of the Constitution refers to the freedom of assembly and association, the concept does not establish pluralism in the trade union organisation. In China, the terminology of collective bargaining is not used in legal acts. In contrast, the Trade Union Law introduces the practice of equal consultations and collective agreements. On the employees' side, the trade union, represented by the trade union chairman, or representatives, elected by the employees, where there is no trade union organised, will act for the employees to conduct collective consultations and conclude the collective agreement.[66] It goes without saying that, for example, ad hoc representatives without any real voice cannot be treated as true partners. It seems that codes introducing, for example, parallel means of organising can constitute neither effective complements nor substitutes for national law. However, the problem here goes far beyond corporate codes of conduct and calls for thorough reforms. Given this context, it should be mentioned that China has not even ratified the Freedom of Association and Protection of the Right to Organise Convention, 1948 (No. 87)[67] and the Right to Organise and Collective Bargaining Convention, 1949 (No. 98).[68]

It seems to be proven under several different circumstances that the role of NGOs cannot be underestimated. NGOs, indeed, engage in detecting infringements, enforcement practices, lobbying for better standards, representing workers and auditing labour conditions in supplier plants. The Worker Rights Consortium is one of the most active of these NGOs. It participated in activities for improving labour conditions at Foxconn, at apparel factories in Bangladesh and at Nike.[69] However, when publicising their 'successes', NGOs should take the necessary measures to overcome the concerns relating to the aforementioned conflict of interests between them and the supplier's workers. Moreover, the idea of publicly rooted monitors (e.g. transnational labour inspectors according to

---

66 Ke Chen, *Labour Law in China* (Alphen aan den Rijn: Kluwer Law International 2011) 104, 114–115.
67 <www.ilo.org/dyn/normlex/en/f?p=NORMLEXPUB:11310:0::NO:11310:P11310_INSTRUMENT_ID:312232:NO> accessed 28 November 2020.
68 ibid.
69 Katz, Kochan and Colvin (n 47) 289.

García-Muñoz Alhambra et al.) also seems interesting. Upon such a foundation, a system that would enable employees to report violations of labour rights could be subsequently developed. Independent international 'observers' could promptly react and more effectively put pressure on corporations highlighting that the situation can result in the increased public awareness of infringements as a consequence of media coverage. Additionally, it is worth noting that periodic training and testing programmes to ensure employee knowledge and comprehension of codes of conduct[70] could be a good idea, especially when employees have little understanding of the concept of rights.

3 Transnational company agreements

Self-regulation through corporate codes of conduct is only one of the pathways of corporate law development. The other one is related to Transnational Company Agreements (TCAs) which can be divided into European Framework Agreements (EFAs) and International/Global Framework Agreements (IFAs/GFAs). As regards the latter, they are negotiated and signed by a multinational company and at least one Global Union Federation (GUF).[71] As Schömann points out, unlike IFAs, which are a global instrument aimed mainly at ensuring international labour standards (especially ILO core labour standards) in all of the target company's locations, EFAs embrace more issues and are regionally limited. The author, however, further adds that this difference is vanishing as it can be observed that, on the one hand, IFAs are becoming much more detailed, and on the other hand, international aspects appear with increasing frequency in EFAs.[72]

There are considerable advantages of TCAs. As pointed out by Schömann, owing to social dialogue with trade unions, these tools are considered as means of promoting industrial peace. Trade unions and workers are involved in drafting, monitoring and implementing TCAs. Trade unions help solve problems related to the implementation of these agreements and provide an alternative dispute resolution mechanism. From the point of view of trade unions, TCAs contribute to involving MNCs in a private standard-setting process with the aim of increasing the quality of working conditions and strengthening the rights of local unions. On the other hand, from the perspective of MNCs, TCAs – similarly to

70 Michael K Braswell, Charles M Foster and Stephen L Poe, 'A New Generation of Corporate Codes of Ethics' (2009) 34(2) *Southern Business Review* 1, 8.
71 Antonio Ojeda-Avilés, *Transnational Labour Law* (Alphen aan den Rijn: Wolters Kluwer Law & Business 2015) 115.
72 Isabelle Schömann, 'Transnational Company Agreements: Towards an Internationalisation of Industrial Relations' in Isabelle Schömann, Romuald Jagodzinski, Guido Boni, Stefan Clauwaert, Vera Glassner and Teun Jaspers (eds), *Transnational Collective Bargaining at Company Level: A New Component of European Industrial Relations?* (Brussels: European Trade Union Institute 2012) 202–203 <www.etui.org/sites/default/files/C5%2012%20 Transnational%20collective%20bargaining%20EN%20Web%20version.pdf> accessed 29 November 2020. See also: Konstantinos Papadakis, 'Shaping Global Industrial Relations' (Geneva: ILO 2011) 2.

other private instruments – help build a good reputation and avoid unfavourable public campaigns.[73] As rightly stated by Ales, due to the fact that TCAs serve the interests of MNCs and their workers, they cannot be seen simply as 'a mere cross-border extension of already existing national collective bargaining systems'. There are some specific MNCs' needs concerning the general priorities that are regulated by national collective bargaining at branch level. Taking into consideration that MNCs operate within several jurisdictions, glocalisation best describes their approach to the employment relationship.[74]

As of November 2019, over 300 TCAs have been signed, including over 100 IFAs.[75] The first IFA was signed in 1988 between the French food company Danone, which could boast of a reputation for social partnership and a progressive attitude to CSR,[76] and the International Union of Food and Allied Workers' Association (IUF).[77] The second one was signed with the ACCOR hotel chain in 1995.[78] In spite of their growing popularity, questions still arise, for example, as to their legal value, legal nature and legal impact as well.[79]

73 Schömann (n 72) 204; see the cited literature.
74 Edoardo Ales, 'Transnational Collective Agreements: The Role of Trade Unions and Employers' Associations' A Thematic Working Paper for the Annual Conference of the European Centre of Expertise (ECE) in the Field of Labour Law, Employment and Labour Market Policies: 'Perspectives of Collective Rights in Europe' (2018) 7 <https://eu.eventscloud.com/file_uploads/185fe09c1a16e079ad008e8927fc6c8a_Ales_Final_EN3.pdf> accessed 29 November 2020.
75 The list of all identified TCAs can be found at: <https://ec.europa.eu/social/main.jsp?catId=978&langId=en> accessed 29 November 2020.
76 Elizabeth Cotton, 'Employment Relations, International Framework Agreements and Global Unions' in Ian Roper, Rea Prouska and Uracha Chatrakul Na Ayudhya (eds), *Critical Issues in Human Resource Management: Contemporary Perspectives* (London: Red Globe Press 2020) 145.
77 Daniela Barrier, 'National Policy Regimes: Implications for the Activism-Policy Nexus' in Peter Utting, Mario Pianta and Anne Ellersiek (eds), *Global Justice Activism and Policy Reform in Europe: Understanding When Change Happens* (New York, London: Routledge 2012) 52. See also: Richard Croucher and Elizabeth Cotton, *Global Unions, Global Business: Global Union Federations and International Business* (London: Middlesex University Press 2009) 34.
78 Jocelyne Barreau and Juliette Arnal, 'Effects of Financialization on Restructuring and Sustainable Development Policy: The ACCOR Group Case' in William Sun, Céline Louche and Roland Pérez (eds), *Finance and Sustainability: Towards a New Paradigm? A Post-Crisis Agenda* (Bingley: Emerald Group Publishing Limited 2011) 268. See also: Dimitris Stevis and Terry Boswell, *Globalization and Labor: Democratizing Global Governance* (Lanham, Maryland: Rowman and Littlefield Publishing Group, Inc. 2008) 112; Bronstein (n 15) 116.
79 Isabelle Schömann, 'Transnational Collective Bargaining: In Search of a Legal Framework' in Isabelle Schömann, Romuald Jagodzinski, Guido Boni, Stefan Clauwaert, Vera Glassner and Teun Jaspers (eds), *Transnational Collective Bargaining at Company Level: A New Component of European Industrial Relations?* (Brussels: European Trade Union Institute 2012) passim <www.etui.org/sites/default/files/Chap%206%20Transnational%20collective%20bargaining%20EN-3.pdf> accessed 29 November 2020.

In fact, despite some doctrinal proposals for an optional legal framework for TCAs[80] and some promising announcements from the European Commission, we are still waiting for a legal framework for TCAs. In 2005, the European Commission stated as follows:

> Providing an optional framework for transnational collective bargaining at either enterprise level or sectoral level could support companies and sectors to handle challenges dealing with issues such as work organisation, employment, working conditions, training. It will give the social partners a basis for increasing their capacity to act at transnational level. It will provide an innovative tool to adapt to changing circumstances and provide cost-effective transnational responses. Such an approach is firmly anchored in the partnership for change priority advocated by the Lisbon strategy.
>
> The Commission plans to adopt a proposal designed to make it possible for the social partners to formalise the nature and results of transnational collective bargaining. The existence of this resource is essential, but its use will remain optional and will depend entirely on the will of the social partners.[81]

In its resolution on the Social Agenda for the period 2006–2010 (2004/2191(INI)) adopted on 26 May 2005, the European Parliament called on the Commission to put forward proposals for a voluntary framework for transnational collective bargaining covering both the intersectoral level and the company and sectoral level.[82] Moreover, on 12 September 2013, the European Parliament adopted a resolution on cross-border collective bargaining and transnational social dialogue (2012/2292(INI)). In this document, the European Parliament asks the Commission to give consideration to the need for an optional European legal framework for European transnational company agreements.[83] As signalled earlier, for now, these initiatives remain unanswered.

4 NGOs' social accountability standards

Social accountability standards are created by NGOs. In 1997, the NGO Social Accountability International established the Social Accountability Standard

80 E.g. Silvana Sciarra, Maximilian Fuchs and André Sobczak, *Towards a Legal Framework for Transnational Company Agreements* (Report to the European Trade Union Confederation) <http://csdle.lex.unict.it/Archive/LW/Data%20reports%20and%20studies/Reports%20%20from%20Committee%20and%20Groups%20of%20Experts/20140424-015608_Report-TCA-EN_lowpdf.pdf> accessed 29 November 2020.
81 Commission of the European Communities, *Communication from the Commission on the Social Agenda*, (COM(2005) 33 final, Brussels, 9 February 2005) <https://eur-lex.europa.eu/LexUriServ/LexUriServ.do?uri=COM:2005:0033:FIN:EN:PDF> accessed 29 November 2020.
82 www.europarl.europa.eu/sides/getDoc.do?pubRef=-//EP//TEXT+TA+P6-TA-2005-0210+0+DOC+XML+V0//EN
83 www.europarl.europa.eu/sides/getDoc.do?type=TA&reference=P7-TA-2013-0386&language=EN&ring=A7-2013-0258

(SA8000) with the aim of implementing international labour standards and national labour laws.[84] More specifically, the Standard mirrors labour provisions laid down in the ILO's conventions and the Universal Declaration of Human Rights. Moreover, it respects, supports and complements national labour laws all over the world. SA8000 is the leading social certification standard for factories and organisations across the globe. Social performance in areas crucial to social accountability in workplaces (child labour, forced or compulsory labour, health and safety, freedom of association and the right to collective bargaining, discrimination, disciplinary practices, working hours, and remuneration) is measured through SA8000. It is anchored by a ninth element, that is a management system that drives continuous improvement in all of the aforementioned areas. Given new and emergent social and human rights issues, regular revisions ensure the Standard's continuing applicability.[85] SA8000:2014 – which replaced SA8000:2008 – is the current version of the Standard. The most important updates to the Standard are related to forced or compulsory labour and health and safety areas. All organisations certified to SA8000:2014 must now ensure that their workers are free from employment fees and costs, and they must establish a Health and Safety Committee responsible for monitoring health and safety hazards, which is composed of management representatives and workers.[86]

As regards the SA8000 certification process, during the first phase the applicant organisation undertakes an online management system self-assessment. Subsequently, it selects and works with one of the independent certification bodies (accredited by Social Accountability Accreditation Services, SAAS) in order to start the full evaluation process. Once the organisation has implemented the necessary actions and improvements to become compliant with the Standard, the certification body grants the SA8000 certificate. Afterwards, the organisation is reviewed through on-site monitoring visits, both announced and unannounced.[87]

As explained by Bronstein, one of the characteristics of standards like the SA8000 is that certification pertains to factories and suppliers of the product and is not directed towards the retailers or the brand itself. Thus, by entering into business only with certified factories, MNCs encourage organisations to obtain certification.[88]

---

84 See: Alexios Antypas, Magdalena Paszkiewicz and Stephen Stec, 'Corporate Social Responsibility and Corporate Accountability: A Historical Overview' in Lez Rayman-Bacchus and Philip R Walsh (eds), *Corporate Responsibility and Sustainable Development: Exploring the Nexus of Private and Public Interests* (Abingdon: Routledge 2016) 25. For more about the ratio of existence of such standards see: Laura Vannucci, 'CSR e Certificazione SA8000' in Adalberto Perulli (ed), *L'impresa responsabile: Diritti sociali e Corporate Social Responsability* (Macerata: HALLEY Editrice 2007) 128 et seq.
85 <https://sa-intl.org/> accessed 29 November 2020.
86 ibid.
87 ibid.
88 Bronstein (n 15) 122.

5 ISO standards

Other private initiatives include the activities of the International Organization for Standardization (ISO). It is an independent, non-governmental international organisation that develops voluntary, consensus-based, market relevant international standards, which give world-class specifications for products, services and systems, to ensure quality, safety and efficiency. They are instrumental in facilitating international trade.[89]

In 2010, the International Organization for Standardization developed the ISO 26000 standard for corporate responsibility. It provides guidance on how businesses and organisations can operate in a socially responsible way, that is, act in an ethical and transparent manner that contributes to the health and welfare of society. It is noteworthy that ISO 26000 provides only guidance and not requirements, so it cannot be certified, unlike some other ISO standards. However, it plays an important role in clarifying what social responsibility is. In addition, it helps businesses and organisations translate principles into effective actions and shares best practices relating to social responsibility, globally. Crucially, it is addressed to all types of organisations irrespective of their activity, size or location. ISO 26000 represents an international consensus since representatives from labour organisations, NGOs, industry, government and consumer groups from around the world were involved in negotiations for five years and contributed to its development.[90]

In the aforementioned context, significant attention should be given to the interrelationship between the UN Sustainable Development Goals (SDGs) and ISO 26000. In other words, how can the ISO 26000 contribute to SDGs? When we think about this question, what first comes to mind is SDG 8: Promote sustained, inclusive and sustainable economic growth, full and productive employment and decent work for all. The case of the Algerian drinks producer NCA Rouiba is a good example of ISO 26000 in action. When it started the implementation of ISO 26000, staff welfare was given high priority. A new employee relations framework was developed with the aim of preventing discrimination and promoting well-being. It was established in association with trade unions and worker representatives. NCA Rouiba updated contracts with suppliers and insisted they implement the same standards. Another example is connected with SDG 1: No poverty. For this one goal, Subclause 6.4.4.2 of ISO 26000 under the core subject 'Labour practices' states:

> An organization should pay wages at least adequate for the needs of workers and their families. In doing so, it should take into account the general level of wages in the country, the cost of living, social security benefits and the relative living standards of other social groups.[91]

---

89 <www.iso.org/about-us.html> accessed 29 November 2020.
90 <www.iso.org/iso-26000-social-responsibility.html> accessed 29 November 2020.
91 ISO 26000 and the SDGs <www.iso.org/files/live/sites/isoorg/files/store/en/PUB100401.pdf> accessed 29 November 2020.

The ISO has also developed a standard that will help organisations to improve employee safety, reduce workplace risks and create better, safer working conditions, all over the world. Here we talk about ISO 45001 Occupational health and safety.[92] Unlike ISO 26000, it is created to be certifiable, to attest the safety and soundness of worker safety procedures. As highlighted by Cooper, organisations have two options: they can accept certification to this standard or adopt it as self-certification in the form of an internal practice. Regardless of the choice made, ISO 45001 is aimed at creating a necessary foundation of worker safety and building integrity standards and conformance that can be accepted all over the world. ISO 45001 furnish all industries, workers, other stakeholders and governmental agencies with operative and useful guidance for improving worker safety.[93]

It all sounds good in theory, but in practice, a dispute arose between the ILO and the ISO, mainly over the ISO 45001 standard on occupational safety and health management systems. The ILO wanted to reserve its exclusive right to create standards protecting workers' safety. It emphasised that its legitimacy results from being a treaty-based organisation, working directly with the nation-states.[94] Admittedly, the Agreement between the ILO and the International Organization for Standardization was signed on 6 August 2013, but the ILO formally notified the International Organization for Standardization on 18 December 2017 of its decision to terminate it (with effect on 8 March 2018). The decision was made after the ILO Governing Body reviewed a report on the ILO's pilot implementation of that Agreement. It was found that the implementation of the said document over four years did not reach the objectives of the agreement. The conflict between the ISO standards and international labour standards was crucial here. According to paragraph 4 of the Agreement,

> Given the broad mandate and action of the ILO to promote social justice and decent work, and ISO's broad mission, ISO standards that relate to issues within the ILO's mandate (ILO issues) should respect and support the provisions of ILS and related ILO action, including by using ILS as the source of reference with respect to ILO issues in case of conflict.

Organisations could not reach a consensus on the question whether development of ISO standards required treating international labour standards 'as the source of reference' or whether the ISO only needed to consider but not to refer to international labour standards. As highlighted by the ILO, the private standards involve the risk of leaving workers without protection in a situation where an international labour standard (concluded through tripartite consensus and given

---

92 <www.iso.org/iso-45001-occupational-health-and-safety.html> accessed 29 November 2020.
93 Scott Cooper, 'Global Supply Chain Governance: ILO, ISO & Worker Safety' (October 2018) 63(10) *Professional Safety* 70, 71–72.
94 ibid 70.

effect for decades) does not constitute the basis for private standards on issues related to the work of the ILO. As stated on the ILO website, according to the decision of the Governing Body, the ILO has no intention of seeking to renew collaboration with the ISO without adequate safeguards ensuring respect of ILO standards.[95]

6 The Dow Jones Sustainability Index (DJSI)

The DJSI was launched in 1999 and is considered a significant standard for corporate sustainability. It provides an instrument to track the financial performance of leading companies across the world, and to measure their progress in sustainability. Created jointly by S&P Dow Jones Indices and RobecoSAM (Sustainable Asset Management), the DJSI selects the most sustainable companies from across 61 industries.[96] From the point of view of MNEs, being listed on the DJSI translates into getting access to significant investment capital. Additionally, taking into account the DJSI's global renown, companies always try to leverage their position on the DJSI in enhancing their own reputation.[97]

As regards reporting under DJSI, it includes three categories that cover the 'triple bottom line':[98] economic, environmental and social. The latter embraces an important aspect for our research, namely human rights, which contains investment, non-discrimination, freedom of association and collective bargaining, child labour, forced or compulsory labour, security practices, indigenous rights, assessment, supplier human rights assessment, and human rights grievance mechanisms. Another reporting aspect is connected with labour practices and decent work. It encompasses employment, labour-management relations, occupational health and safety, training and education, diversity and equal opportunity, equal remuneration for women and men, supplier assessment for labour practices and labour practices grievance management.[99]

However, it is worth stressing that the DJSI keeps itself informed primarily through the SAM questionnaire, which is completed by the companies invited to take part in SAM's Corporate Sustainability Assessment. The second source of information are company and third-party documents, and personal contacts between the analysts and the companies.[100]

95 <www.ilo.org/global/about-the-ilo/newsroom/statements-and-speeches/WCMS_617802/lang–en/index.htm> accessed 29 November 2020.
96 <www.robecosam.com/csa/indices/djsi-index-family.html> accessed 29 November 2020.
97 Michael D'heur, 'Shared.Value.Chain: Profitable Growth Through Sustainable Value Creation' in Michael D'heur (ed), *Sustainable Value Chain Management: Delivering Sustainability Through the Core Business* (Cham: Springer 2015) 57.
98 Joseph Fiksel, *Design for Environment: A Guide to Sustainable Product Development* (New York: McGraw-Hill 2009) 40.
99 Subhas K Sikdar, Debalina Sengupta and Rajib Mukherjee, *Measuring Progress Towards Sustainability: A Treatise for Engineers* (Cham: Springer 2017) 120.
100 Fiksel (n 98) 41.

In the light of these considerations, there is little doubt that the self-reporting method which is not based on observations of a real company's progress in sustainability is not the best one. Besides, the DJSI is favourable towards the world's largest companies and excludes smaller ones. In fact, for example, in 2019, over 3,500 of 'the world's largest companies were invited to participate in SAM's Corporate Sustainability Assessment'.[101]

7 The Global Reporting Initiative (GRI)

The GRI is an independent international organisation, based in Amsterdam, which has pioneered sustainability reporting since 1997. According to its website, the GRI works with the largest companies in the world and contributes to social well-being, better jobs, less environmental damage, access to clean water, less child and forced labour, and gender equality.[102]

The organisation prides itself on the fact that the GRI Sustainability Reporting Standards are the first and the most broadly adopted global standards for sustainability reporting.[103] Developed by the Global Sustainability Standards Board, the GRI Standards give all organisations the possibility of reporting publicly on their economic (the 200 series of the GRI Standards), environmental (the 300 series of the GRI Standards) and social (the 400 series of the GRI Standards) impacts and contributions to sustainable development.[104] For reporting on its material topics, an organisation selects from the set of topic-specific GRI Standards. Interestingly, the 400 series of the GRI Standards can be described as thematically oriented Standards used to report information on an organisation's material impacts exerted on social topics. All Standards included in the 400 series are effective from 1 July 2018 (with the exception of GRI 403, which is effective from 1 January 2021). The Standards are the following: GRI 401: Employment, GRI 402: Labor/Management Relations, GRI 403: Occupational Health and Safety, GRI 404: Training and Education, GRI 405: Diversity and Equal Opportunity, GRI 406: Non-discrimination, GRI 407: Freedom of Association and Collective Bargaining, GRI 408: Child Labor, GRI 409: Forced or Compulsory Labor, GRI 410: Security Practices, GRI 411: Rights of Indigenous Peoples, GRI 412: Human Rights Assessment, GRI 413: Local Communities, GRI 414: Supplier Social Assessment, GRI 415: Public Policy, GRI 416: Customer Health and Safety, GRI 417: Marketing and Labeling, GRI 418: Customer Privacy and GRI 419: Socioeconomic Compliance.[105]

101 <www.finchandbeak.com/1451/the-2019-global-dow-jones-sustainability.htm> accessed 29 November 2020.

102 <www.globalreporting.org/information/about-gri/Pages/default.aspx> accessed 29 November 2020.

103 ibid.

104 <www.globalreporting.org> accessed 29 November 2020.

105 <www.globalreporting.org/standards/gri-standards-download-center/> accessed 29 November 2020.

One can approximate the operation of the Standards using selected examples comprising human rights. Hence, for the purposes of this research, the focus here is on GRI 406: Non-discrimination, GRI 407: Freedom of Association and Collective Bargaining, GRI 408: Child Labor and GRI 409: Forced or Compulsory Labor.

GRI 406: Non-discrimination establishes reporting requirements on the issue of non-discrimination. It can be used by an organisation of any type, size, sector or geographic location that is keen on reporting on its impact in this field (a common feature of all standards). This Standard defines discrimination as 'the act and the result of treating people unequally by imposing unequal burdens or denying benefits, instead of treating each person fairly on the basis of individual merit'. Discrimination includes harassment, which is defined as 'a course of comments or actions that are unwelcome, or should reasonably be known to be unwelcome, to the person towards whom they are addressed'. Importantly, an organisation shall avoid discriminating against any person on any grounds, including discriminating against workers. In order to help understand and apply the Standard, it refers back to ILO Conventions Nos. 100 and 111, and other instruments of the OECD and the UN. Given this context, it should be highlighted that GRI 406: Non-discrimination includes disclosures on the management approach and topic-specific disclosures. 'Disclosure 406–1: Incidents of discrimination and corrective actions taken' establishes reporting requirements. The key point is that in this case a self-reporting method is also used. The organisation shall report the total number of incidents of discrimination during the reporting period, and the status of the incidents and actions taken with reference to: incidents reviewed by the organisation; remediation plans being implemented; remediation plans that have been implemented, with results reviewed through routine internal management review processes; incidents no longer subject to action.[106]

GRI 407: Freedom of Association and Collective Bargaining introduces reporting requirements on the topic of freedom of association and collective bargaining, and makes references to ILO Conventions Nos. 87, 98, 154, ILO Recommendation No. 163, Tripartite Declaration of Principles Concerning Multinational Enterprises and Social Policy, and some instruments of the OECD and the UN. As regards topic-specific disclosures, disclosure 407–1 sets out information that shall be reported by the organisation. First, it shall report operations and suppliers in which workers' rights to exercise freedom of association or collective bargaining may be violated or at significant risk either in terms of:

- type of operation (such as manufacturing plant) and supplier;
- countries or geographic areas with operations and suppliers considered at risk.

106 <www.globalreporting.org/standards/media/1021/gri-406-non-discrimination-2016. pdf> accessed 29 November 2020.

Second, the organisation shall report measures taken in the reporting period intended to support rights to exercise freedom of association and collective bargaining.[107]

GRI 408: Child Labor sets out reporting requirements on the topic of child labour, and makes references to ILO Conventions Nos. 138, 142, 182, Tripartite Declaration of Principles Concerning Multinational Enterprises and Social Policy, and some instruments of the OECD and the UN. According to disclosure 408–1, the organisation shall report three kinds of information. First, it shall report operations and suppliers considered to have significant risk for incidents of child labour and young workers exposed to hazardous work. Second, the organisation shall report operations and suppliers considered to have significant risk for incidents of child labour either in terms of:

- type of operation (such as manufacturing plant) and supplier;
- countries or geographic areas with operations and suppliers considered at risk.

Third, it shall report measures taken by the organisation in the reporting period intended to contribute to the effective abolition of child labour.[108]

GRI 409: Forced or Compulsory Labor sets out reporting requirements on the topic of forced or compulsory labour, and makes references to ILO Conventions Nos. 29, 105, Protocol to Convention 29, Recommendation No. 203, Tripartite Declaration of Principles Concerning Multinational Enterprises and Social Policy, League of Nations 'Convention to Suppress the Slave Trade and Slavery', and some instruments of the OECD and the UN. Disclosure 409–1 requires the organisation to report operations and suppliers considered to have significant risk for incidents of forced or compulsory labour either in terms of:

- type of operation (such as manufacturing plant) and supplier;
- countries or geographic areas with operations and suppliers considered at risk.

Moreover, as in the case of other standards, the organisation shall report measures taken in the reporting period intended to contribute to the elimination of all forms of forced or compulsory labour.[109]

---

107 <www.globalreporting.org/standards/media/1022/gri-407-freedom-of-association-and-collective-bargaining-2016.pdf> accessed 29 November 2020.
108 <www.globalreporting.org/standards/media/1023/gri-408-child-labor-2016.pdf> accessed 29 November 2020.
109 <www.globalreporting.org/standards/media/1024/gri-409-forced-or-compulsory-labor-2016.pdf> accessed 29 November 2020.

8 Concluding remarks

CSR norms are developed beyond the power of the state, cannot be enforced through the court processes and are adopted voluntarily within the private sector, often with the aim of enhancing a company's reputation or getting access to significant investment capital. All this may be perceived as evidence of the limited impact of CSR instruments on labour rights. Within the rich spectrum of CSR instruments that has been discussed, TCAs seem to be attractive mainly because of the benefits of social dialogue and the involvement of trade unions and workers in their drafting, monitoring and implementing. However, as has been raised, their legal nature and impact remain necessary to clarify. Unilateral corporate codes of conduct also present some disadvantages, inter alia, related to their implementation, monitoring and enforcement. Moreover, the self-reporting method inscribed in the nature of CSR instruments (e.g. the DJSI) gives only the illusion of impeccable MNCs' operation. Last but not least, it would be difficult not to mention a dispute that arose between the ILO and the ISO, mainly over the ISO 45001 standard, which is an example of a conflict between public and private organisations. In conclusion, CSR tools can be perceived only as additional value to law, and – as such – can be further developed, mainly because they have a potential to encourage MNCs to raise standards (e.g. to obtain certification in the case of SA8000), to exert a positive impact on the workers' situation (e.g. codes of conduct), and to unite different stakeholders in carrying out one purpose, that is, promoting labour rights.

Bibliography

Alexander Dahlsrud, 'How Corporate Social Responsibility Is Defined: An Analysis of 37 Definitions' (2008) 15(1) *Corporate Social Responsibility and Environmental Management* <https://doi.org/10.1002/csr.132> accessed 28 November 2020.

Alexandra R Harrington, 'Corporate Social Responsibility, Globalization, the Multinational Corporation, and Labor: An Unlikely Alliance' (2011–2012) 75(1) *Albany Law Review* 483.

Alexios Antypas, Magdalena Paszkiewicz and Stephen Stec, 'Corporate Social Responsibility and Corporate Accountability: A Historical Overview' in Lez Rayman-Bacchus and Philip R Walsh (eds), *Corporate Responsibility and Sustainable Development: Exploring the Nexus of Private and Public Interests* (Abingdon: Routledge 2016).

André Sobczak, 'Are Codes of Conduct in Global Supply Chains Really Voluntary? From Soft Law Regulation of Labour Relations to Consumer Law' (2006) 16(2) *Business Ethics Quarterly* 167 <https://doi.org/10.5840/beq200616219> accessed 28 November 2020.

Andrew Herman, 'Reassessing the Role of Supplier Codes of Conduct: Closing the Gap Between Aspirations and Reality' (2012) 52(2) *Virginia Journal of International Law* 445.

Aneta Tyc, 'Corporate Social Responsibility Instruments and Their Impact on Labour Rights' (2020) 29(1) *Acta Iuris Stetinensis*.

Antonio M García-Muñoz Alhambra, Beryl Ter Haar and Attila Kun, 'Independent Monitoring of Private Transnational Regulation of Labour Standards: A Proposal for a "Transnational Labour Inspectorate" System' in Edoardo Ales and Iacopo Senatori (eds), *The Transnational Dimension of Labour Relations: A New Order in the Making? Atti dell'XI Convegno internazionale in ricordo di Marco Biagi* (Turin: G. Giappichelli Editore 2013).

Antonio Ojeda-Avilés, *Transnational Labour Law* (Alphen aan den Rijn: Wolters Kluwer Law & Business 2015).

Arturo Bronstein, *International and Comparative Labour Law: Current Challenges* (Geneva: Palgrave Macmillan, International Labour Office 2009).

Bob Hepple, *Labour Laws and Global Trade* (Oxford: Hart Publishing 2005).

Christine Kaufmann, *Globalisation and Labour Rights: The Conflict Between Core Labour Rights and International Economic Law* (Oxford, Portland OR: Hart Publishing 2007).

Commission of the European Communities, *Communication from the Commission on the Social Agenda,* (COM(2005) 33 final, Brussels, 9 February 2005) <https://eur-lex.europa.eu/LexUriServ/LexUriServ.do?uri=COM:2005:0033:FIN:EN:PDF> accessed 29 November 2020.

Cynthia Stohl, Michael Stohl and Lucy Popova, 'A New Generation of Corporate Codes of Ethics' (2009) 90(4) *Journal of Business Ethics* 607 <https://doi.org/10.1007/s10551-009-0064-6> accessed 28 November 2020.

Daniela Barrier, 'National Policy Regimes: Implications for the Activism-Policy Nexus' in Peter Utting, Mario Pianta and Anne Ellersiek (eds), *Global Justice Activism and Policy Reform in Europe: Understanding When Change Happens* (New York, London: Routledge 2012).

Dimitris Stevis and Terry Boswell, *Globalization and Labor: Democratizing Global Governance* (Lanham MD: Rowman and Littlefield Publishing Group, Inc. 2008).

Edoardo Ales, 'Transnational Collective Agreements: The Role of Trade Unions and Employers' Associations' A Thematic Working Paper for the Annual Conference of the European Centre of Expertise (ECE) in the Field of Labour Law, Employment and Labour Market Policies: 'Perspectives of Collective Rights in Europe' (2018) <https://eu.eventscloud.com/file_uploads/185fe09c1a16e079ad008e8927fc6c8a_Ales_Final_EN3.pdf> accessed 29 November 2020.

Elizabeth Cotton, 'Employment Relations, International Framework Agreements and Global Unions' in Ian Roper, Rea Prouska and Uracha Chatrakul na Ayudhya (eds), *Critical Issues in Human Resource Management: Contemporary Perspectives* (London: Red Globe Press 2020).

Harry Arthurs, 'Private Ordering and Workers' Rights in the Global Economy: Corporate Codes of Conduct as a Regime of Labour Market Regulation' in Joanne Conaghan, Richard M Fischl and Karl Klare (eds), *Labour Law in an Era of Globalization: Transformative Practices and Possibilities* (Oxford: Oxford University Press 2004).

Harry C Katz, Thomas A Kochan and Alexander JS Colvin, *Labor Relations in a Globalizing World* (Ithaca, London: Cornell University Press 2015).

Isabelle Martin, 'Corporate Governance Structures and Practices: From Ordeal to Opportunities and Challenges for Transnational Labour Law' in Adelle Blackett and Anne Trebilcock (eds), *Research Handbook on Transnational Labour Law* (Cheltenham, Northampton: Edward Elgar Publishing 2015).

Isabelle Schömann, 'Transnational Collective Bargaining: In Search of a Legal Framework' in Isabelle Schömann, Romuald Jagodzinski, Guido Boni, Stefan Clauwaert, Vera Glassner and Teun Jaspers (eds), *Transnational Collective Bargaining at Company Level: A New Component of European Industrial Relations?* (Brussels: European Trade Union Institute 2012) <www.etui.org/sites/default/files/Chap%206%20Transnational%20collective%20bargaining%20EN-3.pdf> accessed 29 November 2020.

Isabelle Schömann, 'Transnational Company Agreements: Towards an Internationalisation of Industrial Relations' in Isabelle Schömann, Romuald Jagodzinski, Guido Boni, Stefan Clauwaert, Vera Glassner and Teun Jaspers (eds), *Transnational Collective Bargaining at Company Level: A New Component of European Industrial Relations?* (Brussels: European Trade Union Institute 2012) <www.etui.org/sites/default/files/C5%2012%20Transnational%20collective%20bargaining%20EN%20Web%20version.pdf> accessed 29 November 2020.

Isabelle Schömann, André Sobczak, Eckhard Voss and Peter Wilke, *Codes of Conduct and International Framework Agreements: New Forms of Governance at Company Level* (Dublin: European Foundation for the Improvement of Living and Working Conditions 2008).

ISO 26000 and the SDGs <www.iso.org/files/live/sites/isoorg/files/store/en/PUB100401.pdf> accessed 29 November 2020.

Jack Eaton, *Comparative Employment Relations: An Introduction* (Cambridge: Polity Press 2000).

Jang B Singh, 'Determinants of the Effectiveness of Corporate Codes of Ethics: An Empirical Study' (2011) 101(3) *Journal of Business Ethics* 385 <https://doi.org/10.1007/s10551-010-0727-3> accessed 28 November 2020.

Jerzy Wratny, 'Kodeksy dobrych praktyk jako wyraz społecznej odpowiedzialności korporacji' in Zbigniew Hajn and Dagmara Skupień (eds), *Przyszłość prawa pracy: Liber Amicorum. W pięćdziesięciolecie pracy naukowej Profesora Michała Seweryńskiego* (Łódź: Wydawnictwo Uniwersytetu Łódzkiego 2015).

Jerzy Wratny, 'Korporacyjne kodeksy dobrych praktyk z perspektywy prawa pracy' (2016) 3 *Praca i Zabezpieczenie Społeczne* 2.

Jocelyne Barreau and Juliette Arnal, 'Effects of Financialization on Restructuring and Sustainable Development Policy: The ACCOR Group Case' in William Sun, Céline Louche and Roland Pérez (eds), *Finance and Sustainability: Towards a New Paradigm? A Post-Crisis Agenda* (Bingley: Emerald Group Publishing Limited 2011).

Joseph Carby-Hall, 'Labour Aspects of Corporate Social Responsibility Emanating from the United Nations Global Compact: The Global Case and That of the EU and the United Kingdom' (2016) 5(2) *E-Journal of International and Comparative Labour Studies* 1.

Joseph Carby-Hall, 'Multinationals, SMEs and Non-Profit Organisations Participating in the UN Global Compact' (2020) 10(2) Lex Social: Revista de Derechos Sociales 130 <https://doi.org/10.46661/lexsocial.5067> accessed 28 November 2020.

Joseph Fiksel, *Design for Environment: A Guide to Sustainable Product Development* (New York: McGraw-Hill 2009).

Ke Chen, *Labour Law in China* (Alphen aan den Rijn: Kluwer Law International 2011).

Konstantinos Papadakis, *Shaping Global Industrial Relations* (Geneva: ILO 2011).

Lara Blecher, 'Codes of Conduct: The Trojan Horse of International Human Rights Law?' (2017) 38(3) *Comparative Labor Law & Policy Journal* 437.

Laura Vannucci, 'CSR e Certificazione SA8000' in Adalberto Perulli (ed), *L'impresa responsabile: Diritti sociali e Corporate Social Responsability* (Macerata: HALLEY Editrice 2007).

Lisbeth Segerlund, *Making Corporate Social Responsibility a Global Concern: Norm Construction in a Globalizing World* (Farnham: Ashgate 2010).

Michael D'heur, 'Shared.Value.Chain: Profitable Growth Through Sustainable Value Creation' in Michael D'heur (ed), *Sustainable Value Chain Management: Delivering Sustainability Through the Core Business* (Cham: Springer 2015).

Michael K Braswell, Charles M Foster and Stephen L Poe, 'A New Generation of Corporate Codes of Ethics' (2009) 34(2) *Southern Business Review* 1.

Michael W Toffel, Jodi L Short and Melissa Ouellet, 'Codes in Context: How States, Markets, and Civil Society Shape Adherence to Global Labor Standards' (2015) 9(3) *Regulation & Governance* 205 <https://doi.org/10.1111/rego.12076> accessed 28 November 2020.

Nikita Lyutov, 'Traditional International Labour Law and the New "Global" Kind: Is There a Way to Make Them Work Together?' (2017) 67(1) *Zbornik Pravnog Fakulteta u Zagrebu* 29.

Niklas Egels-Zandén and Jeroen Merk, 'Private Regulation and Trade Union Rights: Why Codes of Conduct Have Limited Impact on Trade Union Rights' (2014) 123(3) *Journal of Business Ethics* 461 <https://doi.org/10.1007/s10551-013-1840-x> accessed 28 November 2020.

Peter Lund-Thomsen and Adam Lindgreen, 'Corporate Social Responsibility in Global Value Chains: Where Are We Now and Where Are We Going?' (2014) 123 *Journal of Business Ethics* 11 <https://doi.org/10.1007/s10551-013-1796-x> accessed 28 November 2020.

Peter Tergeist, 'Multinational Enterprises and Codes of Conduct: The OECD Guidelines for MNEs in Perspective' in Roger Blanpain (ed), *Comparative Labour Law and Industrial Relations in Industrialized Market Economies* (11th edn, Alphen aan den Rijn: Kluwer Law International 2014).

Pun Ngai, 'Global Production, Company Codes of Conduct, and Labor Conditions in China: A Case Study of Two Factories' (2005) 54 *The China Journal* 101 <https://doi.org/10.2307/20066068> accessed 28 November 2020.

Rhys Jenkins, Ruth Pearson and Gill Seyfang, 'Introduction' in Rhys Jenkins, Ruth Pearson and Gill Seyfang (eds), *Corporate Responsibility and Labour Rights: Codes of Conduct in the Global Economy* (London, Sterling VA: Earthscan Publishing Ltd 2002).

Richard Croucher and Elizabeth Cotton, *Global Unions, Global Business: Global Union Federations and International Business* (London: Middlesex University Press 2009).

Richard M Locke, Ben A Rissing and Timea Pal, 'Complements or Substitutes? Private Codes, State Regulation and the Enforcement of Labour Standards in Global Supply Chains' (2013) 51(3) *British Journal of Industrial Relations* 519 <https://doi.org/10.1111/bjir.12003> accessed 28 November 2020.

Richard M Locke, Thomas Kochan, Monica Romis and Fei Qin, 'Beyond Corporate Codes of Conduct: Work Organization and Labour Standards at Nike's Suppliers' (2007) 146(1–2) *International Labour Review* 21 <https://doi.org/10.1111/j.1564-913X.2007.00003.x> accessed 28 November 2020.

Robert J Flanagan, *Globalization and Labor Conditions: Working Conditions and Worker Rights in a Global Economy* (Oxford: Oxford University Press 2006).

Scott Cooper, 'Global Supply Chain Governance: ILO, ISO & Worker Safety' (October 2018) 63(10) *Professional Safety* 70.

Silvana Sciarra, Maximilian Fuchs and André Sobczak, *Towards a Legal Framework for Transnational Company Agreements (Report to the European Trade Union Confederation)* <http://csdle.lex.unict.it/Archive/LW/Data%20reports%20and%20 studies/Reports%20%20from%20Committee%20and%20Groups%20of%20 Experts/20140424-015608_Report-TCA-EN_lowpdf.pdf> accessed 29 November 2 020.

Stefania Marassi, 'Globalization and Transnational Collective Labour Relations: International and European Framework Agreements at Company Level' in Roger Blanpain (general ed), *Bulletin for Comparative Labour Relations* (Alphen aan den Rijn: Kluwer Law International 2015).

Subhas K Sikdar, Debalina Sengupta and Rajib Mukherjee, *Measuring Progress Towards Sustainability: A Treatise for Engineers* (Cham: Springer 2017).

Tom Campbell, 'A Human Rights Approach to Developing Voluntary Codes of Conduct for Multinational Corporations' (2006) 16(2) *Business Ethics Quarterly* 255 <https://doi.org/10.5840/beq200616225> accessed 28 November 2020.

Wolfgang Däubler, 'Corporate Social Responsibility: A Way to Make Deregulation More Acceptable?' in Roger Blanpain and Frank Hendrickx (eds), *Bulletin for Comparative Labour Relations: Labour Law Between Change and Tradition. Liber Amicorum Antoine Jacobs* (Alphen aan den Rijn: Kluwer Law International 2011).

Xiaomin Yu, 'Impacts of Corporate Code of Conduct on Labor Standards: A Case Study of Reebok's Athletic Footwear Supplier Factory in China' (2008) 81(3) *Journal of Business Ethics* 513 <https://doi.org/10.1007/s10551-007-9521-2> accessed 28 November 2020.

7 Conclusions

Back in 1992, when Francis Fukuyama published his famous book entitled *The End of History and the Last Man*, the Western world believed in such a scenario, as indicated by the first part of this title. Free trade was to be the path to one global system of rules, happiness and prosperity. However, the times we live in prove something else. It seems that a reorganisation of the world order is inevitable in the face of a current fundamental crisis of trust in the principles of global trade and labour governance systems.

The example of China, which was admitted to the WTO on 11 December 2001, shows how much that country has made use of globalisation. Millions of cheap hands to work have appeared in that system and the large corporations, not infrequently American ones, have made big profits. At the same time, it was believed that China would be transformed into a liberal democracy and would respect human rights, but those hopes have proved to be illusory. China has never intended to resign from its communist regime but has intended to derive an advantage from a mass influx of technology and knowledge that has allowed it to make tremendous technological progress. China has been rising and the rest of the world has tolerated its totalitarian system for decades.

This book recalls that one of the primary goals of the creation of the ILO was to ensure fair competitive conditions in international trade. International labour standards were meant, inter alia, to equalise production costs in the member states, thus preventing an unfair competition manifesting itself in the lowering of wages and the deteriorating working conditions. The Chinese example shows that the original goals of the organisation have nothing to do with reality. Moreover, a long-standing protective umbrella over China has allowed for wiping out competition from the other countries through subsidies, among other things. Therefore, not only workers' rights have been violated, but also the WTO rules.

Coronavirus has turned the Sino-US trade wars into propaganda wars, and what we experience now is a technological war. The latter race between China and the US plays a crucial role since the winner will create new supply chains, in large part replacing those that were cut by the COVID-19 pandemic. The country with the latest technologies, for example, artificial intelligence, technical possibilities of harvesting energy from space, leadership in quantum communications,

5G or 6G, will establish the new, global division of labour and maybe the new economy as well.

COVID-19 has affected the free movement of goods, services, capital and people. It has also exerted an impact on the free flow of data and free movement of ideas and technology, and all this will be of great importance for the world to come. Even before the pandemic, Vietnam and Mexico had become the winners of the trade wars between Washington and Beijing. Currently, American politicians from both sides of the political spectrum call for shifting production from China to the US. 'Decoupling' from China would mean a reconfiguration of the global supply chain that has been formed since the 1980s by multinational corporations and Chinese authorities together with local business partners. But can the goal of bringing manufacturing 'home' be reached? It must be noted that business does not seem interested in such a solution. According to the 'American Chamber of Commerce Shanghai 2020 China Business Report', jointly released on 9 September 2020 by the American Chamber of Commerce in Shanghai and PricewaterhouseCoopers, 70.6% of respondents said they would not move production out of China.[1] Moreover, it would be difficult to replace several hundred million Chinese workers with workers from Mexico or Vietnam etc. Another weak point of the US is that China enjoys a great number of engineers and technicians. This is related to a wider problem, namely that the Chinese teach children math and physics, while the Western world focuses on social sciences. Importantly, China has also a very modern infrastructure which ensures the speedy and punctual delivery of manufactured goods. In addition, the construction of a number of new transport corridors is envisaged – it is even enough to mention the New Silk Road project.

On the one hand, the US wants to shorten supply chains by moving manufacturing back home from China, thus reducing dependence on that country. On the other hand, Xi Jinping announces a 'dual circulation' model, in which pressure will be put on 'internal circulation', namely 'the domestic cycle of production, distribution, and consumption'. By contrast, 'external circulation' will play a supportive function. It should be underlined that the 'dual circulation' economic approach promises to form a crucial part of the government's five-year plan (2021–2025).[2] Undoubtedly, in the longer run, it could also help China in reducing its dependence on overseas markets and US technology. The latter goal could be additionally supported by 'China Standards 2035'.[3] All of this

1 <www.tellerreport.com/business/2020-09-09-report-of-the-american-chamber-of-commerce-in-shanghai–78–2%25-of-respondents-in-china-and-us-companies-made-profits-last-year.SJcqqglIVv.html> accessed 29 November 2020.
2 Kevin Yao, 'What We Know About China's "Dual Circulation" Economic Strategy' *Reuters* (15 September 2020) <www.reuters.com/article/us-china-economy-transformation-explaine/explainer-what-we-know-about-chinas-dual-circulation-economic-strategy-idUSKBN-25Z3C9> accessed 29 November 2020.
3 Arjun Kharpal, 'China Has a 15-Year Plan to Shape the Future of Tech: But Some Call It Hype' *CNBC* (22 June 2020) <www.cnbc.com/2020/06/22/

falls within the Xi Jinping's aim to achieve the 'great rejuvenation of the Chinese nation' by 2049, that is, by the 100th anniversary of the founding of the People's Republic of China.[4]

The implementation of the aforementioned plans is not one of the easiest tasks. However, if it turns out that the world powers continue to move in the outlined directions, regionalisation may become a spectre of the future. For example, Foxconn had already relocated some of its production to India and Vietnam. Admittedly, about 70% has remained in China,[5] but there are further serious plans to open a new factory, this time in Mexico. Taking into account that in light of the USMCA, more locally sourced inputs for tariff-free exports to the US are required,[6] Foxconn's example confirms the trend of regionalisation.

In this context, and considering the disruption of multilateral mechanisms and the WTO crisis, it seems appropriate to advocate for international trade agreements, bilateral, trilateral or plurilateral, believing that they would be the best guarantee for improving the situation of workers across the world. The findings presented indicate that a significant increase in free trade agreements has been observed since the crisis of 2008. Undoubtedly, one should not be indifferent to the role they can play in alleviating the consequences of the current recession, especially since the impact of coronavirus on millions of workers is devastating. According to the *ILO Monitor: COVID-19 and the world of work* 4th edition, in the second quarter of 2020 a decline in working hours of around 10.7% relative to the last quarter of 2019 is estimated, which is equivalent to 305 million full-time jobs.[7]

The USMCA is a solution which inspires hope in the parties to the agreement. It is believed that it would speed up the post-COVID-19 recovery[8] and – in combination with reshoring jobs from China – would maintain the trajectory

---

china-standards-2035-tech-plan-could-face-challenges-to-live-up-to-hype.html#close> accessed 29 November 2020.

4 See more: Julia G Bowie, 'Introduction: Scrambling to Achieve a Moderately Prosperous Society' in Julia G Bowie (ed), *Party Watch Annual Report 2019: Scrambling to Achieve a Moderately Prosperous Society* (Washington DC: Center for Advanced China Research 2019) 1 <https://97da3d29-d157-40bc-9f03-6b6ab7c8dd7f.filesusr.com/ugd/183fcc_02a68a69 47cd44e89b129af042d0c202.pdf> accessed 29 November 2020.

5 Isabella Weber, 'Could the US and Chinese Economies Really "Decouple"?' *The Guardian* (11 September 2020) <www.theguardian.com/commentisfree/2020/sep/11/us-china-global-economy-donald-trump> accessed 29 November 2020.

6 Sumeet Chatterjee, Yimou Lee and Anthony Esposito, 'Exclusive: Foxconn, Other Asian Firms Consider Mexico Factories as China Risks Grow' *Reuters* (24 August 2020) <www.reuters.com/article/us-mexico-china-factories-exclusive-idUSKBN25K17X> accessed 29 November 2020.

7 <www.ilo.org/wcmsp5/groups/public/-dgreports/-dcomm/documents/briefingnote/wcms_745963.pdf> accessed 29 November 2020.

8 Sergio Chapa, 'USMCA, Overshadowed by Pandemic, Seen Speeding Post-COVID Recovery' *Houston Chronicle* (13 September 2020) <www.houstonchronicle.com/business/texas-inc/article/USMCA-overshadowed-by-pandemic-seen-speeding-15553482.php> accessed 29 November 2020.

of job growth.[9] Obviously, it would not be wise to expect immediate effects, but the USMCA's innovative provisions are of great promise. Compared to its predecessor, namely NAFTA, the new model agreement uses stronger language. It should be emphasised that the USMCA clearly provides that each Party shall 'adopt and maintain' the rights, as stated in the ILO Declaration on Rights at Work, i.e.:

- freedom of association and the effective recognition of the right to collective bargaining;
- the elimination of all forms of forced or compulsory labour;
- the effective abolition of child labour and, for the purposes of the USMCA, a prohibition on the worst forms of child labour; and
- the elimination of discrimination in respect of employment and occupation.

As regards the language, the new agreement also firmly stipulates that each party 'shall adopt and maintain statutes and regulations, and practices thereunder, governing acceptable conditions of work with respect to minimum wages, hours of work, and occupational safety and health'. This wording represents a significant advance in the approach to labour rights when compared to the NAFTA and to many other trade agreements concluded so far.

Some other pertinent provisions in the USMCA's 'Labor' chapter include nine 'greater certainty' clauses, among which we can find a clarification related to the right to strike. Footnote 6 expressly states that this right 'is linked to the right to freedom of association, which cannot be realized without protecting the right to strike'. Consequently, it eliminates any uncertainty that has so far been expressed against the background of many other trade agreements and makes the right to strike an explicit commitment.[10] Overall, it is apparent that the USMCA proves how footnotes matter. Other significant examples include footnotes 8 and 9 that were shaped under the influence of the US–Guatemala CAFTA labour arbitration ruling of 2017.

It would also be impossible not to mention momentous regulations introduced into the USMCA and concerning: the goal of eliminating all forms of forced or compulsory labour, including forced or compulsory child labour (Article 23.6);[11] exercising labour rights in a climate that is free from violence against

---

9   Kalley Huang, 'Borderland Business Leaders: Trade Deal Provides Needed Economic Certainty During COVID-19' *El Paso Times* <https://eu.elpasotimes.com/story/news/2020/07/01/coronavirus-el-paso-juarez-usmca-trade-deal-economy-jobs-covid-19/5358128002/> accessed 29 November 2020.

10 See also: Jeffrey Vogt, Janice Bellace, Lance Compa, Keith D Ewing, Lord Hendy QC, Klaus Lörcher and Tonia Novitz, *The Right to Strike in International Law* (Oxford: Hart Publishing 2020) 133.

11 The provision clearly states that the parties shall 'prohibit' the importation of goods produced by forced or compulsory labour into their territories. This reflects a significant progress comparing to some other trade agreements, for example, the Trans-Pacific Partnership,

workers (Article 23.7); the recognition of the vulnerability of migrant workers with respect to labour protections (Article 23.8); and the goal of eliminating discrimination in employment and occupation; and promoting equality of women in the workplace (Article 23.9).

Additionally, recent experience related to the US–Guatemala case has taught the parties to the agreement that they should introduce a provision according to which in a dispute arising under the 'Labor' chapter, panellists (other than the chair) shall have expertise or experience in labour law or practice. This is reflected in Article 31.8 of Chapter 31 on dispute settlement.

Among the significant provisions of the USMCA are also those of Annex 23-A entitled 'Worker Representation in Collective Bargaining in Mexico' (an annex related to labour law reform in Mexico); and Annex 31-A 'Facility-specific rapid response labor mechanism'. The latter assumes the formation of a 'Rapid Response Labor Panel', whose competencies include, among other things, conducting on-site verifications at the facility in question. As we have seen, such a solution is absolutely unprecedented in comparison to previously concluded trade agreements. The same is true for a new 'Labor Value Content' rule, which entails the payment of average wages of US$16 per hour. However, we can argue that an adjustment should be made as regards 'average' wages, which should be changed into 'minimum' wages. Moreover, one of the main points of interest should be the USMCA Implementation Act of 2020, which requires the US president to establish 'the Interagency Labor Committee for Monitoring and Enforcement' equipped with important powers.

In view of all the aforementioned advantages, the USMCA could serve as a model when concluding new trade agreements.[12] However, one should remember that the USMCA's provisions cannot be just blindly and uncritically copied into another trade agreement because it may simply bring unexpected results. Instead, when taking into account a 'copying' method, one shall first assess all contextual differences.[13]

It must be realised that following the pathway of using the USMCA as a template for trade agreements to be negotiated in the future, may further accelerate regionalisation and reduce the role of the WTO. However, a question arises as to the usefulness of this Organization in the protection of workers' rights. The analysis in this book shows limitations of the trade-labour nexus based on the WTO. If these limitations existed at a time when the WTO dispute resolution

---

Article 19.6, which only states that each party shall 'discourage . . . the importation of goods from other sources produced in whole or in part by forced or compulsory labour, including forced or compulsory child labour'.

12 For example, Scherrer highlights, in particular, the usefulness of the Labour Value Content clause relying on the payment of average wages of US$16 per hour, as well as monitoring and sanctioning instruments for Mexico for ensuring internationally recognised labour rights. See: Christoph Scherrer, 'Novel Labour-related Clauses in a Trade Agreement: From NAFTA to USMCA' (2020) 11(3) *Global Labour Journal* 291, passim.

13 ibid 300–301.

system could be named 'the jewel in the crown of the WTO', most of them are all the more true in an era in which COVID-19 deepens problems faced by the WTO. In fact, the current situation of the WTO does not instil optimism. Efforts made to date to reinstate the WTO's Appellate Body have not been successful. The Organization is in a deep crisis and it seems that it has lost its current position in the international arena. In this context, it would be very difficult to apply in reality the institutional approach or the integrated legislative approach, which have been presented in this book. Considering also the lack of political will, integrating core labour standards into the WTO through changes to law or enhancing cooperation on labour rights between the ILO with the WTO seem unrealistic, even if these ideals are high and fine.

All things considered, our attention must naturally focus on the ILO. Although it is attracting much criticism from many commentators, it shall continue to constitute one of the important keystones of global labour governance. In these uncertain times, it is important to keep this mainstay of safety for workers in the best condition possible.

As regards the criticism mentioned, to a large extent it refers to the fact that the ILO has a strong capacity for setting international labour standards, but unfortunately, it lacks the ability to ensure their implementation and compliance with them. The number of ratifications of the ILO conventions leaves much to be desired and there is no apparatus to exert pressure on member states to make them ratify ILO instruments. It must be added that it is simply a symptom of hypocrisy that not all ILO core conventions have been ratified by all members holding non-elective seats in the Governing Body.

Likewise, the procedural aspect of compliance involving the fulfilment of the reporting requirement has proven to be far from perfect. The administrative problems faced by some member states prevent them from performing their reporting duties. Others often just want to avoid being assessed by the CEACR. It is also hard to be optimistic regarding the substantive aspect of compliance, namely whether member states have fulfilled obligations set out in an ILO convention. The Myanmar case confirms that the ILO mechanism in the form of Article 33 of its Constitution is not as effective as it will need to be. Unfortunately, the other available instruments to ensure compliance with the ILO's standards include only dialogue, diplomacy, publicity, moral persuasion, technical assistance and naming and shaming. While some authors point out that 'It would be wrong to underestimate the impact of the moral suasion and "naming and shaming" approach on countries failing to implement reasonable labor standards',[14] others argue that all this is not enough to ensure effective enforcement of labour rights. One can, of course, wonder about the wording of Article 419 of the Treaty of Versailles and speculate if such a provision would be used today, that is, if 'measures of an economic character' would be recommended. If so, would those measures achieve

---

14 Steve Hughes and Nigel Haworth, *International Labour Organisation (ILO): Coming in from the Cold* (London, New York: Routledge 2011) 71.

the intended goal, or the outcome would be uncertain? Charnovitz uses an apt quote from Oliver Wendell Holmes Jr. that 'the life of the law has not been logic: it has been experience'.[15] One thing is certain: the removal of sanctions in 1946 eliminated the possibility of gaining experience.

Moreover, Charnovitz establishes his own interesting thesis on the unwillingness to resort to sanctions in the 1920s. The underlying reason was that the ILO Constitution as it then stood did not introduce 'scales of penalties' with the aim of avoiding 'excessive penalty'. According to the author, if the sanctions process had evolved the extent that a Commission of Enquiry or the Permanent Court of International Justice indicated 'appropriate' economic measures, 'legal standards for appropriateness would have developed through caselaw'. He points out that the Commission of Enquiry would have submitted any recommendations on economic measures to the Permanent Court of International Justice, which could have heard the parties and the assessors on the most appropriate type of sanction. The Court would have been able to apply the principle of proportionality in order to 'quantify the sanctions indicated'.[16]

However, all this did not happen, and persuasion is the key point about the concept of compliance with international labour standards. In this context, there is no doubt that support should be given to the idea of strengthening the ILO's supervisory system, which is the oldest in the UN. The ILO Centenary Declaration for the Future of Work of 2019 puts it clearly that: 'The setting, promotion, ratification and supervision of international labour standards is of fundamental importance to the ILO. International labour standards . . . need to . . . be subject to authoritative and effective supervision'. In fact, according to the report of the Committee of Experts on the Application of Conventions and Recommendations of 2019, 'the Centenary year was . . . an opportunity to continue to reflect on ways to strengthen the supervisory system with courage and ambition, based on a better grasp of constituents' needs and priorities and a more user-friendly, clear and concise presentation of findings and recommendations'. 'The Standards Initiative: Implementing the workplan for strengthening the supervisory system' of 2018 is one of the manifestations of the quest for improvements in the area and may contribute to the increased impact of both supervisory bodies.[17] Other examples might include: a practice of 'urgent appeals' that was established by the CEACR in order to strengthen supervision of ratified ILO conventions and measures approved by the Governing Body concerning the operation of the

---

15 Oliver Wendell Holmes Jr, 'The Common Law' (Little Brown 1881) 1. Quoted from: Steve Charnovitz, 'The Lost History of the ILO's Trade Sanctions' in George P Politakis, Tomi Kohiyama and Thomas Lieby (eds), *ILO 100 – Law for Social Justice* (Geneva: International Labour Office 2019) 255 <www.ilo.org/wcmsp5/groups/public/-dgreports/-jur/documents/publication/wcms_732217.pdf> accessed 29 November 2020.

16 Charnovitz (n 15) 251.

17 The Committee of Experts on the Application of Conventions and Recommendations, *Application of International Labour Standards 2019* (Report, ILC.108/III(A), 108th Session of the International Labour Conference, Geneva 2019) 10–11.

representations procedure under Article 24 of the Constitution. This book contains more paragons of improvement of the Organization from within.

It should, however, be remembered that the previously mentioned global supply chains are governed in a somewhat different way. Often the role of the ILO in those organisational structures is perceived as ineffective.[18] Admittedly, there are rational proposals to increase this role, for example, by establishing a transnational labour inspectorate system with the ILO as an entity responsible, inter alia, for providing a list of transnational labour inspectors, but it remains only in the sphere of postulates.[19]

One of the chapters of this book focuses on some key tools within the CSR that exert an impact on workers in the global supply chain. These include corporate codes of conduct, transnational company agreements, NGOs' social accountability standards, ISO standards, the Dow Jones Sustainability Index and the Global Reporting Initiative.

There is evidence in research which shows that implementing private codes of conduct equipped with global labour standards in supply chains may lead, inter alia, to a strengthening of the norms promoted by the ILO, a generation of enforcement pressure that is lacking in the ILO, a revision of domestic labour laws and an improvement in the tangible working conditions. Unfortunately, it has also been proven that codes of conduct exert limited impact on less tangible rights, for example, freedom of association and the right to collective bargaining. In fact, according to the recent Principles for Responsible Investment's report concerning agricultural supply chains, 91% of companies admitted that freedom of association is included in their supplier codes of conduct as one of the expectations, but only 12% of them were able to describe how they work on this subject with suppliers. It is also sad to find out that none of the companies reported that they analyse trends or collect data on the issue.[20] There is no question that all of the three generations of corporate codes of conduct have their shortcomings, among which are also problems related to their implementation, monitoring and enforcement.

However, it does not mean that they should be abandoned or should not be taken seriously, particularly in such difficult times. It is important to recognise

---

18 Huw Thomas and Peter Turnbull, 'From Horizontal to Vertical Labour Governance: The International Labour Organization (ILO) and Decent Work in Global Supply Chains' (2018) 71(4) *Human Relations* 536, passim <https://doi.org/10.1177/0018726717719994> accessed 29 November 2020.

19 Antonio M García-Muñoz Alhambra, Beryl Ter Haar and Attila Kun, 'Independent Monitoring of Private Transnational Regulation of Labour Standards: A Proposal for a "Transnational Labour Inspectorate" System' in Edoardo Ales and Iacopo Senatori (eds), *The Transnational Dimension of Labour Relations: A New Order in the Making? Atti dell'XI Convegno internazionale in ricordo di Marco Biagi* (Turin: G. Giappichelli Editore 2013) 275–277.

20 Principles for Responsible Investment, 'From Farm to Table: Ensuring Fair Labour Practices in Agricultural Supply Chains' (2020) <www.unpri.org/download?ac=10533> accessed 29 November 2020.

that the current COVID-19 pandemic has brought new risks to workers all over the globe, including those related to core labour standards, such as child or forced labour. A number of negative economic phenomena, for example, fluctuations in commodity prices, significant changes in demand or cancellations of orders, wield influence on the most vulnerable groups. For this reason, any tools, even imperfect as corporate codes of conduct, shall be taken in consideration when addressing how to reduce vulnerabilities, especially in the context that MNCs' supply chains in a post-pandemic world, to some extent, will differ from the current ones. This book presents certain ways in which codes could be transformed to more effectively address workers' rights.

Undoubtedly, transnational company agreements are also among the instruments that merit appreciation and support. For reasons of social dialogue with trade unions, they are perceived as means of promoting industrial peace. As demonstrated in this book, TCAs work for the benefit of both workers and MNCs. It can only be suggested that attention be directed towards the creation of a legal framework for TCAs. In the EU, the European Commission and the European Parliament have already made certain announcements in this regard. Further research should also consider this problem.

Some of the CSR instruments discussed, such as the GRI or the DJSI, use a self-reporting method that can be described as not too much reliable. Besides, some of them are favourable only towards the world's largest companies (e.g. the DJSI) and have not been able to coexist without conflict with the ILO (the ISO).

As a matter of principle, it must be understood that (voluntary) CSR norms are not within the power of the state and cannot be enforced through court action. Above all, it is domestic labour law that applies to all companies in a given country so it shall be drafted in a way protecting the rights of all workers. CSR initiatives should enhance labour standards, thus providing additional value to law.

Finally, a unilateral mechanism in the form of GSP schemes constitutes an important component of a multilevel approach adopted by the author. The concept in which very poor countries have preferential access and export to rich economies assumes, inter alia, linking trade liberalisation with the protection of workers' rights. Its vital aspect implies that the US government has the possibility of withdrawing customs duties exemptions to imports coming from countries that do not comply with internationally recognised workers' rights and the EU can withdraw three preferential arrangements for any of the reasons mentioned in the Regulation (EU) No 978/2012, including serious and systematic violation of principles laid down in the core human and labour rights UN/ILO Conventions. Similar to the CSR practices, the GSP programmes have both advantages and drawbacks that were discussed in this book. This is true not only for the US scheme but also for the EU's one.

Overall, the results indicate that in former years there were many cases where the threat of blocking imports to the US was sufficient to trigger law reforms in a country that infringed labour rights. GSP supporters recall that it had not only a positive effect on the US labour movement and international labour solidarity but also on research related to, for example, corporate codes of conduct, social labelling programmes and other forms of international standard setting, monitoring or enforcement of labour laws. Also, in the case of the EU, it was found that its GSP has exerted a beneficial effect on social development and human rights in developing countries. The most recent version of the EU GSP has particularly contributed to the promotion of sustainable development and good governance. That is due in particular to the EU's closer monitoring of the implementation of the international conventions relevant to GSP+. Looking at these positive outcomes should strengthen our belief that GSP programmes are worth operationalising. They also perfectly fit into the aforementioned postulate related to the conclusion of FTAs. Indeed, the EU GSP specifies the target aspirations in terms of conventions that should be ratified and implemented by future FTA partners. Thus, the GSP may be often perceived as a stepping-stone to the conclusion of a FTA.

Bibliography

Antonio M García-Muñoz Alhambra, Beryl Ter Haar and Attila Kun, 'Independent Monitoring of Private Transnational Regulation of Labour Standards: A Proposal for a "Transnational Labour Inspectorate" System' in Edoardo Ales and Iacopo Senatori (eds), *The Transnational Dimension of Labour Relations: A New Order in the Making? Atti dell'XI Convegno internazionale in ricordo di Marco Biagi* (Turin: G. Giappichelli Editore 2013).

Arjun Kharpal, 'China Has a 15-Year Plan to Shape the Future of Tech: But Some Call It Hype' *CNBC* (22 June 2020) <www.cnbc.com/2020/06/22/china-standards-2035-tech-plan-could-face-challenges-to-live-up-to-hype.html#close> accessed 29 November 2020.

Christoph Scherrer, 'Novel Labour-Related Clauses in a Trade Agreement: From NAFTA to USMCA' (2020) 11(3) *Global Labour Journal* 291.

The Committee of Experts on the Application of Conventions and Recommendations, *Application of International Labour Standards 2019* (Report, ILC.108/III(A), 108th Session of the International Labour Conference, Geneva 2019).

Huw Thomas and Peter Turnbull, 'From Horizontal to Vertical Labour Governance: The International Labour Organization (ILO) and Decent Work in Global Supply Chains' (2018) 71(4) *Human Relations* 536 <https://doi.org/10.1177/0018726717719994> accessed 29 November 2020.

Isabella Weber, 'Could the US and Chinese Economies Really "Decouple"?' *The Guardian* (11 September 2020) <www.theguardian.com/commentisfree/2020/sep/11/us-china-global-economy-donald-trump> accessed 29 November 2020.

Jeffrey Vogt, Janice Bellace, Lance Compa, Keith D Ewing, Lord Hendy QC, Klaus Lörcher and Tonia Novitz, *The Right to Strike in International Law* (Oxford: Hart Publishing 2020).

Julia G Bowie, 'Introduction: Scrambling to Achieve a Moderately Prosperous Society' in Julia G Bowie (ed), *Party Watch Annual Report 2019: Scrambling to Achieve a Moderately Prosperous Society* (Washington DC: Center for Advanced China Research 2019) <https://97da3d29-d157-40bc-9f03-6b6ab7c8dd7f.file-susr.com/ugd/183fcc_02a68a6947cd44e89b129af042d0c202.pdf> accessed 29 November 2020.

Kalley Huang, 'Borderland Business Leaders: Trade Deal Provides Needed Economic Certainty During COVID-19' *El Paso Times* <https://eu.elpasotimes.com/story/news/2020/07/01/coronavirus-el-paso-juarez-usmca-trade-deal-economy-jobs-covid-19/5358128002/> accessed 29 November 2020.

Kevin Yao, 'What We Know About China's "Dual Circulation" Economic Strategy' *Reuters* (15 September 2020) <www.reuters.com/article/us-china-economy-transformation-explaine/explainer-what-we-know-about-chinas-dual-circulation-economic-strategy-idUSKBN25Z3C9> accessed 29 November 2020.

Principles for Responsible Investment, 'From Farm to Table: Ensuring Fair Labour Practices in Agricultural Supply Chains' (2020) <www.unpri.org/download?ac=10533> accessed 29 November 2020.

Sergio Chapa, 'USMCA, Overshadowed by Pandemic, Seen Speeding Post-COVID Recovery' *Houston Chronicle* (13 September 2020) <www.houstonchronicle.com/business/texas-inc/article/USMCA-overshadowed-by-pandemic-seen-speeding-15553482.php> accessed 29 November 2020.

Steve Charnovitz, 'The Lost History of the ILO's Trade Sanctions' in George P Politakis, Tomi Kohiyama and Thomas Lieby (eds), *ILO 100 – Law for Social Justice* (Geneva: International Labour Office 2019) <www.ilo.org/wcmsp5/groups/public/-dgreports/–jur/documents/publication/wcms_732217.pdf> accessed 29 November 2020.

Steve Hughes and Nigel Haworth, *International Labour Organisation (ILO): Coming in from the Cold* (London, New York: Routledge 2011).

Sumeet Chatterjee, Yimou Lee and Anthony Esposito, 'Exclusive: Foxconn, Other Asian Firms Consider Mexico Factories as China Risks Grow' *Reuters* (24 August 2020) <www.reuters.com/article/us-mexico-china-factories-exclusive-idUSKBN25K17X> accessed 29 November 2020.

Index

Note: Page numbers followed by "n" indicate a note.